SPIKED

Church-State Intrigue and
The Rose Tattoo

Gerard Whelan
with Carolyn Swift

**NEW
ISLAND**

SPIKED: CHURCH–STATE INTRIGUE AND *THE ROSE TATTOO*

First published November 2002

New Island
2 Brookside
Dundrum Road
Dublin 14
Ireland

ISBN 1 902602 92 7

The moral right of the authors has been asserted.

British Library Cataloguing in Publication Data
A catalogue record for this book is available
from the British Library

New Island receives financial assistance from The Arts Council
(An Chomhairle Ealaíon), Dublin, Ireland.

Cover design: Jon Berkeley
Interior layout: New Island
Printed in Ireland by Colour Books Ltd

Contents

This book is respectfully dedicated to all of the children of Alan Simpson, in the hope that it will remind the world what an extraordinary man, in his time and place, their father was.

It is also dedicated to David Alexander Conrad Whelan Ziere, who between the ages of six and eight must occasionally have felt that *The Rose Tattoo* had swallowed his daddy too.

'Sorry about all your trouble over *The Rose Tattoo*.
Bastards, bastards …'
Samuel Beckett, in a letter to Alan Simpson, August 1957

Preface

Ever since the first policeman darkened the doorway of the Pike Theatre in May 1957, I have been asking myself the same question: why?

In the awful year that followed, everyone asked me this question: Why were my husband and I being threatened? Why were the full forces of the State ranged against our tiny theatre? Why were our lives being destroyed? Why *The Rose Tattoo* – and why *us*?

As the spuriousness of the State's case became evident, a second question joined the first: who? Who was behind it all? Some powerful politician who objected to himself or his political party being lampooned in one of the late-night Pike revues? The Knights of Columbanus? The Catholic Church? Archbishop John Charles McQuaid himself?

When asked about this, I could only shrug helplessly. Over the succeeding years both our marriage and our theatre broke up under the strain of it all, and I found it hard to talk about the whole episode without breaking down myself. I grew weary of constantly having to explain that there was no nudity in the play, nor was a contraceptive (at that time illegal) dropped on the stage; that there was no chorus line of women in corsets; that Alan had not been showing blue movies; that the play was considered completely in accord with Catholic teaching by various priests, monsignors and theologians ... and so on. Still, with three young daughters to raise on my own, I had to get on with my life. I began a new career as a script editor with the recently founded RTÉ Television and, despite the fact than an anonymous writer complained at RTÉ employing a pornographer, I

9

tried to put *The Rose Tattoo* and everything connected with it out of my mind.

Obstinately, both play and case kept forcing themselves back into my consciousness, as they were dragged up by journalists every time there was an incident involving the law, or the Church, and the theatre. When the Dublin Theatre Festival of 1958 was cancelled over objections to the inclusion of plays by Seán O'Casey and James Joyce, for instance, the Pike duly came up for mention, as it did when *The Ginger Man* was withdrawn from the Gaiety. It surfaced again in the 1970s when a councillor protested that the Gay Sweatshop should not be allowed to perform in the Project Art Centre. In fact, whenever anything even *remotely* connected with theatre censorship cropped up, media attention focused again on *The Rose Tattoo*. Of course such a return was only natural, since it was the single occasion in which the State had behaved in this manner – a fact which had always made many feel certain that the case had quite specific political causes.

Every time the matter was mentioned, however, journalists got the facts concerning the Pike case wrong, stating that the theatre was closed down by the police – which it was not – because a contraceptive was dropped on stage – which was equally untrue. Each time, I had to relive the whole traumatic episode while I wrote furious letters to the newspapers concerned, trying in vain to set the record straight. I clung to the hope that the State papers on the case would be released after thirty years, as is normally the case, and that then at least everyone would know why the Pike Theatre had been singled out and harried. But 1987 came and went without a whisper, as did the many years that followed. I had given up hope of ever learning more when, in January 2000, the Attorney General's and Justice Department's papers on the case were finally released. Ironically, I discovered this only because the case was, once more, misreported in the newspapers.

Again I found myself writing angry letters of denial, as well as trying to put the record straight on the *Joe Duffy Show* on RTÉ

Radio 1. Still I was unable to answer Joe Duffy's questions as to why the State had acted as it did, just as the previous year I had been unable to answer Gay Byrne's similar questions on his radio programme about the 1950s, and just as I had always been unable to answer such questions. There was only one thing to do. Though neither a detective nor investigative journalist, I would have to search for the reason myself. Then maybe I could find out what the journalists had missed and get the truth set in print. But it seemed an undertaking far too big for one 77-year-old, even an obstinate and determined one. That is when I turned for help to my friend Gerard Whelan.

It soon became clear that only one of us could do the actual writing and that that person should be Gerard. As someone who was not even born when most of these things took place, he could write about events more dispassionately than I ever could. He had grown up in a different Ireland and could see more clearly when something that seemed self-evident to me needed setting in its historical or sociological context, in order that present-day readers would accept that such things were possible. Although the words are entirely his, and I might sometimes have expressed things differently, his chronicle of events is based on our combined research, my recollections and papers, and on documentary evidence which we have both examined. I guarantee its accuracy in so far as it is possible for a fallible human being to guarantee anything. Moreover, his conclusions entirely satisfy me.

At last I trust that my search is over. Unless or until State papers are released that change my opinion, I believe I now know why the *Rose Tattoo* case happened and why the State was so vicious in its consistently inexplicable prosecution of Alan Simpson.

Carolyn Swift
Summer 2002, Dublin

Introduction: The Pornographer in the Lane

On the evening of May 23rd 1957, shortly after 7.30 in the evening, a man was arrested by the police in a back lane near the Grand Canal in Dublin. In itself, of course, this was hardly unusual – police everywhere arrest people all the time and for all sorts of reasons. Since the suspect offered no particular resistance, the arrest itself might have been expected to pass off quietly – a paragraph in a sidebar, perhaps, on the bottom of an inside page of the newspapers.

There were, admittedly, some peculiar features about the arrest, perhaps the oddest being the fact that it took place at all – over a year later, after the ensuing legal case had gone through every court in the land, a judge in Dublin District Court would conclude that a simple summons would have been not only more appropriate but also far more normal. But this was only the first of several oddities. The arresting officers, for instance, were not ordinary uniformed Gardaí, but very large, tough-looking men in plain clothes – as well they might be, since they were senior members of Ireland's Special Detective Branch, a unit normally used to apprehend dangerous and frequently armed criminals, including what would nowadays be called terrorists. The form of arrest warrant used was also uncommon, since it was a so-called summary warrant: one which precluded the granting of bail and was normally used to ensure the immediate detention of those suspected of armed crime or political subversion – people who might reasonably be expected to flee the jurisdiction if given an opportunity.

With an active IRA campaign in progress on the border and draconian State measures being planned to subdue it, neither measure would have been remarkable if the arrested man's supposed offence had been a political or even a merely violent one. But this was far from being the case here: not only was the 'offence' neither political nor violent, it was so uncommon as to be completely unheard of – quite literally at this point, since the arrested man would only later learn the charge on which he was being detained. It was for the great crime of 'producing for gain an indecent and profane performance', an unprecedented charge that might well in itself have merited a passing mention in even the preternaturally careful Irish newspapers of the day. Ireland, with a controversial censorship system governing all forms of publication, was well-used to having printed matter deemed obscene – indeed, it was internationally notorious for it. But an indecent *performance* was another matter entirely: there was, after all – officially at least – no stage censorship in Ireland.

Another odd aspect of the incident – and it was a *very* odd aspect – was the nature of the arrested man himself. The son of a Protestant clergyman (whose parish lay just around the corner), the suspect was a respectable family man, a captain in the Irish army and a successful theatre owner and producer who had, in recent weeks, found himself hob-nobbing with celebrities and being sought out by eager State dignitaries at official receptions all over Dublin – hardly the stuff of which the public perception of pornographers was made, nor the sort of person whom Irish policemen tended to manhandle. Neither (as the judge in the resulting court case would later point out) was he the type of man who might reasonably be expected to flee the country, leaving his careers, business, property, wife and three children behind him.

The May 23rd arrest was meant to be quick and quiet. Some publicity was bound to result, but the Irish media – which consisted, by and large, of the newspapers – knew far better then than to query too closely the peculiarities of State behaviour, especially when – as in this instance – the incident was generally felt to have the fingerprints of the Catholic Church all over it. And, ordinarily, that would have been that: one more would-be corrupter of Ireland's world-famous sanctity taught a lesson and a grateful citizenry safe in their chaste beds. In spite of the odd circumstances the whole incident would, with even a little bit of luck, have been quickly forgotten.

Unfortunately for those behind the arrest, that all-important bit of luck failed to materialise. Apart from anything else there was the very public nature of the 'offence': the 'indecent' performance was a play, being produced by one of the city's most fashionable theatres as a central part of an officially sponsored, state-subsidised and widely publicised international theatre festival. Nor was this a matter of preventing some obscure piece of pornography from polluting the boards of an innocent Irish stage: the production was the European English-language première of a major work by a world-famous American playwright, then at the height of his fame. At the time of the arrest the play had already been showing to capacity audiences – which had included members of the Government and international dignitaries and celebrities – for over a week and the production had received wide coverage and rave reviews both at home and abroad. In fact it was the acknowledged highlight of the festival and was being touted as such by official Government publications overseas.

Finally (and crucially) there was the sort of people the authorities were dealing with: theatre people – people who, in the Ireland of the time, were more aware than most of the value of publicity. Worried sick by the anticipated arrest, the theatre's owners had seen publicity as their best (indeed their only) defence against what they could only think had to be some enormous official mistake. They had contacted the press in advance and delayed the arrival of the suspect until the newspaper people were present in force. In other words, they'd effectively stage-managed the whole incident. As a result the arrest took place in front of a gaggle of

reporters and press photographers, who captured the entire incident not only for posterity but – of more immediate importance
to all concerned – for the front pages of the next day's newspapers.

The rest, as they say, is history. Instead of being relegated to a
few lines in a sidebar of a newspaper, the arrest became front-page
news. Instead of being limited to a little local matter, the whole affair received extensive international coverage. The events in the
laneway would lead to a marathon court case, which went as far as
the Irish Supreme Court and focused unwelcome international attention on the realities of Irish life. For the police, it led to being
laughed at in open court. For the State, it led – in those innocent
days when such things were possible – to much embarrassment. For
Irish theatre in general and for the few beleaguered proponents of
freedom of thought and expression in the Irish Republic, it resulted
in what has always been seen as an extremely important victory
against an authoritarian and proudly philistine State.

But what about the arrested man, his wife (and business partner)
and their theatre – to what, for them, did the whole sorry process
lead? Well, for the alleged pornographer and his wife – professional
stage people whose tiny theatre, founded and run on a shoestring,
had become the toast of the Irish theatrical world and who had
seemed on the brink of serious international fame – it led to fear,
social ostracism, disillusion and eventual ruin. The strain that the
next thirteen months would place on their relationship destroyed it:
within a couple of years both their private and their business part-
nerships dissolved. For their theatre, which in its brief life had
brought cultural glory to Ireland and entertained a great number of
Irish people, as well as becoming a *de rigueur* port of call for visiting
foreign critics and celebrities, the financial and other hardships
caused by the court case led to eventual closure, even though the
obscenity case itself was eventually thrown unceremoniously out of
court without even coming to trial. No vindication is without its
cost and even the most victorious battle has its casualties.

Yet there is no doubt that the outcome *was* a vindication and even the process itself a victory: for the man, whose reputation was cleared in court; for the theatrical world in Ireland, which feared that a successful prosecution would lead to the introduction of a censorship for which many in Ireland had been calling; and for freedom of expression itself in a country where it was a rare, precious and frowned-upon commodity. Instead of a small, sleazy incident doomed to well-deserved obscurity, the affair became a landmark in the often-sorry history of the struggle for civil and artistic freedoms in Ireland. But it became something else, too: in the absence of any realistic explanation of the State's action the affair became a puzzle, a legend and a mystery whose roots, it was long assumed, would never *really* come to light. The arrest and attempted prosecution seemed another in the long list of Irish solutions to Irish problems, one which (like every other item in that category) raised far more questions than it ever answered.

In this particular case, however, the real mystery was never the arrest itself, bizarre though that was: the truly baffling matter was the question of what exactly the arrest was meant to achieve. If it wasn't really meant to stop the performance of an obscene theatrical production, then what *was* it meant to do? The desire to stop the play was certainly real – a warning that performances must immediately cease had preceded the arrest and it was only when the theatre owners refused to comply that the matter was taken further. The authorities clearly had not expected the theatre owners to do what in fact they did – refuse to play along with the authorities' script. They refused to do this partly because they didn't know this script existed ('We were so terribly naïve!' as the arrested man's then-partner says today) but also for more admirable motives: from a genuine belief that the production was an important work of art and in no sense obscene but also because they were theatre people to their fingertips and believed utterly in that at once hackneyed yet sacred theatrical commandment, which the judge who eventually quashed the charges would himself cite in his final judgement: 'The show must go on.'

The show did go on, or rather the theatre's show went on briefly (but – contrary to subsequent myth – to the end of its advertised run) and then the government's circus took over for a much longer run, before a much larger audience and with much longer-lasting effects for all concerned. And it really was a circus of a kind, complete with unintentional clowning and acrobatics devoid of logic, as well as darker, more shadowy acts. The whole affair became so strange, even by the frequently Kafka-esque standards of Ireland at the time, that it would remain in the public consciousness for decades afterwards, a hardy perennial that would surface again and again in books and articles, feature in radio and television programmes and give rise to a body of often contradictory legend and myth that would in itself fill a book. And it was not only in Ireland that the memory stayed alive – in 1982 the London *Times* noted the 25th anniversary of the arrest. Five years later again the BBC would commission a full-length television script on the case from the writer Hugh Leonard (who as a young man had attended the court case and written about it for *Plays and Players* magazine). The events in the lane and of the courtcase that followed would be mentioned – almost invariably inaccurately – in dozens of books and held up as a classic example of 'the bad old days'. The case would be used over the years, by many whose interest lay in talking up various new, improved Irelands, as an example of how very far the country had progressed, so that nothing similar could happen there nowadays. It would be used to fulfil, for a variety of persons, a variety of not-always-straightforward purposes, but still the story of how it had ever happened remained a mystery. No serious observer may have believed the Government account of the matter; but no more credible story ever emerged. And it was, perhaps, this very mystery that did most to keep the matter alive.

The 1957 arrest took place at number 18a, Herbert Lane, the site of the Pike Theatre Club. The arrested man was Alan Simpson, the noted theatre director who, with his wife Carolyn Swift, had founded the Pike only five years before. By 1957 the theatre, though tiny in size, was already famous as (among other things) the theatre which had discovered Brendan Behan and for its warm relationship with Samuel Beckett (whose *Waiting for Godot* had had its Irish première in the Pike two years earlier). The 'indecent' play – which has lent its name to the entire affair – was Tennessee Williams's *The Rose Tattoo*. The actual facts of that May evening – of how it ever happened in the first place and, more importantly, why – have, since 1957, remained obstinately obscure. The prime movers in the matter – the Irish State – had nothing to add to the charges laid in court and later attempts to raise questions about the matter in the Senate were peremptorily quashed. As the decades passed, so, one by one, many of those most closely associated with the matter died. Still silence reigned. Irish Government files are automatically sealed for 30 years, but the year 1987 passed with no sign of the release of the relevant State papers. So did 1988 and, for that matter, 1989. So did the entire decade of the 1990s.

A selection of Government papers on the *Rose Tattoo* case was finally made public by the Irish State in January 2000, some thirteen years after the due date. Though these papers did seem to offer an explanation of sorts, it was not one that really stood up to scrutiny. The release, however, did prompt Alan Simpson's former wife and business partner, Carolyn Swift – by now elderly and unwell – to make one final attempt to investigate the matter. Her motives were straightforward and perfectly understandable: having dwelt on the case in her own mind for more than 40 years, she simply wanted to understand what had really made an Irish Government effectively destroy her own and her then-husband's lives. It is, one must admit, the sort of thing one might well wonder about. This book is the result of two years' research undertaken by the present writer in collaboration with Ms Swift. This research took the released papers – woefully incomplete though they obviously were – as its starting point. It followed trails found in those papers through the archives of the former archbishop of Dublin,

John Charles McQuaid, by then also open to scrutiny. It was here, among the carefully preserved papers of that extraordinary man, that the story of how the whole affair ever started was finally tracked down. That story, for what it is worth, is told fully here for the first time.

'For what it is worth'? Indeed. For the story of the case's genesis, surprisingly, did little to explain the case itself. When we began our research we thought of it (as we later realised) as that classic type of mystery, the 'whodunit': we believed, almost axiomatically, that discovering how the matter started would bring us to an understanding of why it happened at all, a belief encouraged by the State's obvious reluctance to disclose anything about the case's origins. In the event we were wrong: even a full discovery of how *The Rose Tattoo* came to the Government's attention left the State's decision to act against the Pike as baffling as ever. The *how* of the matter was one thing; the *why*, it turned out, quite another. Quite apart from the decision to take action, the nature of that action was baffling in itself. The case might, legally, have been baseless, as the presiding judge eventually found it to be; but there was nothing frivolous about the way the State pursued it. The Attorney General of the day even threatened – unofficially, through Simpson's legal team – to pursue the accused further no matter what the court decided and bring him to trial under his own steam. If the obscenity accusations were groundless, what threat could a play in a converted coach-house represent to deserve such heavy-handed attempts at repression?

On this subject the released State papers are silent. As so often in the history of the Irish State, the written record fails to tell the whole story, while tantalising hints of hidden conspiracies lack documentary evidence. Documents have been lost or misplaced, while others remain unreleased, and it is certain – for such was most assuredly the custom – that some important but delicate decisions were never recorded on paper in the first place.

This silence on the central question is, of course, a kind of eloquence in itself. This book is, above all, the result of an attempt to answer that single question and to provide a plausible explanation for State behaviour which, viewed with the more informed eyes of the 21st century, appears even more bizarre than it did in 1957. Significant gaps in the available documentation mean that the final theory advanced in these pages must remain speculative, but it is very highly informed speculation, based on an enormous amount of new evidence. It will concentrate on the two most important and baffling aspects of the case – why the State decided to take any move at all against the Pike and why its actions took the bizarre form that they did. The explanation given here may not be 100 per cent correct; but at any rate it fully satisfies Carolyn Swift, who has lived in the shadow of these events for almost 50 years without ever finding a credible explanation for them. As such, it fulfils the author's main objective in taking up the issue.

In the mythology of the *Rose Tattoo* case Alan Simpson has, by some, been canonised as a sort of martyr to free speech. The story told here suggests that this is, in a roundabout way, perfectly true; but in *this* story he – and the Pike Theatre – are more properly seen as martyrs to political expediency. In an almost insulting way they emerge as – to use perhaps the most obscene of all military terms – collateral damage: acceptable casualties among bystanders, incurred in the course of a bigger struggle. This book will suggest that Alan Simpson was, through an unlikely concatenation of circumstances and timing, caught up in something that was not his fight. Like many martyrs before him, he had wandered into the arena without entirely meaning to, only to look up and find himself surrounded by lions. When he realised where he was, it was a living nightmare for him. He had a very great deal to lose and he found himself in confrontation with a State that, once committed to the fight, seemed determined that he should in fact lose every bit of it. But he and his wife fought as best they could, with such weapons as they could muster and among these were a belief (certainly to some degree naïve) in justice and a simple certainty that they would win because they had done nothing wrong. They were obviously not students of Irish history. This book is, among other things, the story of a fight between David and Goliath. As in all the best stories, Goliath loses; but, since this is not a fairy story, the price that David pays is very high – and his victory is most definitely pyrrhic.

PART ONE

THE RIDDLE OF *THE ROSE TATTOO*

'I suppose you could say it was a storm in a teacup. But you have to understand that we all *lived* in a teacup in Ireland then.'
Kate Binchy to the author, June 2001

1. The Good Daughter

Late in 1999 Maureen Simpson, the eldest of Alan Simpson and Carolyn Swift's three daughters, flew into Dublin on a pre-Christmas visit to her mother. Maureen had been living in Britain for many years, but she visited Ireland frequently and, on all of her visits, was used to finding Swift – now in her late seventies – as busy as ever, pursuing one facet or another of the varied career that she had carved out for herself in journalism and the arts since the 1960s. At various times (and often simultaneously) Swift had worked in the drama department of the then Telefís Éireann, as an arts journalist and reviewer of drama and (an old love of hers) dance, as a radio broadcaster and scriptwriter and at enough other things to fill (it seemed to me sometimes) a small telephone book. In the early 1980s she'd played a groundbreaking role in the establishment of Irish-published children's literature. By 1999 this had become a thriving field and in that year Swift had received a special award in recognition of her pioneering part in it. But age and ill health had in recent years taken their toll on Swift and her general worldview hadn't been helped by a run of plain bad luck.[1] All in all, Maureen had sensed a loss of energy in her mother that worried her more than any bad medical news would have done. While this particular visit home wasn't motivated solely by concern, concern was certainly an element of it.

What she found at her mother's home in Leeson Street – the house Swift and Alan Simpson had moved into in the heady days of 1955, when the Pike Theatre had seemed on an unstoppable roll – confirmed Maureen Simpson in her view that there was indeed something to be concerned about. A stranger, or even a friend less intimate with Swift, might have missed the signs, but to Maureen they were unmistakable. For as long as she could recall, her mother had always been working on *something* – always writing, always making plans, always looking to the future. As a single woman bringing up three daughters in 1960s Dublin, after she and Alan Simpson separated, Swift had simply *got on with it*; and she had been just getting on with it ever since. Now though, Swift complained of constant mental and physical tiredness. She lamented the effect age was having on her pin-sharp memory and on her keen mind. And – a downright frightening sign to her daughter – Swift wasn't *writing* anything except for some bread-and-butter reviews. In fact she even spoke of a belief that she would write no more – that her days as an author were done.

Above all Swift seemed concerned with the old Pike days and with the continuing mystery surrounding the theatre's being singled out for the treatment it received. Even during her illness she had continued to act as guardian of the Pike's memory, patiently writing to newspapers (or 'making a bloody nuisance of myself' as she puts it) when the details of the *Rose Tattoo* case were (as invariably happened) misreported, despairing anew each time some supposedly definitive history or theatre book got the most basic facts about the case wrong (*The Irish Times Book of the Century* had just appeared, repeating the same old errors). The Pike Theatre was now a matter of history – it had been closed for almost 40 years and its general archives, as well as its trove of correspondence with Samuel Beckett, had recently been acquired by the library of Trinity College. Yet the root cause of the theatre's premature demise – the roots of the *Rose Tattoo* case – remained a mystery.

Maureen Simpson knew that, physically, her mother was in as good a shape as a recovering cancer-patient in her late seventies had any right to expect. However, Maureen concluded that Swift had begun to believe that the truth of the *Rose Tattoo* case would never emerge. The late 1990s had seen a whole succession of

Swift's long-time friends die. Her own brush with mortality, it seemed to Maureen, had brought her mother face to face with the fact that time would pass and she too would die. There would be no one to correct the misreporting, no little voice to pipe up and wonder what the actual mechanisms had been which resulted in the inexplicable destruction of a bright spark in Irish cultural life. What had happened to the Pike Theatre had been patently unjust and there had been nothing accidental about it. Neither Simpson nor Swift had ever been so naïve as to expect recompense; but they had always presumed that, somewhere along the line, they would at least receive some kind of an explanation. Alan Simpson himself had died in May 1980, a week short of the 23rd anniversary of his arrest; he could never now know the full story of his early dream's destruction. It seemed to Maureen that Swift was convinced the same fate awaited her. The Ireland of 1999 was a slightly less secretive place than that of the 1950s, at least about things that were safely past: but still no information about the *Rose Tattoo* case had emerged.

While the events dealt with in this book were actually occurring, Alan Simpson and Carolyn Swift made superhuman efforts to protect their children from the worst effects of their own ordeal. These efforts had been largely successful and Maureen herself had been a teenager before she began to understand exactly what her parents had gone through during her childhood. Three decades later, she fully understood her mother's abiding interest in the roots of the matter and shared her belief in its importance. Even so it was at first mainly as an effort to spark some activity in Swift that Maureen suggested she should spend time researching the case – surely by now *something* had emerged? There were all sorts of papers available in the National Archives whose release would, even a few years before, have been unthinkable. There were still plenty of people around who recalled the events of those times, and the power of the forces which everyone assumed had been behind the case had waned somewhat: surely *something* could be discovered now, at the dawn of the 21st century? Swift demurred: she just didn't have the energy any more, she said, to pursue the matter. She'd always kept a close eye on newspaper reports of the Government papers released annually to the National Archives. Nothing about *The Rose Tattoo* had ever been among them. And she was just too *tired* to go trawling through archives in search of stray references that were unlikely to tell her anything useful.

But Maureen Simpson was the product not only of her mother's own pigheadedness, but of her father's too: she was, if anything, even more stubborn than Swift herself. Why, she asked, could Swift not *share* the work? There must be lots of people who'd like the opportunity of working with her: wasn't there anyone she herself would like to work with? After much probing, Swift could think of only one, a younger author she'd become friends with over the past couple of years and who'd shown great interest in her Pike days. That author was myself, then just out of my thirties and thus far too young to actually remember Swift as a theatre owner, though I knew of the important part she and Alan Simpson had played in Brendan Behan's career. Like all of my generation in Ireland, however, my own first experience of Carolyn Swift (though of course I hadn't known it at the time) had been through her work on the television series *Wanderly Wagon.* When I'd first visited her home and been shown her archives, my attention had not focused on the Beckett or Behan material at all but had been drawn straight to the neatly filed shelf of scripts in which O'Brien, Judge, Rory and Godmother still had the adventures that I – and every other person of my age in Ireland – had followed as a child. Swift and I had spent long hours discussing those days in her life, as well as just about everything else. Her multifaceted career, and her work itself, fascinated me and our friendship had grown to the point where she was due to spend that coming Christmas with my family. She admired my writing, but our friendship was first and foremost a personal one. But, she warned her daughter, the idea of asking me to help was a nonstarter: between my family and my burgeoning writing career, I was a very busy man. I couldn't be expected to take time out to help her on what she was sure would be a wild-goose chase. No amount of persuasion by Maureen could persuade her otherwise: the matter was not to be mentioned to me, period.

Maureen Simpson is a dutiful daughter; but she is, again, her parents' child: on her return to London she immediately got in touch with me and recounted her discussions with her mother. As she'd more or less expected, I jumped at the idea of working in any capacity with Swift. My fourth book in four years had just been published and I was looking for a project that would involve a complete change. The prospect of spending a few months help-ing someone I liked and admired so much to research a subject that meant a great deal to her was a very attractive one. Then too, the whole story of *The Rose Tattoo* had come to fascinate me also. It seemed a classic product of that period which I had come to think of as 'Holy Catholic Ireland' – that factory of mysteries and grievances, the tail end of which I had been born in. In the course of many years of reading about Irish history, I had always tended to avoid going into that period in any great depth. Its manifest hypocrisies were too blatant; the gulf between its public pieties and private squalor was too great. I had seen too much of its humbug as a child to have any great respect for it and known too many of its seemingly endless victims to think it would make for comfortable investigation. Throughout the 1990s the stories of some of the period's more ordinary secrets had gradually begun to emerge: nothing revealed by an investigation of the *Rose Tattoo* case could possibly be as cruel or as twisted as some of the facts which had already come to light – even assuming any new infor-mation about the case could be discovered at all. For I had already learned most of the known details of the matter from Swift herself: to the eyes of a generation which had grown up with Watergate the whole thing stank purely and simply of politics, which meant that the truth of the matter was likely to be buried somewhere very deep indeed. Still, the idea of working with Carolyn Swift was attractive: apart from anything else there was something very *neat* in the idea of working as an adult with somebody one had admired (albeit sometimes unknowingly) since childhood.

When Swift heard what her daughter had done, she was both pleased and angry. My own obvious pleasure at the prospect of working with her, though, soon mollified the anger. During her Christmas visit we discussed the matter and tried to plan a course of action. Although she felt it would be useless to search in the National Archives, it still seemed the only sensible place to begin. And since the Catholic Church and its lay allies must be presumed to have had *some* hand in the matter – censorship of all kinds was, after all, one of their major concerns – a second and perhaps more likely avenue of research also suggested itself. This was the enormous archive of the former Catholic Archbishop of Dublin, John Charles McQuaid, a man whose endless energy and interventionist drive had made his very surname a sort of shorthand for that entire period. Whatever we might find in the National Archives, it went without saying that anything therein would have gone through a long vetting process before it was released; McQuaid's vast trove of papers, which had been made available as they stood, seemed much more likely to contain any potential revelations. Swift and I parted that Christmas with plans made to visit both archives as soon as the millennium celebrations ended and life returned to normal in the city.

As it happened, the 'normality' to which that life returned would, for our search, be quite a new one: on Tuesday, January 4th 2000, as I sat reading Alan Simpson's own description of the *Rose Tattoo* case, I had a phone call from my wife. On a break from work, she had turned on her car radio and heard Carolyn Swift being interviewed. 'It's something to do with *The Rose Tattoo*,' my wife told me. 'The Government released some files or something.'

The Government had indeed done exactly that: over four decades after the event, the Irish State had finally seen fit to release to the National Archives of Ireland a part of the file relating to the arrest and attempted prosecution of Alan Simpson. Among other documents allowed into the public domain were files on the Irish Government's reaction to the outbreak of the Northern Troubles. It says a great deal for the longevity of public interest in the *Rose Tattoo* case that, even though vying for attention with such major historical documents, the papers on Simpson's arrest received a great deal of publicity – not least on RTÉ radio, where the matter featured for three days running on the highly popular *Joe Duffy Show*. Callers and interviewees (including Swift herself) rehashed the events of the time and at least one caller – the widow of one of the police witnesses – still insisted, all these decades later and in spite of what the District Court had found, that the play had been *filthy*.

In the immediate aftermath of the release it was difficult to know whether the emergence of the papers had been a providential aid to our planned investigation or had simply done away with all need for it. Newspaper accounts of the file's contents were quite clear on one point: the papers revealed, all the reports said, that the Government of the day had acted out of fear of a public statement on *The Rose Tattoo*, condemning the lack of State action against it, from Archbishop McQuaid. This notion accorded very well with the mythology and with suggestions that had been made many times since 1957. Yet to anyone even vaguely familiar with the realities of Church–State relations in the period, it seemed, even then, an odd explanation for the events of 1957. The Government which pursued Alan Simpson was the last led by Eamon de Valera, a figure who jigged to nobody's whistle – least of all, as McQuaid knew to his chagrin, the Archbishop of Dublin's. And though many down the decades had indeed pointed the finger at McQuaid as the ultimate author of Alan Simpson's woes, none had had anything more than suspicion to go on.

As it happened, Swift herself had always defended McQuaid against such charges. Her belief in his non-involvement was based on an incident reported to her by the late Dr Rory O'Hanlon, whose father was a close friend of the Archbishop's. O'Hanlon junior, then a young man, had actually called on McQuaid to deliver a message from his father on the very day of Alan Simpson's first court appearance – quite possibly while Simpson was actually in court. He'd found the Archbishop reading the newspaper reports of Simpson's arrest. Flinging down the papers, McQuaid bitterly announced his certainty that he would be credited with the police actions, which – he assured O'Hanlon – he'd known nothing about until reading the newspapers. The implication was also clear that, until then, the Archbishop had never even heard of *The Rose Tattoo*. McQuaid, Swift maintained, might have been a master of sophistry, casuistry and half-truths; but he was not, she was convinced, an actual liar.

Swift, almost unable to believe that her dearest wish had seemingly come true, had already made a visit to the Archives to see the papers. She'd been accompanied then – in a manner that even now seems extremely historically apt – by Katy Simpson, Alan Simpson's eldest daughter from his second marriage. They had gone through the released file, but, while there were many surprises there still, the papers had seemed to say just what the media reports suggested – that the real cause of the State's actions against the Pike had been fear of Archbishop McQuaid. In the end there seemed only one thing for it: Swift and I would return to the National Archives and examine the released papers in detail. This was a fateful decision. It would lead not to the few months of research I had imagined but to two years of haunting libraries and archives, reading endless old documents, clippings and books and to our becoming far more familiar than we ever wanted to be with the thought processes of both 1950s Irish politicians and their Catholic Right contemporaries. Maureen Simpson's original idea, though it succeeded, was very quickly forgotten as we – a small, fat, bespectacled female Holmes and her equally small, fat and bespectacled male Watson – picked our way through the tangled undergrowth of those thankfully departed times. And, since writing things down is my personal way of trying to understand them, I began to write about what we found. This book is the ultimate result of that writing. It recounts the story – the stories, rather – we uncovered and the conclusions that we reached. For we did reach conclusions, though whether the theory we arrived at is 'the' truth or not I cannot know. We found no documentary evidence for it: indeed had we done so it would indicate extreme laxness on somebody's part. This is not to say that such evidence does not exist, only that it is not in the public domain. For the file released by the State on the *Rose Tattoo* case is, even on internal evidence, pitifully incomplete; though we found shocking documents aplenty, none explicitly made the connection we believe provides the only sane explanation for the behaviour of the State in 1957.

This book begins with the first ever full and in-depth account of the events of the *Rose Tattoo* case itself, devoid of myth and based on contemporary records as well as the separate accounts given in their respective books by Alan Simpson and Carolyn Swift. It is a striking story in itself and it is hoped that, now that the actual details are in print, it will end at least some of the mis-reporting which Swift has been at such pains to correct over the years. The book next examines the papers released by the State in January 2000 and attempts to work out what they actually say – as distinct from what they only seem to say. Following this it moves to matters unearthed in what will be, for many years to come, the mother lode for those researching Church–State relations in mid-twentieth-century Ireland: not the National Archives of Ireland, but the McQuaid Papers in the archives of the Catholic Archdiocese of Dublin. For much of the book we move away from the Pike Theatre completely: something which seems entirely appropriate since (however strange it may seem) the genesis of the *Rose Tattoo* affair would seem to have had remarkably little to do with the Pike or with theatre at all. Much of this part of the book will deal with what is on the face of it another censorship issue entirely – a crisis which involved very serious players indeed in Holy

33

Catholic Ireland and dirty linen which had the potential to undermine the credibility of the then Irish State itself.

A critical part of this other, largely unknown and never fully explored crisis overlaps – with quite uncanny precision – the central events of the *Rose Tattoo* affair. On the Government side, a startling number of its central figures also figure prominently in the released *Rose Tattoo* papers; while opposing them were some of the most influential people in the Ireland of the day – including literally all of the forces which have, at one time or another, been held responsible for the pursuit of Alan Simpson. It is quite a remarkable story.

The book will end by returning to May 1957 and recasting the story of the *Rose Tattoo* case in the light of our new discoveries, offering something that has never previously been available: a plausible explanation of not only why the State moved against the Pike Theatre in the first place but of why those moves took the form that they did. In its thirteen months in court the *Rose Tattoo* case took on something of a life of its own and touched on many matters which the State never intended it to go near. It is not our intention to go into all of these, though it will be both instructive and even necessary to touch on a few; but for the most part we will concentrate on what we have identified as the one central question of the entire case – how on earth Alan Simpson came to find himself, on the morning of May 24th 1957, in the dock of a Dublin court, facing an unheard-of indecency charge brought by an Irish Government with little publicly stated interest in censorship, following an arrest which would have been more appropriate for an armed criminal.

2. Genesis

The distinguished critic Brian Fallon, writing of Irish theatre in the 1950s,[1] has this to say of our book's theatrical subject:

> Undoubtedly, most of the laurels for the decade belong to the gallant little Pike: for its staging of Behan's masterpiece, for mounting Beckett's *Waiting for Godot* the following year and for its 1957 performance of Tennessee Williams's *The Rose Tattoo* which led to the actors appearing in court under a police prosecution for indecency.

Lionel Pilkington, meanwhile, in his more recent *Theatre and the State in Twentieth Century Ireland*, recounts how Alan Simpson was arrested and charged 'following an anonymous complaint from a member of the public concerning the alleged dropping of a contraceptive on stage'.[2]

These quotations, with their mixture of undoubted fact and basic error, typify the state of knowledge about the Pike Theatre even in supposedly informed circles in Ireland. Pilkington even repeats as fact the two most frequently heard errors – that there had been a complaint about the show and that a condom was, at least allegedly, dropped on stage. Both errors stem from a 1972 interview with Anna Manahan – no complainant, anonymous or otherwise, was ever mentioned as having gone to the police about *The Rose Tattoo* and nothing was dropped on the stage of the Pike during its production.

The errors, however (as these quotes would appear to indicate), seem ineradicable and crop up again with each new publication that mentions the Pike. The catastrophe that was the *Rose Tattoo* case has been swaddled in rumour, myth and misinformation and this misinformation has been perpetuated and become accepted as fact. If nothing else, it is hoped that the present book will finally dispel at least the worst of these myths.

In early 1957, the point at which its catastrophe befell it, the Pike Theatre was widely regarded as one of the most significant outposts of modern culture in Ireland. Admittedly Ireland at the time was not overburdened with such outposts and since many powerful forces in the country both disliked and mistrusted modern culture, there were certain risks attendant even on cultural involvement, never mind prominence. It is difficult now, when the arts are accorded a place of pride by the State, to appreciate their status (or lack of it) in Ireland for decades after independence.[3] Reading – at least of literature – was a decidedly minority interest. Theatre, however, especially in the post-war years, had a much more significant role. In an age without television, in a country where printed matter (newspapers and magazines as well as books) was subject to a censorship whose strictures – particularly in the early 1950s – were an international byword for excess, theatre provided Irish audiences with a rare window on a wider world which was everywhere in social and cultural ferment. One has only to read the theatre reviews and articles of the time to become aware that a large number of ordinary Irish people, officially cut off from the mainstream of modern thought and hungry to experience its fruits, saw theatre in precisely this way; and one has only to count the articles devoted to drama and read even a few of them to realise how just seriously theatre was taken.

The theatre-going public in Dublin was, in spite of the attractions of cinema (also, of course, censored), simply enormous by modern-day standards. Most, naturally, sought entertainment; but many sought something more. At the same time powerful forces – most notably the Church and its teeming lay agents and auxiliaries – had spent over 30 years in a largely successful attempt to keep dangerous modern ideas out of Ireland,[4] and many of the notions and world-views encountered in the post-war arts, and particularly in the convulsively changing world of 1950s theatre, were especially offensive to them. Precisely because theatre was not officially censored, it was an object of particular interest to some of these forces. This was, in Ireland, the golden age of what Seán Ó Faoláin has usefully termed the 'lay cleric' and one of the concerns of such lay clerics – in organisations such as the fretful and sometimes half-crazy Irish League of Decency, the frankly sectarian and seriously disturbing Maria Duce and the socially prestigious and Church-approved Knights of Columbanus – was to keep a close eye on what went on in Dublin theatres, either overtly or through one of the front-organisations which the Knights of Columbanus in particular were wont to found. The Knights were closely linked to the authoritarian Catholic Archbishop John Charles McQuaid, but though McQuaid's interest in censorship was close and of long standing he seems to have been surprisingly disinterested in theatre censorship himself.[5] Nor were some organisations content merely to monitor individual suspect works: calls for the introduction of a general theatre censorship were constant throughout the decade, while complaints to the police about particular theatrical performances were common (if seemingly invariably fobbed off) and organised demonstrations both inside and on the streets outside theatres were a hazard faced by all but the most respectable institutions. Indeed, that respectability often depended precisely on their avoidance of controversial productions.

Since objection could be taken to things that even at the time seemed highly unlikely to the average punter, this situation made for a somewhat timorous attitude in some Irish theatrical circles. It was not simply plays, which even today are regarded as slightly risqué, which attracted the attention of the amateur censors: the musical *Guys and Dolls*, for instance, provoked widespread protests against its 'irreligion', while the anti-Communism which the Church shared with McCarthyite America[6] led Maria Duce to stage what amounted to mini-riots in protest against visits to Dublin by such arch-Communists as Orson Welles, Danny Kaye and the harmonica-player Larry Adler.

For the most part, however, the eyes of the righteous found little worth truly fretting about. In the early part of the century Ireland had developed a world-wide reputation for great theatre, thanks largely to the work of Yeats's Abbey Theatre and, in the 1930s, the modernist brilliance of MacLíammóir and Hilton Edwards at the Gate. But the Abbey, once the jewel in Ireland's cultural crown, had since the death of Yeats settled into somnolence under the directorship of the dour northerner, Ernest Blythe, an impeccably Establishment figure. Artistically the great creation of the Literary Revival had fallen on lean times and (at Blythe's insistence) paid far more attention to people's ability to speak Irish than their ability to write, act or direct actual plays.[7] The theatre survived largely on a diet of Synge and O'Casey revivals (reduced after 30-odd years to comfortable familiars) and much-derided Irish-language pantomimes rather than developing any challenging new talent. It would be hard to imagine it now as a home for cutting-edge drama and hard to imagine Blythe as the sort of person who would either stage the modern-day equivalents of O'Casey and Synge, as Yeats had, or – again like Yeats – stand up to the baying mobs of religious or nationalistic bigots who had rioted over *The Plough and the Stars* and *The Playboy of the Western World*. Even the Abbey's productions of classic 'Abbey' plays were, many said disgustedly, mere travesties: in 1946 the highly regarded poet Valentin Iremonger had, with fellow writer Roger McHugh, staged a walkout during an Abbey performance of *The Plough and the Stars* after publicly protesting against what he saw as the risible production on offer. Addressing the audience before he walked out, Iremonger said:

> When the poet Yeats died, he left behind him to the Irish nation as a legacy his beloved Abbey Theatre, then the first theatre in the world in acting, in production and in the poetic impulse of its

tradition. Today, eight years after, under the utter incompetence of the present directorate's artistic policy, there's nothing left of that fine glory.[8]

Many at the time felt that Iremonger had let the Abbey off lightly. By the early Fifties, however, things had worsened. Eric Bentley, writing of the theatre in *Poetry Magazine*, spoke for many who had swallowed the myth of Abbey greatness:

> What a comedown for the visitor to Dublin to see performances that would scarcely pass muster in a German *Stadttheater*! He feels himself the victim of a hoax, a gigantic hoax that has been written into the history books and engraved in the general mind.[9]

When the Abbey burned down in 1951, it was popularly joked that the fire was the first flame of any kind to light the place up for many years. The theatre's move to a temporary home in the Queens Theatre saw no improvement. Whatever the merits or otherwise of its revivals, real cutting-edge theatre had long passed from the Abbey's grasp and even to some extent from that of its still-occasionally-glittering rival, the Gate Theatre, where differences between the Edwards/MacLíammóir camp and Lord Edward Longford had led to the outright split which saw two completely separate companies using the same theatre. Longford Productions had a taste for the light and classical and tried to meet its costs by renting out the Gate (itself physically crumbling) to other companies. MacLíammóir and Edwards depended largely on foreign tours for their survival, while at home they perpetually teetered on the verge of bankruptcy and were kept afloat by the tireless efforts of Terence de Vere White, who on more than one occasion literally kept the bailiffs from their door. Neither of the Gate's companies was deemed worthy of government support, which was concentrated on a grudging grant given to the Abbey and (more understandably in terms of then-current pieties) to Galway's Irish-language Taidhbhearc theatre.[10]

In the decade after the Second World War, progressive theatre in Dublin lay mainly in hands other than those of the big guns of former times. Such thought-provoking drama as an idea-hungry public could locate was to be found on what would nowadays be called the theatrical fringe,[11] in a variety of small, cash-strapped and often impermanent theatres which owed their existence to the frustration felt by some theatre people with the blandness and lack of opportunity prevalent in established theatrical circles.

The small theatres of mid-century Dublin – theatres such as the Studio Theatre Club run by Madame Bannard Cogley in Mount Street, Barry Cassin's and Nora Lever's 37 Theatre Club in Baggot Street and Godfrey Quigley's Globe Theatre Club in Dún Laoghaire – are largely forgotten in Ireland now outside (and increasingly even inside) theatrical circles. Poor, impermanent, confined by the absence both of money and of suitable buildings to whatever work-spaces they could find, the little theatres were worked in by actors who lived hand to mouth or supported themselves elsewhere and often acted for no greater reward than the opportunity for self-expression it gave them. Failing artistically perhaps as often as they succeeded and frequently disappearing whether they failed or not, such theatres walked a fine line between existence and non-existence, liable – if they honestly reflected what was being written in the world outside and what a growing number of Irish people wished to see and hear discussed – to find themselves the object of scrutiny by a Catholic Church for which the world beyond Ireland was a dangerous place. Even their legal status was dubious and most called themselves 'clubs' to avoid the necessity of applying to the Government for a theatre licence which they could ill-afford and in all probability would not get. Yet for many actors the little theatres of Dublin represented a first opportunity to practise their art and their craft and many who first learned their stagecraft in a small Dublin theatre, with makeshift scenery on a rudimentary stage, went on to distinguished international careers.

In 1957 it seemed that the work done by the little theatres of

Dublin was finally to receive some official recognition. It was announced that an international theatre festival was to be held in Dublin as part of An Tóstal, the national 'Springtime Festival'. An Tóstal, inaugurated in 1953, had been founded with the hope of attracting foreign (specifically Irish-American) visitors and their money to Ireland and was one of the Irish State's experiments in the new post-war field of mass tourism. From its inception An Tóstal had attracted much derision in Ireland itself, not least because few people saw much to celebrate about the country. The proposed theatre festival was an attempt to give some cultural clout to an occasion which had previously been better typified by religious processions, sporting events and – in general – activities which might have well graced a County Fair but seemed bathetic as the backbone of a national festival.

Eight theatres had been chosen for inclusion in the Dublin Theatre Festival and two of these were leading lights among the little theatres. One – Dún Laoghaire's Globe Theatre Club, run by Godfrey Quigley – had even ventured close to a good old-fashioned Irish theatrical controversy the year before, when its production of *I Am a Camera*[12] had led to walk-outs and complaints to the police. The other small theatre included on the festival bill was a remarkable 'pocket' theatre which had rapidly established itself as a cultural powerhouse and was already attracting a great deal of foreign attention: the Pike.

3. Progress

The Pike Theatre Club, run by the husband-and-wife team of Alan Simpson and Carolyn Swift, joined the ranks of small theatres in Dublin in 1953. Simpson, the son of a Protestant clergyman, was a captain in the Irish Army Engineers and had been involved in theatre since his college days; Swift, London-born daughter of a Jewish businessman, had first been brought to Ireland by one of the grandest grand old men of Irish theatre, the brilliant, irascible (and now almost semi-legendary) apostle of the touring theatrical company, Anew McMaster. Swift and Simpson had met in 1946 at the Gate Theatre, which McMaster was using at the invitation of his brother-in-law, Micheál MacLíammóir. After their marriage, Simpson and Swift drifted through the bohemian Dublin arts scene nostalgically immortalised in any number of memoirs of the period, dreaming of producing the sort of adventurous plays they wanted to mount and which they were convinced would be a success in Dublin. Simpson's full-time army career kept him busy, while Swift had her hands full raising three daughters, although both did theatre work whenever they could.

As with everyone else interested in modern drama in Ireland, Swift and Simpson found opportunities for such involvement few and far between. Apart from the need to keep a wary eye on the various Catholic vigilantes, who in their turn kept a suspicious watch on goings-on in the arts, the chronic problem for anyone wishing to present new drama in Ireland was the lack of a suitable venue. For all their energy, theatres such as the 37 Theatre Club were forced to mount their performances in ordinary rooms in various houses, without any of the theatrical machinery available to purpose-built theatres. Alan Simpson, a director with very definite ideas of what he wanted to do on the stage, insisted that someday he would have this and more.

Sometime in the very early 1950s, at first as a joke, Simpson came up with an idea of how he and Swift might achieve this end: they'd build their own theatre. It seemed not so much a dream as a delusion. With his army pay, Simpson was more solvent than many denizens of the sub-world to which official indifference condemned the arts but, then as now, an army captain's pay hardly ran to theatre building. No financial institution would lend money for such a dubious project at the best of times; in the dark economic days of 1952 in Ireland, the very idea must have sounded insane. Simpson, however, had skills beyond those of stage-manager and director, namely his engineering qualifications and – perhaps most important of all – the cunning which anyone working in the hand-to-mouth Irish arts world had to learn in order to survive. After a six-month search he and Swift found and bought an old, broken-down coach-house at 18a Herbert Lane, off Baggot Street near the Grand Canal. Months of backbreaking work, assisted by friends and Simpson's army colleagues and using materials begged, borrowed or downright stolen from a variety of unlikely sources, transformed the unprepossessing wreck into something that, when it opened as the Pike Theatre Club in September 1953, completely charmed Dublin's theatre critics. R. M. Fox, writing in the *Evening Mail*, spoke warmly of the delights awaiting future audiences at the new theatre:

> They will be entering a theatre quite unlike anything with which they are familiar. Dublin's latest Little Theatre … the newest in point of time but the oldest in atmosphere, is a cameo of the late Regency and early Victorian theatre. It is, in fact, the spirit of the theatre personified. It has the red plush (or what looks like it) of tradition and the indispensable complement of red plush – gilt. The gilt is on charming period wall-brackets and on the lighting

in the auditorium, for electricity has been subdued to the convo-
lutions of the ancient chandelier and even persuaded to emerge in
the shape of a candle flame.[1]

The prettiness of the theatre – as well as its minuscule size –
would often be mentioned in future writing about the Pike.
Though Simpson would go on to more celebrated triumphs, the
Pike Theatre itself was in a real sense his first great display of the
stage-manager's power to deceive. Its plush seating was cobbled
together from dumped tram seats and Dunlopillo and covered in
canvas which had started life as army latrine covers; much of the
material used in both costumes and hangings had been converted
by Carolyn Swift from old curtains begged from well-wishers; the
reflectors forming a vital part of the Pike's elaborate lighting system had been hammered from empty biscuit tins by a moonlight-
ing army sergeant. In a real sense the entire Pike was, like the
backdrops later designed for its tiny ten-square-foot stage by
Pauline Bewick, a stage set. Like any such set its purpose was to
direct attention to what was happening on the stage itself; and it
was the events on that tiny stage, where Alan Simpson finally
came into his own as a director, that would make the Pike famous.

Between 1953 and 1957, as the Irish economy foundered and
the country's population drain grew to terrifying proportions, the
Pike Theatre mounted a string of productions which spread its
fame first nationally and then internationally. Its first really big hit
wasn't a play at all but a revue show – *The Follies of Herbert Lane*,
which opened in the winter of 1953. Downright daringly, in the
context of the time and place, the *Follies* introduced to Dublin – a
city which basically shut up shop at eleven o'clock every night –
the continental concept of late-night revue (the fact that the show
would run till after midnight was one of the main points of advance press interest) coupled with biting satirical cabaret of a type
which Ireland had never seen before. The show was an immediate
hit, not least because delighted Irish audiences were completely

unused to witnessing direct public jeering of Establishment sacred cows, such as in the *Follies*,[2] written largely by Swift. Public utterance in Ireland then was above all careful: they might jeer the same things among themselves in private, but it was unheard of to see them wittily derided in public. Audiences lapped it up. The revue ran to packed houses and ecstatic reviews for four solid months; its success spawned a series of sequels which became a Pike tradition and remained, for at least a couple of years, the thing for which the theatre was best known. But Simpson and Swift were just getting started and their ambitions, for that time and place, were enormous.

Though the Pike had impressed journalists and punters alike, Simpson and Swift had always seen it as no more than the best they could do with their limited resources and a stepping-stone to bigger things. The question of packed houses leads immediately to the Pike's central difficulty – its tiny size. Since this would play a small but influential part in the events of 1957, it bears comment here. When one speaks of a 'packed house' at the Pike, one is still speaking of very small audiences indeed. The Dunlopillo seats might, in those austere days, have struck some observers as the last word in luxury but, as became clear right from the theatre's opening night,[3] there were never enough of them. The little coachhouse, however tarted up, could squeeze in no more than perhaps 65 paying audience members, including those standing. This meant that even the most popular play at the Pike – especially if it had a large cast – always risked losing money. A maddening feature of the theatre's biggest commercial successes was the stream of disappointed would-be punters who had to be turned away at the makeshift box office – in actuality a shed at 6 Herbert Lane, across the street from the Pike, which the ticket sellers shared with Dolly, the pony owned by local carter Ned Doyle.[4]

The space problem never went away and attempts to overcome it form a leitmotif running through the Pike's entire lifetime. Behind the on-stage dramas would always lie the ongoing struggle to reach larger audiences, a search which increasingly led Simpson and Swift to stage outside productions in bigger theatres and, in the case of their 1956 Irish première of *Waiting for Godot*, to take the extraordinary step of bringing that totem of the European avant-garde on a highly successful (and frequently surreal) tour of Irish provincial towns. It would be precisely an attempt to gain bigger audiences for a hit play which led Simpson and Swift to plan, in May 1957, on transferring their production of Tennessee Williams's *The Rose Tattoo* to the Gate when the play's hit Theatre Festival run ended. And it would, quite specifically, be the Government's decision to prevent this transfer that led to the beginning of the *Rose Tattoo* case.

As a commercial theatre dedicated to artistic principles the Pike had its failures as well as its successes, but even some of its commercial misfires – such as the first ever English-language production of a Ionesco play in 1956 – were artistic landmarks which placed Ireland on Europe's cultural map and were seen as so doing within and outside Ireland. It was not for failures on any level, however, that the Pike was mainly known. While the *Follies* rapidly established itself as a Dublin institution,[5] the theatre soon afterwards demonstrated its commitment to straight, challenging modern drama by staging *Summer and Smoke*, the first-ever performance in Ireland of a play by Tennessee Williams, then internationally regarded as one of the world's major playwrights. This successful 1954 run was completely overshadowed, however, by the production which followed it in Herbert Lane: the world première, in November 1954, of Brendan Behan's *The Quare Fellow*, which Simpson and Swift rescued after the play had been comprehensively rejected by both the Abbey and the Gate. Retitled by Simpson and revised and edited by Swift,[6] *The Quare Fellow* was a huge success in Dublin and launched Behan's international career.

The following year the Pike's status was solidly cemented when, after a pursuit lasting almost three years, it finally managed to stage the first Irish production of Samuel Beckett's *Waiting for*

Godot, a production which ended up becoming one of the longest-running shows mounted in Ireland up to that time and which pleased Beckett (with whom a warm relationship developed) enormously. It was Beckett (referred to by Quidnunc in the *Irish Times* as the Pike's 'honorary Paris liaison officer')[7] who steered Swift and Simpson towards Ionesco, and the Pike's production of *The Bald Prima Donna*, though a commercial disaster with baffled Dublin audiences, attracted the attention of senior British critics such as Claude Cockburn, who would become a firm friend of the Pike and a much-needed supporter during its coming tribulation. Beckett had also been instrumental in securing the rights of Jean-Paul Sartre's *Nekrassov* (which Simpson staged at the Gate), while another Sartre play, the anti-racist *The Respectable Prostitute*, gave the Pike yet another commercial success in 1956.

1957 dawned with the Pike on a seemingly unstoppable roll. The successes of the previous year had, even taking into account the theatre's tiny size, added considerably to its finances as well as its reputation. This was vital for Simpson's and Swift's long-term plans, which involved a transfer to much larger and more centrally located premises in Fownes Street, in what is now Temple Bar. They had been working towards such a move from the outset and architect's plans for converting the building they'd chosen into a 300-seat theatre had already been drawn up. The September 1956 number of the *Pike Newsletter*, regularly issued to Pike Theatre Club members, had announced the launch of a building fund to which there had already been a good response. Less than five years after opening, the Pike seemed on the brink of theatrical bigtime. The latest edition of the *Follies* – *Say It With Follies*, launched on New Year's Eve – was the series' greatest critical and commercial success yet and would run to packed houses until the summer. And the best – it seemed – was yet to come: 1957 saw the Pike receive a seal of official approval from the State when it was announced that the theatre had been chosen for inclusion in the official Theatre Festival. On a more practical level, Theatre Festival productions were to be backed by a financial indemnity against loss: with such backing, both Simpson and Swift felt that the Pike couldn't fail.

Originally Alan Simpson had hoped to produce the English-language première of Samuel Beckett's second play, *Fin de Partie,* as the Pike's festival contribution. But Beckett was still working on the translation of the play and when it became obvious that this would not be finished in time Simpson and Swift turned instead to another they'd longed to produce for several years. It's a measure of the confidence inspired by the government indemnity that this was the sort of large-scale production which Simpson loved working on but which, after a near-disastrous financial experience with *The Quare Fellow,*[8] he and Swift had reluctantly decided to abandon as potentially ruinous for the Pike. They'd been scrimping and saving for years as they tried to build up money for the planned new theatre: one of the greatest benefits even of *Waiting for Godot,* from a cost point of view, had been the small size of its cast. The Festival indemnity offered them a chance to pull out all the stops and show just what the Pike could do. For the first Dublin Theatre Festival, they would produce a major work by an international playwright, with a cast bigger than any they'd used since *The Quare Fellow*: they would stage Tennessee Williams's *The Rose Tattoo.*

4. Omens

Simpson and Swift had first seen *The Rose Tattoo* in a French production several years before. They'd been struck at the time by the appeal they were sure it would have for Irish audiences.[1] The *Rose Tattoo* tells the story of Serafina Delle Rose, an Italian-American widow whose obsession with the idealised memory of her dead husband has made her turn her back on life and love in the real world. Serafina's refusal to allow her daughter Rosa to grow up threatens to destroy their family, especially when Rosa falls in love with a naïve young sailor, Jack Hunter. Serafina's mistrust of Hunter's intentions – she is convinced he is interested only in sex – completely alienates her daughter. Serafina herself is reluctantly attracted to a newcomer in town, the amiable Alvaro Mangiacavallo, but her idealised memory of her husband stands between her and a chance at regaining happiness. The climax of the play comes when she is forced to confront the fact which (it is suggested) she has always subconsciously known: that her husband was not the cherished figure of memory but an unfaithful low life who was carrying on with a card-dealer at the local roadhouse. Traumatised by this, Serafina re-emerges into the world freed of the lies that have been paralysing her ability to live and love.

For the Theatre Festival production of *The Rose Tattoo* the Pike assembled a sterling cast. Alvaro Mangiacavallo was played by Pike regular Pat Nolan, Jack Hunter by Brian Phelan. The vital role of Rosa, Serafina's daughter, was played by Kate Binchy, the 19-year-old daughter of a Circuit Court judge, whose youth, combined with an acting ability which would astonish critics, made her perfect for the difficult part of the 15-year-old Rosa. For the central and absolutely vital role of Serafina, Simpson and Swift had only one actress in mind: Anna Manahan, whom they'd known since 1949 and who had taken part in several previous Pike productions. Manahan was then a highly respected character actress who'd worked with the Gate and the Globe, but Simpson and Swift were convinced she had the makings of a great leading actress of international calibre. From the first time they saw *The Rose Tattoo* in France they'd been convinced that the role of Serafina would be a powerhouse vehicle for her talents and could provide a major career breakthrough for her. As Manahan herself has always been first to admit, they proved to be perfectly right: her part in *The Rose Tattoo* would give her a chance to show exactly what she could do and would unlock the door to international celebrity.

Taking care of business, Simpson visited Lord Longford at the Gate and arranged to transfer the play to the larger theatre for an extra week at the end of what he was certain would be a successful festival run. The Gate's experiences with previous Pike productions – Sartre's *Nekrassov*, the comedy *The Little Hut* and even a week of *Godot* – had proved beneficial to both camps and Longford was delighted to oblige this time too. The Gate Theatre building itself had been found wanting by safety inspectors and was to close after the festival for major repairs. Longford, who'd been supporting the Gate financially out of his own pocket for almost 20 years, had put himself in debt and walked the streets of Dublin with a collection box to raise money for the work. A successful run that didn't involve production costs for himself would provide a welcome addition to his own fund. The Pike's week would begin once MacLíammóir and Edwards's Theatre Festival production of *The Old Lady Says No* ended. With each full house at the Gate being the equivalent, in terms of audience capacity, of a fortnight's worth of packed houses in Herbert Lane, a week there with a hit play would also bring the Pike's own new theatre measurably closer.

Rehearsals for *The Rose Tattoo* began on April 30th, the day after the 100th performance of *Say It With Follies*, which was still
packing them in after four full months. From the first there was
only one thing in the Williams play that posed a real (if entirely
non-theatrical) problem. This was a stage direction in Act Three,
when Alvaro, the leading male in a play populated mainly by fe-
males, is described as accidentally dropping 'a small cellophane-
wrapped disk' from his pocket onto the floor. Although the object
is never named, it is obvious that what he has dropped is a condom. Fearing that his intentions will be mistaken (or, for that
matter, correctly perceived) Alvaro quickly kicks the condom under a sofa but is too late to avoid Serafina noticing it.

Serafina's reaction to the sight is everything that a Catholic
bishop could hope for: she turns on Alvaro in a fury, informs him
that '*Io, non sono puttana*'[2] and tells him to leave immediately. The
scene is critical since it initiates a sequence of events leading to
Serafina's telephone confrontation with her cheating husband's
former mistress and to her realisation that the women who had
earlier revealed the affair to her had not (as she'd insisted on
thinking) been maliciously lying.

There was no question of Alvaro's kicking a condom – or anything else – under a sofa on the stage of the Pike, because there
wasn't room for a sofa on the stage. As it happened, however,
there was just as little question of the condom's being kicked under the chair that would replace the sofa in the Pike production.
Ultimately the Pike's problem didn't stem from the condom: what
it stemmed from was the time and place of the play's staging. In
the Ireland of 1957 condoms were exotic items. The sale of contraceptives was strictly illegal and the exact problem faced by the
Pike was how to stage the scene in any sensible way without one.

Finding what one is tempted to call a black market condom
was out of the question: the mere production of such an item on a
public stage would call the immediate wrath of both Church and
State down on the theatre concerned. Besides, the management of

the Pike didn't have the slightest idea of how they might lay hands on a condom in Dublin even had they wanted to. As Swift recalls in her autobiography, she knew only too well the difficulties involved: some years before, she and Simpson had been warned, after the premature birth of their first child, that it would be life-threatening for Swift to conceive for at least eighteen months. Despairing of finding contraception in the south, Simpson had sent his wife north, to decidedly non-Catholic Ulster, in pursuit of prophylactics. Swift – completely ignorant not only of Northern Ireland's geography but also of its complex patchwork of sectarianism in all things – had arrived in Belfast, wandered into the first chemist's shop she saw and asked for condoms, only to have a decidedly Catholic chemist harangue her bitterly on the evils of artificial contraception. Dazedly wandering away from this assault, she had next found a Protestant chemist's, only to have the proprietor deliver an equally vehement diatribe against the iniquity of the priest-ridden South. For Swift it had been a deeply humiliating experience and there was no way on earth that she was going to undergo any further trouble with prophylactics – at any rate not of her own free will.

So the problem remained. With rehearsals progressing well and the cast's performances gelling into what everyone concerned knew in their bones was a very impressive production, only the little matter of the condom remained to be dealt with. Attempts to substitute various objects of the requisite size and shape – stand-ins, one might say – proved unworkable. As a last resort experiments were made with a little disk of roughly the correct shape and size, dutifully cut from a sheet of paper by Kate Binchy. This proved as useless as anything else: Pat Nolan, who played Alvaro, was an experienced actor, but he wasn't an acrobat – he simply could not guarantee to get the kick right first time in every performance and anything less was unacceptable. Finally, as Swift and Simpson had from the first suspected might be necessary, it was decided simply to mime the whole thing and let the audience understand what had happened from the context and the ensuing dialogue. It was a small, risky point (dramatically speaking), but under the circumstances they saw no alternative. With this last difficulty resolved, rehearsals continued apace.

Though it had broken much new ground in Irish theatre, the Pike had largely escaped the attentions of the lay clerics who kept an eye on the Dublin stage. No theatre working in the modern field, of course, could escape them entirely, but the Pike had done better than many. An article in the Catholic weekly *The Standard* – subsidised by the Knights of Columbanus, but normally quite supportive of the Pike – had taken the theatre very severely to task over some of the sketches in *Further Follies* in 1955. At the time Swift and Simpson had actually taken legal advice on the article. The advice they received says a great deal about Ireland in 1955: they were told that the article was plainly libellous, but were advised not to sue since no jury – whatever its members' private feelings – would dare to find publicly for a theatre in a case against a Catholic publication, especially one associated with the powerful Knights.

A year later the Pike had discovered the wonderful world of Catholic hate mail during its successful production of Sartre's *The Respectable Prostitute*, which – although it concerned racism in the American South – had drawn the ire of people who had never seen it both because of its title and because of its author: Sartre's work was on the Catholic Church's Index of Forbidden Books and his novels were banned in Ireland. The hate mail had been distressing, but the production had been a great critical and commercial success, confounding the concerned warnings published by the pseudonymous newspaper columnist Candida when the production was announced:

> A man called Jean Paul Sartre, with a somewhat progressive outlook, wrote a play about the racial war between whites and blacks in the Southern States of America.
>
> I don't know what Jean Paul Sartre called his opus originally. He writes about a white girl defended by a Negro against a white

man; the Ku Klux Klan boys swing the accusation the other way and a Negro is lynched. The wrong Negro at that.

Remembering Sartre's last effort a few years ago – they put black streamers cutting out the title on the posters – I fear for the Pike...

By the time the respectable folk are finished with the Pike next month they'll all be trying to rise from the ashes.[3]

'Sartre's last effort a few years ago' referred to the occasion in the early 1950s when a visiting Northern Ireland troupe had put on his *Huis clos* in the Royal Irish Academy. The Academy's governors, fearing that the mere name of Sartre would provoke attack from vigilantes, had insisted that the playwright's name should be left off all publicity material for the production – including the programmes and even the posters. If times had changed between 1952 and 1956, still they hadn't changed that much: Candida's own newspaper feared to print the title of *The Respectable Prostitute* in the Pike's advertisements and even in its review – though Fianna Fáil's *Evening Press* had no such qualms. At least both dared to print Sartre's name, which one supposes was – by Irish standards – a kind of progress.

In spite of the admittedly unpleasant hate mail, the Sartre play had encountered no public controversy: there had been no demonstrations, complaints or walk-outs, all of which were a normal part of life for all but the most somnolent Dublin theatres. Simpson and Swift had been grateful for this. Unlike some of the smaller theatres, who sometimes seemed to treat controversy as a form of cheap publicity, they were not deliberate controversialists. When Pat Nolan – whose genuinely devoted Catholicism was known and respected in the theatre world – expressed some unease about some of the implications he saw in *The Rose Tattoo*, they were happy for him to consult his confessor (as was his habit on such occasions) and relieved and amused when he reported the priest's opinion that not only was the play not morally dubious, but it would be liable to make conversions.

It came as both a surprise and distraction, therefore, when a concerned Brendan Smith, director of the Theatre Festival, contacted the Pike at the beginning of May. Smith had received an alarming letter from a group calling itself the Irish League of Decency (of whom Simpson and Swift had never heard) claiming that the Pike's Theatre Festival production actively promoted the use of 'artificial' birth control. Simpson and Swift hastened to reassure Smith that nothing could be further from the case, pointing to the continued presence of Nolan in the cast as proof. Smith, a theatrical producer himself, knew Nolan well – the actor's moral qualms had actually caused him to turn down parts in plays Smith was producing as family fare in Butlin's holiday camp. At Simpson and Swift's suggestion, Smith spoke with Nolan, who repeated his own confessor's assurances. Smith was mollified. Simpson and Swift returned to work, puzzled by the incident but – in the hectic activity of preparing a play for the Festival while simultaneously running a nightly revue – soon forgetting about it.

The letter from the League has since been lost and this is unfortunate. At the time its main effect on Swift and Simpson was puzzlement. The incident with the condom was the only thing in *The Rose Tattoo* that could by any stretch of even the Irish Catholic imagination be related to contraception, and the appearance of the condom (which would in any case be imaginary in the Pike production) was greeted in the play with the sort of reaction even a priest would have thought appropriate. Besides, *The Rose Tattoo* had never had an English-language performance in Europe: how could anyone know what it did or did not promote? The book, of course, was available in Dublin bookshops – but would anyone, even in Ireland, be obsessive enough to vet the texts of Festival plays in advance, searching for dirt? It is perhaps a measure of their naïvety that Simpson and Swift discounted such a notion as fantastic. They had more than enough on their plates. With the Festival due to start in a few days, they set to work building the new scenery that would be needed to mount the play on the much larger stage of the Gate. They'd watched *The Rose Tattoo* coming together in rehearsal and were more confident than ever that it would be a success. If nothing else, the actual performance of the play would demonstrate to even the most suspicious mind that there was nothing objectionable in it. Or so they thought.

5. An Inspector Calls

The first International Dublin Theatre Festival opened on the evening of May 12th 1957. *The Rose Tattoo* was its opening play and it was obvious from the first night that it was going to be a sensation. Gabriel Fallon, the most respected of Irish theatre critics, positively rhapsodised about the production in the next day's *Evening Press*. 'Last night', wrote Fallon, 'the directors of the Pike Theatre opened the International Theatre Festival by presenting the English-speaking European première of Tennessee Williams's *The Rose Tattoo*. Play and presentation were well worthy of the occasion.'

Fallon's review divided its extravagant praise between the play itself and the Pike's production of it. The play was 'a brilliant example of what today's major playwright can do when he attempts to work in a tragic vein'. It was 'filled with lightning flashes of "felt life", of scenes and sounds that linger beyond curtain-call, of figures that come and go upon the stage with mercurial reality'. Serafina Delle Rose, the central character, was 'undoubtedly one of the major creations of modern drama' and the Pike's presentation 'was distinguished by the magnificent performance of Anna Manahan in the part ... It is difficult to believe that Miss Manahan was merely following the author's stage directions. What she gave to the part in looks and voice, in emotion and gesture, not only answered Mr Williams's characterisation, but went gloriously beyond that.'

Fallon's praise for the production did not end with Manahan – far from it: 'Alan Simpson's production and lighting and the setting designed and painted by Reginald Gray, come next in order of praise. Nineteen characters on that diminutive stage call for a touch of genius in the director. Every one of these characters is finely played, though one must single out Pat Nolan's Alvaro and the very moving performance of Kate Binchy and Brian Phelan for special praise.' The review concluded with the observation that 'the Pike must be highly recommended for giving Dublin a remarkable piece of theatre'.[1]

Well might Alan Simpson regard the review 'with not a little self-satisfaction',[2] not least because the *Press* was the acknowledged mouthpiece for the governing Fianna Fáil party, which ultimately held the purse strings of the entire festival. But Fallon's review was only the overture to a chorus of critical praise from at home and abroad. On May 14th reviews of *The Rose Tattoo* appeared in both the London *Times* and the *Manchester Guardian*, as well as in the *Daily Telegraph*. At the weekend a downright rapturous review appeared in the *Sunday Times*. In the *Telegraph*, eminent reviewer A.V. Coton yet again singled out Manahan's performance: 'Anna Manahan ... underplayed nothing of the animal qualities of the character, but when the light touch was necessary she gave it delicately yet decisively.'[3]

The ultimate accolade – certainly from Simpson and Swift's point of view – came with an article in the *Sunday Times* by Harold Hobson, doyen of English theatre critics and (with Kenneth Tynan) the man who had turned around the fortunes of *Waiting for Godot* in Britain after the play received an extremely hostile reception when it first opened. Merely to be noticed by Hobson would be a triumph for any Irish theatre; but Hobson did far more than just mention the Pike's production – he all but worshipped it. In the course of what was theoretically an overview of the entire festival, Hobson singled out the Pike for special praise. Indeed, apart from a final paragraph which praised MacLíammóir's acting at the Gate in Denis Johnson's *The Old Lady Says No*, the article was in effect a paean to the Pike rather than a review of the Festival: Hobson wrote that he hadn't even gone to the Abbey or the Olympia.

Instead, he wrote:

> I was immediately drawn to the Pike because it is giving the English language European première of Tennessee Williams's *The Rose Tattoo*.
>
> It is giving it well. Jammed together tight as bricks in a wall, sweating, sticking our elbows into our neighbours, digging our knees into the people in the row in front, sore from the knees of the people in the row behind, we were hit wherever we were most susceptible by the heat, the squalor, the strident passions and the emotions that scream in Mr Williams's story of the fat and blowsy Sicilian immigrant into [sic] America who is swept off her shambling feet by a truck-driver with the body of an Apollo and the head of a clown, who tattoos a rose on his chest in order to rouse her.
>
> The spectacular part in this play is, of course, that of the slatternly middle-aged woman. Anna Manahan plays her with a vulgar beauty and a shameless pride. There is something strangely touching in the scene in which, obese and dishevelled, she tries to button herself up in a pair of corsets and then flings them away in an impatient, irritated despair. This is a fine performance; but I was as much, or even more impressed by that of Pat Nolan as the truck driver … Mr Nolan is not precisely helped to the creation of beauty by having to blow his nose on his dirty shirt or by having to drop on the floor (unless I am mistaken) something not mentionable in Ireland. But he gives to this hoodlum fortune-hunter, whose ambitions are so sympathetically genial and limited, a compelling, fundamental tenderness and a soft, surprised music of speech.
>
> This is a distinguished production, directed with outstanding discrimination by Alan Simpson.

His review again singled out Manahan, describing her performance as 'a *tour de force* of sustained intensity' before going on to praise 'the well-judged mixture of fire and pathos' which Kate

Binchy brought to the role of Rosa and noting that Pat Nolan 'serves his author well'. The *Guardian* too had noted Binchy's 'impeccable performance'.[4] It lauded the performances of Brian Phelan (as Rosa's sailor boyfriend, Jack Hunter) and Michael McCabe (as the doctor) and was also impressed with Reginald Gray's 'cunning' staging.

Subsequent events would make Harold Hobson rue the day he wrote this encomium. Until his death he held himself partly responsible for them, believing that – in some way – his mention of 'something unmentionable in Ireland' had drawn the attention of some very ugly customers to the Pike and had called down the wrath of the Establishment on a theatre for which he had only the greatest affection and respect.[5] If anything, of course, Hobson's reference is a tribute to Nolan's skilful mime. While Carolyn Swift has always believed that the article did in fact do some damage to the Pike, it was in quite a different sphere. By belittling the Gate (at least in the ever-vigilant eyes of MacLíammóir and Edwards) and pointedly ignoring the other theatres, he had 'made us the hate-object of every other theatre management in Dublin'.[6] When Nemesis came, Simpson and Swift would meet with much sympathy from individual theatre people; but they would also meet with hostility and *schadenfreude* and the theatrical Establishment in general would be singularly unsupportive, even though the attack on the Pike was generally interpreted as an attack on Dublin theatre as a whole.

But all that was in the future, although behind the scenes the wheels that would crush the Pike had been set in motion before the play even opened. For the moment – for ten heady days – the Pike and its people were the toast of the Theatre Festival and thus of Bord Fáilte, which was ultimately behind the entire Festival idea. The theatre's success in impressing foreign critics and the glowing reports that those critics were writing abroad were exactly what the tourist board had hoped for from the Festival: a stark contrast to the damp squibs of former Tóstals and a badly needed face-lift for Ireland's miserable public image abroad. The Pike, as the success of the Theatre Festival, was something to show off to important visitors, and Simpson and Swift had to get used to daily calls from Bord Fáilte's PR Department reserving seats for VIPs and foreign dignitaries, curious to see for themselves this odd little theatre that was causing such a stir. The odd little theatre itself was of course delighted to oblige, so long as the guests were prepared to squeeze themselves in like everyone else: in a theatre as small as the Pike there was no room for special treatment for even the most VI of Ps.

Socially, meanwhile, Simpson and Swift found themselves much in demand for official parties and receptions and (a rare experience for members of a profession held in such suspicion) were sought out at these by the great, the good and the respectable. The Festival passed in a blur of hard work, good reviews and parties. Carolyn Swift recalls one such occasion, when she spent most of an evening dancing with the up-and-coming young Government TD Charles Haughey, whom they already knew from the notorious back room of Groome's Hotel, where Fianna Fáil politicians and theatre people habitually drank till the small hours, happily ignoring the licensing laws. 'When we weren't drinking cocktails with the diplomatic corps', wrote Simpson, already sounding semi-disbelieving only a few years later, 'we were being shaken warmly by the hand by Government ministers and Tourist Board officials.'[7] There was no mistaking what was happening to them: it was success and the politicians (in a manner much more familiar nowadays than it was then) could smell it. By this stage even Simpson and Swift caught the aroma and it smelled very sweet indeed. They may, as Swift writes, have been full of themselves but they had every reason to be.[8]

Between supervising nightly performances of *The Rose Tattoo* itself, then the *Follies* show that followed it each night (and in which Simpson, incredibly, also took part) and the whirlwind of socialising in which they also found themselves caught up (not to

61

mention the more mundane demands of raising three small children), Simpson and Swift were both permanently exhausted. But it was the heady, champagne tiredness of success and if it all went to the couple's heads still they can surely be forgiven. They had – by dint of hard work, skill and perseverance – done the seemingly impossible: they'd become the toast of Official Ireland in the 1950s, yet they'd done it in a DIY theatre, staging cutting-edge, world-class work in a suspect trade. It was, by any standards, a great achievement.

And then the sky fell.

'On the second Tuesday after we had opened', Alan Simpson wrote in 1962, 'I was upstairs in the men's dressing-room of the Pike, discussing the financial arrangements for the Gate Theatre with a member of the cast.' [9] It was the evening of May 21st 1957 and the audience for that evening's show was already arriving. Simpson's negotiations were interrupted by Swift with the news that there was a policeman outside demanding to see him. Thinking that it was some minor matter, Simpson took his time. The presence of policemen at the Pike was no new thing – the residents of the lane were by and large accommodating, but those in the more respectable Herbert Street (particularly the owners of a nursing home) had complained about late-night noise and about theatre patrons' cars blocking access. But when Simpson eventually went outside he sensed immediately that this was different.

It was. Simpson found waiting for him not a lowly beat Garda but a uniformed Inspector. The policeman, Inspector Ward, immediately produced a document which he said had been issued by Garrett Brennan, the Deputy Police Commissioner. He then read the contents of the document aloud. It had been brought to the attention of the police, it said, that the play being performed contained 'objectionable passages'. That evening's performance must not proceed unless these passages were removed. If this were not done, both Simpson and Swift would be liable to prosecution. [10]

To say that Swift and Simpson were stunned is an understatement: coming after their recent experiences, this was quite simply unreal. It is perfectly easy to believe Swift when she says that it was a genuine struggle to take in what Ward was saying. When asked, the Inspector refused to reveal what the supposedly 'offensive' passages were; nor would he reveal the source of the complaint. Though there was a lingering temptation to laugh at the absurdity of it all, it was clear now to both Simpson and Swift that the policeman meant what he said. His refusal to point out the offensive lines meant that – whatever Simpson and Swift might decide – no change could be made in the play; in effect Ward was simply ordering them to cancel a show whose opening was, by now, ten minutes overdue, with a full house waiting.

'Do you intend to continue presentation of this play?' Ward asked Simpson – somehow managing to make the word 'play' (Simpson notes) sound like a dirty word.[11] Simpson and Swift exchanged glances. They were theatre people with an audience waiting for the curtain to rise. As Ward concentrated on Simpson, Swift slipped into the Pike and told the stage manager, Dahna Davis, to raise the curtain. For better or worse, the die was cast.

Simpson told Ward that he'd have to get a solicitor's advice – something he recalled hearing people say in films. The brave-sounding words were rendered somewhat hollow by the fact that he and Swift had no solicitor as such, but Simpson phoned Con Lehane, the lawyer who'd bested the Pike in its breach of contract case against Brendan Behan a couple of years before. At the time Lehane had told Simpson that, while the Pike had the better case, Behan had the better lawyer and expressed some regret that he hadn't been acting for the Pike. A former IRA man and a founder-member of Clann na Poblachta, Lehane had a reputation as a tough, canny lawyer, unusually unafraid of the authorities; Simpson, recalling him now, at least had the wit to suspect that he might need someone like that.

When Lehane arrived he asked to see Garrett Brennan's document and was in his turn astonished when Inspector Ward refused to show it to him. Then Lehane asked who had complained about the play, but again Ward refused to answer. After prompting from Lehane, the Inspector did agree to read Brennan's statement aloud again while Lehane copied it down. Lehane assured him forcefully that he would be in touch with the Attorney General the next day to demand identification of the 'offensive passages'. Only when this had been clarified would the Pike respond. Ward left.

Discussing the bizarre incident, Simpson, Swift and Lehane could only conclude that it was all some horrendous mistake. It is hard to see what other conclusion they might have reached. Native politicians and visiting dignitaries were at that precise moment sitting, a few metres away, watching the 'objectionable' *Rose Tattoo* – to which no one at all, so far as they knew, had actually raised any objection. The production had generated a great deal of excellent publicity for Ireland, precisely as the Theatre Festival had been supposed to do. Politicians had spent the better part of the previous fortnight courting Simpson's and Swift's company. Above all, *The Rose Tattoo* was simply not obscene. Ward's visit could *only* be a mistake. Even Lehane, who (having dealt with the police from both sides of the law) had few illusions on the subject, could think of no other sane explanation. The important thing now was to stop the whole thing before it went any further – before the newspapers heard of it. If the story got out of hand it could cause enormous embarrassment for the Festival and indeed for the police and the Government. And causing embarrassment to an Irish Government, however innocently, was a singularly unwise thing to do. Simpson tried to contact Bob Briscoe, Lord Mayor of Dublin, long-time Fianna Fáil stalwart and Chairman of the Tóstal Council, the Theatre Festival's sponsors. Briscoe, he was sure, would immediately see the danger of the situation and he'd have the clout to sort the matter out promptly. But Simpson failed to reach Briscoe by telephone and had to postpone the attempt till the following day.

There was nothing more to be done that night. Shock or no

shock, Simpson was due to perform in *Say It With Follies*, which would begin shortly after *The Rose Tattoo* ended. The police visit was frightening but he'd sort it out with Briscoe next day. The Pike was on a roll: it wouldn't be halted just yet.

6. A New World

It was early next day, when Simpson began his efforts to sort out the mess, that he started to get a seriously bad feeling about the whole matter. When he finally reached Bob Briscoe, he didn't know whether to be alarmed or surprised by the Lord Mayor's reaction: Briscoe immediately attacked him, refusing to listen to Simpson's explanations and demanding to know how the Pike dared present such a play in the Council's name. Simpson was flabbergasted. What was going on? Throughout the day he and Swift, with increasing frustration, tried to contact anyone else who might be able to help. But something was very obviously wrong: the politicians and dignitaries who had been courting them for the past fortnight were suddenly unavailable or unsympathetic. It was as though, somewhere in Official Ireland, an invisible door had begun to close.

Simpson's and Swift's increasingly frantic attempts to find out what was really going on were fruitless. Dr Michael ffrench O'Carroll, a former Fianna Fáil Senator who'd been in college with Simpson, did try to find out but failed. He offered, though, to go bail for Simpson if necessary – not something Simpson and Swift wanted to think about and perhaps the first indication they'd had of how bad the situation might get. They contacted their friend Florrie O'Riordan,[1] third secretary in the Department of External Affairs (as it then was). O'Riordan thought the whole thing was preposterous and was confident that he could have it sorted out. For a while they were relieved, but when O'Riordan got back to them later in the day he was, Swift recalled later, 'much shaken':

'I can only tell you that it comes from the very top,' O'Riordan said. 'Dev himself wants action taken against you.'[2]

For many years Swift would think this really had to be ridiculous. Though she trusted O'Riordan implicitly, still he couldn't possibly be right: what had Dev to do with them or they with Dev?

Amidst the growing confusion and anxiety, one thing seemed clear to both Simpson and Swift: for the moment, at least, it was still best to keep this thing quiet. The Government would surely relent if the right people could simply be alerted to the potentially ghastly situation; but to back down in public would make the authorities lose face and one simply did not do that with Irish governments, which had a highly developed sense of their own importance. Still they continued to contact anyone who might have some influence in the matter or who would at least be able to tell them what was really going on. But there was nothing doing: the doors they had sensed closing were now firmly shut.

That night *The Rose Tattoo* and the *Follies* ran to the usual appreciative audiences. Next day, but rather desperately now, Swift and Simpson continued to look for information. Lehane could discover nothing either. In spite of their decision to keep the matter quiet, Simpson and Swift felt it only fair to make one person in particular aware of what was going on: Lord Longford, at the Gate, should be warned that there was something funny happening. Simpson called on Longford at the Gate on Thursday afternoon. But even the shocks of the past day and a half hadn't prepared him for the surprise that he got on this visit: Longford seemed actually *amused* by his problem. More to the point, the peer announced that he was cancelling the transfer and would put cancellation notices in the newspapers that very day.

Simpson, incredulous, mentioned the fact that they had a contract. Longford told him he was free to sue the Gate – knowing full well, as Swift would somewhat bitterly recall, that Simpson was in no position to do so. When Simpson pointed out that the

Pike had already incurred costs in preparing new scenery suitable for the Gate stage, Longford told him that he would repay the costs involved (although in fact he never did). Simpson, still hoping to avoid publicity and knowing that Longford's cancellation notices would attract press attention, begged him to at least wait for a couple of days before inserting the ads. Longford refused.[3] Simpson was by now definitely frightened; the sensation of being way out of his depth was overwhelming and the fact that he had no idea of how or why only compounded it.

By now too it was obvious that the situation, however unreal it might seem, was deadly serious. It still never struck Simpson or Swift for a moment that there might be any justification for the police action; but that was, in the short term at least, irrelevant. The behaviour of their political contacts – especially Florrie O'Riordan's claim about de Valera – was extremely disturbing, suggesting that the matter had been politicised. If this was the case, then it would be a waste of time trying to find out what was really going on, never mind trying to influence it. It was time to stop thinking about official embarrassment and to start thinking of how to defend themselves against whatever was happening.

The trouble was that, if the Government itself really was (for whatever reason) behind events, a little theatre up a back lane – even a celebrated little theatre up a back lane – didn't really have many options for defence against it. Longford's cancellation notices would make it impossible to keep a lid on the matter. After the previous two weeks the Pike's public profile was particularly high: news of an obscenity allegation against the highlight of the Theatre Festival would be headline stuff. Worse again, the cancellation notices would make it seem that the Pike was in some way at fault. The only sensible thing Swift and Simpson could do, it seemed, was get their version of events in first by courting the publicity they had thus far been keen to avoid.

By previous arrangement they brought their daughters that afternoon to the zoo, to celebrate the eldest child's – Maureen's –

recent birthday. While the children and their friends took a ride in a donkey-cart, Simpson and Swift put together a press statement in what seems, in retrospect, like an eminently suitable place – the Monkey House. The statement gave an account of what had taken place on Tuesday night and reaffirmed their belief in the innocence of *The Rose Tattoo*. Before distributing the statement Simpson brought it to Lehane so that the solicitor could check it out and Lehane had his secretary make typed copies. He himself had already written to Deputy Police Commissioner Garrett Brennan, complaining about the irregularities of the police visit and demanding to know what specific changes in the text were being called for. Brennan's reply arrived by special messenger while Simpson was in the office. It was far from encouraging. Completely ignoring Lehane's questions, Brennan simply informed him that the matter was 'being dealt with by the proper authorities and that in view of [Simpson's] refusal to take off the play the matter would be dealt with according to the law'.[4] Lehane read this as meaning that the police meant to arrest Simpson and warned him that there might be trouble at the Pike that night. As Simpson struggled to take this in, Lehane's secretary called over the intercom. 'A Mr Brady is downstairs to see you,' she said. It was the Dublin representative of the *Daily Express*, who had got wind of the fact that something was brewing: the press had begun to sniff at the story already.

Simpson left to distribute copies of the Pike statement to the newsrooms of the Dublin papers, handing a copy to the *Express* reporter as he went. When he reached home afterwards, he found that Swift had already left for the Pike. Then he got a call from the theatre to say that plainclothes policemen were keeping watch at both ends of Herbert Lane. Simpson remembered Lehane's words: they could only be there to arrest him and maybe Swift too.

There seemed no point in evading them: it was too late for that. It's uncertain at this point who came up with the idea of stage-managing the arrest, but this was the course of action the

Pike decided on. Simpson contacted Lehane, and then phoned every reporter he could think of. When the newsmen had had time to reach Herbert Lane, Simpson himself would call to friends whose house fronted on the Grand Canal; then he would just walk down their back garden and, completely bypassing the police, go through the door in the back wall and simply emerge outside the Pike.

This is precisely what he did. By the time he arrived at the theatre a group of reporters and cameramen – the latter, on Simpson's advice, having hidden their cameras as they went by the detectives – had assembled in Herbert Lane. Simpson informed them that the police would shortly be arresting him. Then he and Swift – who'd said nothing as yet to the cast, hoping to settle the matter without needing to alarm them – called a cast meeting and told everyone the full story, mystifying though it was. They themselves were determined to continue with the play; conceding now would look like an admission of guilt. But in the last analysis they felt the decision should rest with the cast, who might, after all, be endangering themselves by performing. It wasn't only that the actors might ultimately be arrested themselves: simply being accused of involvement with 'indecency' carried heavy risks in 'respectable' Irish society. Anna Manahan, speaking decades later, still remembered that cast meeting well:

> I must say on first hearing the news (remember this was the first time any of us in the cast knew anything about the whole affair) we were stunned, shocked even, but against all the odds the cast unanimously agreed to continue with the performance. In the end there was no question of us not doing so. And some people in the cast were placed in a difficult position by their decision ... I remember Pat Nolan was understandably concerned about losing his job with Dublin Corporation ... but there was no question then of him leaving the production.[5]

At that moment Simpson and Swift were the only ones who'd actually been threatened – although next day everyone involved with the Pike would be individually (and misleadingly) warned by the police of their liability to immediate arrest. None would crack under the deliberate pressure, even when policemen lined the back wall of the thronged Pike during performances or threw the doors open during intense moments in the play.[6] If Simpson is to be admired for his stand, then so too are the cast who stood by him.

Having secured the cast's agreement to continue, Simpson and Swift oversaw a last, symbolic raising of the curtain on *The Rose Tattoo* and then went outside to where the newsmen still clustered. Simpson sent Swift to inform the police that he was at the Pike. Two detectives came down the lane where they were obviously taken aback to find reporters and cameramen. One of them even retreated, but the other – shielding his face with his arm – strode on and demanded that Simpson accompany him to the end of the lane – out of sight of the press – to speak to an Inspector Scanlan. Simpson refused and the policeman went back to confer with his superior. After some delay an unmarked police car drove down Herbert Lane and four detectives (including Scanlan) emerged and surrounded Simpson, conspicuously ignoring the pressmen. The detectives were very large men – even in photographs they are all at least a head taller than the almost-six-foot Simpson – and they looked distinctly uncomfortable before the audience of newsmen in the lane. Scanlan asked Simpson to accompany them into the Pike box-office, where they might speak privately. Simpson had no interest in privacy at this point and refused point-blank. Two of the detectives thereupon grabbed him and hauled him, struggling, into the box-office. Swift and Aidan Maguire, manager of the Pike, tried to follow them in. When Maguire tried to stop the police from closing the box-office door, one of them slammed it on his wrist, injuring him.

Once the door was closed, Scanlan immediately got down to business. He informed Simpson that he was under arrest and must go with the police to the Bridewell prison. There was no point in resisting. Simpson accompanied the detectives to the police car and they took him away. At the Bridewell he was formally charged with 'presenting for gain an indecent and profane performance'.[7] This was the first time that Simpson had heard which law he had supposedly broken and the first time he'd ever known that such a charge existed.[8] He then had to go through the usual (but for Simpson new and intimidating) routine of emptying his pockets and having all sharp instruments confiscated for the duration of his stay. Then he was taken to a dimly lit basement cell from where, after a while, he was brought out to see Con Lehane who'd missed the arrest itself. Lehane was both puzzled and worried. He was certain now that there was far more going on here than met the eye.

'They're giving you the full works,' he told Simpson. 'They've arrested you on a summary warrant.'[9]

Simpson had no idea what a summary warrant was, but Lehane explained: summary warrants were used to detain people who might flee the jurisdiction and excluded the possibility of bail before the suspect had appeared in court. This was perhaps the most bizarre element yet of the whole affair. Even Lehane (no stranger to political trials) had never heard of a summary warrant being used except in cases of terrorism or armed robbery. Simpson had a business, a wife and three daughters in Dublin: where (and why) was he expected to flee?

The use of a summary warrant had other implications too, Lehane explained. Simpson would be allowed to speak to no one except his lawyer – not even to Swift, whom Simpson expected to be frantic with worry. Under the terms of his arrest, Simpson's rights were by and large confined to the right to buy (at his own expense) a meal. Right now all Lehane could do for him was to give him some cigarettes and matches and promise to go to the Pike to reassure Swift. After Lehane left, Simpson settled down as best he could. He was due to appear in court next morning; but it was going to be a very long night.

7. In the Bridewell

Even with all that was to follow, Alan Simpson would always re-call that night in the Bridewell as the worst of his entire life. A 'surly' warder got him a meal on request and Simpson ate it 'with-out relish', as much to kill time as anything else. There was a great deal of it to kill and as each hour passed so each minute grew longer. Later the surly warder was replaced by a friendlier one, who asked whether it was 'naked women' that Simpson was 'in for'. When Simpson reassured him that it wasn't, the man re-marked 'sadly' that 'they' were 'very funny in this country about them things'. He then got Simpson a welcome – and by now badly needed – Baby Power.[1]

The small touch of comic humanity was as appreciated – and as rare – as the whiskey that night. Understandably Simpson didn't sleep. Instead he spent the hours of darkness mulling over his situation. Lehane had estimated that the maximum sentence he might receive would be two years. But his punishment, if he were convicted, would go far beyond any jail sentence. For a start he would lose his army rank: he would be cashiered immediately, with loss of pension rights. And then there were the realities of Irish life to deal with: 'The nineteenth century neurosis of the Irish people would immediately bracket me in the category of sex criminal. To be caught embezzling, or drunk in charge of a vehi-cle, is a matter for sympathy or even open laughter; and to be im-prisoned for political offences is regarded as an honourable ap-prenticeship to public life. But a man or woman convicted of any-thing even remotely involving sex is treated as a social pariah and an outcast and his crime can only be discussed by dark hints in lowered voices.'[2]

And what would happen on his release? Work in Ireland would be impossible; even life there would be difficult – emigration might be the only solution. What would become of Swift and their children if he were sent to prison? It seemed unlikely she too would be charged, even though she was co-owner of the Pike, but in an affair that seemed to have no sense about it at all, the possibility could not be discounted. What would become of the children then? Downright crazy thoughts went through his mind: but it was a mad situation, even by the standards of the day.

It is unsurprising that, by the time morning came, Simpson's morale was so low as to be almost non-existent. Just before eleven, after a breakfast of a piece of bread and a mug of 'dubious' tea, he was brought from his cell to 'a dimly-lit, subterranean, iron-barred ante-room directly beneath the court'. There he was put in the charge of a detective who was 'very pleasant' and the two fell to discussing the relative working conditions in the police and the army. In the course of the discussion it emerged that the detective had actually seen *The Rose Tattoo*, but when Simpson tried to discover the man's views on the play 'he shut up like a clam'.[3]

Lehane arrived just before Simpson was led up the stairs into the dock. He looked 'even gloomier and sterner' than the night before. He brought very peculiar news: the State wanted to make a deal. Lehane had engaged James Heavey, a mutual friend, to act as Simpson's barrister. Heavey had been discussing the case with the Chief State Solicitor and the latter had told him that, if Simpson would give an undertaking in court that there would be no more performances of *The Rose Tattoo*, the State would simply drop the charges against him. Along with the offer, however, came a threat: if Simpson refused, then the State would not only proceed with the case but would also oppose bail. This could mean that Simpson would have to stay in jail at least until the date of the first hearing, which could be anything up to six weeks away. Simpson was appalled: six weeks in jail, with no proof that he was guilty of anything at all!

All Simpson had to do to avoid this fate was, to put it in the simplest possible terms, to admit that the Pike had done something wrong and to promise not to do it any more. What could be easier? But it was there in that dank room that, whatever his many qualities as a theatre director, a husband, a father or a man, Alan Simpson became something slightly more than any of these things. One hesitates to call him a hero, because that makes him sound far more special than he ever thought himself to be. But, for whatever reason, it simply stuck in Simpson's craw to admit wrongdoing when he didn't for one moment believe that it was true. In the context of Irish society at the time this was an extremely unusual way of thinking. But whether from his background, his principles, his personality or even pure contrariness – of which he evidently had a strong and, in the circumstances, useful streak – Simpson found himself hesitating.

'What do you advise?' he asked Lehane.

Lehane was impassive.

'As your solicitor', he said carefully, 'I must advise you to give the undertaking.'

Simpson thought he caught a slight emphasis on the first three words. *As his solicitor*, he realised, Lehane's job was to have him freed, full stop: clearly the obvious way to do that was for Simpson to give the required undertaking.

'But as a friend?' Simpson asked.

'I am here', Lehane pointed out, 'as your solicitor.'

Simpson thought he detected 'a flicker of a smile' in Lehane's eyes. He considered his options. To give the required undertaking would, it seemed to him, be tantamount to an admission of guilt and would certainly be taken as such by the public. It would also be to accept the State's right to interfere unjustly in Irish theatre simply because – for whatever reason – it felt like it. The whole thing had now gone too far. To Simpson now the only way in which he could keep his own integrity intact and stand by his belief in *The Rose Tattoo* was to put his faith in the legal system and trust that – since he'd done nothing wrong – his name would be cleared in court. He had no doubt at all that Swift would stand by the decision.

'Tell them I will give no such undertaking,' he said to Lehane.

Lehane smiled.

'I thought you might say that,' he said. 'But I didn't want to influence you.'[4]

Lehane left to deliver Simpson's response to the authorities. Simpson himself could only sit and wait to be called into court. He had cast the die now; he would follow through to the end. After another while he was led upstairs and found himself blinking in the sudden brightness. He was in the dock of Dublin Circuit Court. The court was crowded and when his eyes adjusted to the light he was cheered to see that among the crowd were Swift, several of the Pike's backstage crew and almost the entire cast of *The Rose Tattoo*, as well as a large number of theatrical well-wishers.[5] These were joined by a gaggle of fascinated pressmen representing Irish and British newspapers and by Canon Walter Simpson, Alan's father. The attempted prosecution of Alan Simpson (and, of course, of the Pike Theatre, *The Rose Tattoo* and, as many then and later saw it, of freedom of speech in the Republic of Ireland) was about to begin.

8. In the Dock

The presiding judge on that first day in court was District Justice Alfred Rochford. The sitting opened with the State, in the person of Mr W. Conway, Assistant State Solicitor, again offering Simpson the deal he had already refused: if he agreed that 'further performances would not be repeated, all State charges against him would be dropped'.[1] Again Simpson refused and the gloves came off. The State's position and tone were established from the outset by Conway, who relied entirely on a simple repeated assertion of Simpson's guilt. As Simpson would later recall it, 'Words like "lewd", "indecent", "offensive", "corruption" and "morality" spat from his mouth like machine-gun bullets.'[2] Conway repeated the charge, which he said was an offence under Common Law. In fact there were three separate charges, relating to three separate performances of the play on three dates in May. Carrying out the threat conveyed earlier and again adverting in public to an offer that he would certainly have preferred to have had accepted in private, Conway said that his instruction was 'to oppose bail unless an undertaking was given that the performances would not be repeated by the defendant or on his behalf on any stage or at any place'.[3]

Séamus Heavey, for the defence, was less concerned about a trial date than with the question of Simpson's staying in jail until it arrived. The charge was unusual, he said, and the defence would require a considerable time to prepare its case. He therefore asked District Justice Rochford to deal first with the matter of bail. His side denied that any offence had taken place and so could not sen-

77

sibly give the required undertaking. A request had been sent two days before asking the Garda Commissioner 'to indicate what parts of the play were regarded as objectionable and in what parts the law was alleged to have been infringed'.[4] No satisfactory reply had been received, so the accused had had no option but to run the play exactly as it had been running (without a single complaint from the public) for nearly two weeks.

Conway's response to this was syllogistic. It was, he said, the Attorney General's duty to protect the public and *therefore* to close *The Rose Tattoo*. If bail were granted, there was every reason to believe that the accused would continue to run the play and *therefore* bail should not be granted. Such arguments of course relied entirely on an acceptance of his own initial assertion that *The Rose Tattoo* was obscene and this Simpson's side flatly denied. In a sly aside, no doubt meant for the ears of the cast-members present – they certainly took it as such – Conway pointed out that any further performance would constitute a further offence, not only on Simpson's part but on the part of 'everyone associated with it'.[5] In the public gallery, the Pike people heard and understood the insinuation. 'It looked', Swift wrote, remembering, 'as if we were all headed for Mountjoy Gaol.'[6] But it was merely one further piece of rhetoric, since it had not been proved that any performance was in fact illegal.

Heavey repeated his point that no one had told the accused what was objectionable in the play. To this Conway, consistent at least, simply said the Attorney General held that *The Rose Tattoo* was 'lewd, indecent and offensive and [that it] tends to corrupt minds, morality and good order'.[7] This, of course, was not evidence: this was name-calling.

Justice Rochford ordered a recess. At the end of fifteen minutes he returned with an announcement that seemed to startle the prosecution considerably.[8] He had found, he said, a colleague who was free to hear the case that very day. Conway's threat of an immediate six weeks in jail was simply neutered. Conway, visibly flustered, demanded a further recess so that he could consult with the Attorney General. Rochford granted the request. When the court reconvened Conway admitted that the State could not proceed that day. Its witnesses, he said, were not available nor could the Book of Evidence be ready in time. In that case, Rochford said immediately, he would adjourn the case until July 4th. 'As there was no evidence that the defendant was guilty of any offence',[9] Simpson would be granted bail. There would be an independent surety of £50 and Simpson's own bail of £50 – £100 in all.[10] Was there anyone present, Rochford asked, willing to sign the bail bond on Simpson's behalf? Canon Simpson, Alan's father, rose to his feet but before he could put himself forward Commandant Séamus Heron, Legal Officer of the Irish Army's Eastern Command, offered himself as guarantor. Heron had been sent to the hearing as an official observer by Eastern Command but signed Simpson's bond as his friend.[11] Nonetheless this public indication that the army was standing by one of its officers seemed significant.

Outside the court Simpson, still in shock, found himself the centre of the 1957 version of a media scrum. Cameramen posed him at the centre of a group of beaming Pike workers and supporters. In some of the photographs his dazed features stand out among the beaming smiles of his friends and one imagines he looks pale even in the old monochrome pictures. One shot, occurring in several versions, shows a Pike group set out like a winning football team. On the left stands Canon Simpson, the very figure of solid Protestant rectitude, there to show his faith in his talented son. Pat Nolan, Aidan Maguire and Brian Phelan beam at the camera, as do the radiant Kate Binchy and the shock-haired designer, Reginald Gray. Swift, her arm linked with her husband's, positively glows. In the middle of them stands Simpson, his raincoat draped over his arm. Perhaps it is imagination, but his smile looks watery and forced, as though, with the first round won, he wondered what would come next.

What would come next was already becoming clear by the time

the joyous Pike party reached the city centre. In O'Connell Street the early editions of the evening papers were going on sale and the events in Herbert Lane and the District Court were the day's main news. 'INDECENT PLAY CHARGE'[12] screamed the headline of the *Evening Press*, over a full report of the morning's proceedings. 'DIRECTOR CHARGED WITH PRESENTING LEWD PLAY'[13] said the *Herald*, while the *Evening Standard* contented itself with 'ROSE TATTOO MAN ACCUSED'.[14] 'Each story was accompanied by large and easily recognisable photographs,' Simpson wrote. 'I felt people looking curiously at me. When I caught their eye, they would hastily look away. It is the business of everyone in the theatre to court publicity on every possible occasion for professional reasons, but this was different. This was notoriety.'[15]

Swift too remembered that look well. 'It was not the instant admiration accorded to film stars but something furtive and shameful.'[16] In his Bridewell cell Simpson had tormented himself, imagining the pariah status he might receive as a convicted sex-offender. Now he was receiving his first intimation that, in the pluperfectly respectable public Ireland of 1957, actual conviction might not be necessary.

At a full cast meeting in Herbert Lane, Simpson and Swift left the final decision about whether to continue the production up to the actors and backstage staff of the Pike. The meeting ended with a unanimous decision to continue, though most of those present felt sure they would end up in jail before the curtain next fell. The only person who did not carry on was Kate Binchy: her father, himself a judge, felt that her continued involvement under the circumstances would put him in an impossible position. Simpson and Swift, parents themselves, agreed with him. Binchy herself actually planned to leave home and stay with friends while continuing to take part in *The Rose Tattoo*. Aware of the terrible publicity that would result, Swift and Simpson hastily dissuaded her from the plan. She must stay off-stage till all this was over: a reluctant Swift would take her place on-stage.

That night, again shortly before curtain time, the police appeared again to the Pike. Once more they were led by Inspector Scanlan. They seemed astonished to find the theatre getting ready to put on a show and Scanlan demanded to speak to the players. He informed each individually that they would be liable to prosecution the moment they stepped on-stage. Frustrated by the equanimity with which they seemed to take the news, he confronted Swift.

'You understand', he asked, 'that the minute you take up the curtain on this production you also may be charged?'

Swift nodded. She tried to enlighten him.

> '[Y]ou see,' I explained patiently, 'If you arrest me, Brian Phelan, the stage-director will carry on and, if you arrest him, the stage-manager will take over.'
>
> 'Then he will also be liable to prosecution.'
>
> 'She,' I corrected … 'But in that case the assistant stage-manager, Michael McCabe will run the show.'[17]

Scanlan must have felt that he was dealing with lunatics: authority rarely met with such a response in Ireland then. Alan Simpson himself wasn't at the Pike that night: Lehane had advised him that he must on no account hang around and risk a second arrest, which – however unjust – would look damning. Instead Simpson spent the evening on tenterhooks in the city centre – much of it in Groome's hotel, having drinks with Joe Groome, the Fianna Fáil party treasurer – until he was sure that, for better or worse, the performance of *The Rose Tattoo* must be over. When he got back to Herbert Lane he discovered that he had missed truly extraordinary scenes. After the court appearance he and Swift had wondered whether anyone would even dare to come and see the play; in fact the cast had played to a jam-packed and enormously supportive house. They'd gone on stage fully expecting to be arrested or – in the case of Swift, who'd been mortified (as a 35-year-old mother of three) to be playing a 16-year-old – almost hoping to be. But the police had done nothing, though detectives had posted themselves at the back of the auditorium and outside in the lane and remained there throughout the performance.

The truly extraordinary event of that evening, though, was the arrival in Herbert Lane of a crowd of demonstrators who turned out spontaneously to support the Pike. Estimates of the size of the crowd vary wildly: the London *Times* put the number at 500, while other newspapers reported 50 (the *Daily Express*), 100 (the *Irish Press* and the *Irish Times*) and even 600–700 (the *Telegraph*).[18] What is certain is that most of them were in no mood to let anyone at all be arrested and some were prepared to use force to prevent this. These included the erstwhile Pike playwright Brendan Behan, who threw beer bottles at the police in the lane while exhorting the rest of the crowd to do likewise. They also included a group of Simpson's army comrades who made no bones about the fact that they planned to ensure that anyone – official or otherwise – who laid hands on their fellow army officer was going to have immediate cause to regret it.[19] Also present were a large group of actors from various theatres and companies, Tomás MacAnna of the Abbey, Barry Cassin of the 37 Club, Séamus Kelly of the *Irish Times*, the poet (and Pike regular) Patrick Kavanagh and even a judge – District Justice (and playwright) Donagh McDonagh.[20]

Whatever its size, the importance of that evening's demonstration in Herbert Lane should not be minimised. The presence of Catholic vigilantes demonstrating *against* productions was a common phenomenon in Dublin; one of Simpson's and Swift's chief worries had been that some vigilante group might arrive and perhaps riot in the lane. The spontaneous arrival of large numbers of people to publicly *support* a notorious play (as *The Rose Tattoo* had now become) was completely unprecedented.

The bravery of the *Rose Tattoo* cast (and backstage workers) in the face of prosecution threats and intimidating police behaviour was extraordinary. All went on-stage expecting arrest. But while it does not detract from their dedication, it should be noted that

Scanlan's warnings were essentially a bluff. While he left each in-dividual with a very clear perception that he or she would be ar-rested if they took part in the play, what Scanlan in fact *said* to them was that should they go on-stage they would be *liable* to prosecution: no more or less than the prosecutor, Conway, had said in court that morning.

In the event the play went on – as Swift is very proud to recall – to finish its scheduled run two nights later. Indeed, one of the aspects of the *Rose Tattoo* mythology which she finds most dis-tressful is the common statement that the play was taken off – for it was, of course, precisely her own and Simpson's refusal to take it off which caused them so much grief. On both of the remaining nights there were police in the auditorium and supporters in the lane. The audiences were utterly supportive – and in the atmos-phere of 1950s Ireland, anyone who turned up to see *The Rose Tattoo* at all after Alan Simpson was arrested must be counted by definition as a supporter, just as much as those who came to dem-onstrate in the Pike's favour outside the theatre.

The final night of the play's run was booked out. Even at the height of the *Godot* run, the Pike had never had to turn away so many customers. On that last night Simpson and Swift managed to find space for two specially invited guests. They felt it impor-tant that Séamus Heavey should see what he was defending; hav-ing seen the play, Heavey declared himself fully satisfied. Simpson and Swift also very much wanted Alan's father to see with his own eyes that his son was not a pornographer. The old man had never doubted this but he was deeply moved by the play itself and said as much afterwards to his son and daughter-in-law. It was all the satisfaction the senior Simpson would get: he died seven months later, with the State still attempting to imprison his son.

9. Tribulations

The six weeks until Simpson next appeared in court on July 4th were understandably tense times, but they were not without their positive moments. The publicity over *The Rose Tattoo* led to an invitation to bring the play to Belfast and stage it at the Belfast Opera House. Aware that many in Northern Ireland would happily seize on the case as yet further proof that the South was a priest-ridden Catholic tyranny, Simpson and Swift were at first reluctant to provide any opportunity for propaganda. But in the end, looking at the personal and financial losses they and the cast had already incurred, they decided that the Irish State had given them no particular reason to be sensitive about its feelings. The Belfast trip would partly make up to the cast for the incomes they'd lost through the Gate cancellation. It was also important to Simpson and Swift to let as many people as possible see the play itself, which so obviously did not warrant the accusations made against it.

The short Belfast run (to Swift's great relief) marked the return of Kate Binchy to the cast. Binchy's father, as a sort of insurance, had had her give the text to her Jesuit confessor, who declared it to be 'excellent'.[1] Even Con Lehane – a keen amateur actor – took a small part in the play in Belfast, replacing an actor whose day job kept him in Dublin. Simpson and Swift later came to believe that the familiarity this gave Lehane with the play helped enormously in court, where Heavey (who was being instructed by Lehane) would use Lehane's close working knowledge of it to rebut every false impression of *The Rose Tattoo* given by the police evidence.

In Belfast the RUC, mindful of possible controversy, checked the play out during rehearsals and afterwards 'roared with laughter at the idea that there might be anything offensive in the play, describing it as suitable for a Sunday school picnic'.[2] RUC officers also attended the opening night but only to keep a wary eye out for religious bigots (of whatever stripe) who might get ideas. They were, however, not the only policemen present: in the audience Swift recognised, to her surprise, several Dublin detectives whom she'd last seen in more threatening circumstances in Herbert Lane. The purpose of their being in Belfast quite escaped her.

Reviews for the Belfast shows were in the main overwhelmingly positive, with only Catholic papers (predictably enough) demurring at all. C.F. Corbett, in the course of a laudatory review in the *Belfast Telegraph*, hoped 'that last night's enthusiastic reception … helped Alan Simpson for his Dublin disappointment. His thoughtful production is worthy of the long applause it received.'[3] Of more practical help than any good review was the defence fund founded in Britain by *Envoy* magazine. The letter announcing the fund was signed by Seán O'Casey, Peter Hall, John Osborne, John Gielgud and Wolf Mankowitz among others. A flood of supportive letters began to arrive at the Pike, many from noted cultural figures but also very many from ordinary people, at home and abroad, who were outraged at the evident stupidity of the accusations and the injustice of the case. Foreign newspapers had taken an interest from the start and it was already clear that the State's attempt to quash the play quietly had backfired badly.

By no means all of the reaction was so supportive. While many members of the Dublin theatrical world felt great sympathy for the Pike and felt it was being scapegoated, others were far less understanding. As early as the night of Simpson's arrest, the actor Godfrey Quigley – who had, in the immortal phrase, 'drink taken' at the time – told Swift that Simpson had brought down the wrath of the law on Dublin theatre, adding that he hoped Simpson was sent to jail. Even to this day Swift finds it unbelievable that such sentiments should have come from the man whose own production of *I Am a Camera* at the Globe the year before had been seen as (successfully) courting controversy. At the time of the remarks Swift, shocked and emotional, had to be restrained from physically attacking Quigley. Less direct insults, however, were harder both to respond to and to endure. 'Quite a large number of people tended to avoid both myself and my wife', Simpson wrote later, 'and ... [o]rdinary citizens tended to shun us in shops and elsewhere.'[4]

This was putting a good face on it. In fact many erstwhile companions and bosom pals had, from the start of their trouble, treated Simpson and Swift as highly infectious moral lepers. With Simpson busy in his army job and surrounded by the support of his fellow-soldiers,[5] the brunt of this treatment (as Simpson himself later admitted) fell on Swift, who had to get used to acquaintances and even supposed friends avoiding eye-contact or sometimes crossing the street when they saw her approach. Then there were the public insults from complete strangers anxious to demonstrate their abhorrence of filth. While Swift nowadays resists all prompting to identify specific individuals ('It's long ago,' she says. 'People were frightened then. Things were different.') it is clear from hearing her speak for even a short time about this aspect of the matter that these personal slights and insults seared her in a way which the State's more threatening but also more impersonal assaults simply failed to do. She still refuses to have detail on these matters given here.

Deeply hurt though Swift was by such treatment – which she and Simpson risked whenever they appeared in public – she could do nothing about it. The household had to be run, the children had to be fed, the shopping had to be bought. But if even the simplest shopping trip risked becoming an occasion for wounding, it also provided – oddly enough – an opportunity for occasional uplift. Swift did much of her shopping in the working-class street market in Moore Street and the Dublin working class, then as ever, had little reason to cherish illusions about Irish law. Whenever Swift turned into Moore Street with her shopping bags, cries of 'Up *The Rose Tattoo*' would rise from some of the market traders and she frequently found her money being refused as stallholders loaded her shopping bags with free fruit and vegetables. It is one of the few memories of the time she still treasures, as is the case of the surgeon who refused payment for an operation on her daughter Gráinne, stipulating that the refusal was his contribution to the *Rose Tattoo* defence fund.

The doctor's preference for a private gesture, however, was in all likelihood caused by more than simply modesty. Even among the Pike's supporters, many felt wary of public involvement. When the Irish defence fund was set up by Jim Fitzgerald, director of Globe Theatre Productions, only two Irish newspapers would even print the letter announcing its launch. Fitzgerald had great trouble finding people who, however privately supportive of the Pike, dared associate their names with it in public by signing the letter for publication. When he sent a list of contributors to the Pike, Fitzgerald felt obliged to warn that the list must on no account be circulated, as many of those contributing were terrified that public knowledge of their support would lead to personal or business repercussions. Some even forbade Fitzgerald to give their names to Simpson himself. It is a sobering comment on Ireland in 1957 that neither Simpson nor Swift saw anything odd in this. 'Given the atmosphere of the time', Swift wrote later, 'many people might have suffered unpleasantness or even loss of employment or business, had they been seen to encourage us by financial support. So it was generous of them to give at all.'[6] In a society where even TDs who wrote letters mildly censorious of Church practices to the newspapers often felt obliged to use pseudonyms, such fear was not only to be expected; it was often a matter of simple common sense.

Every penny in the Pike fund was going to be needed. When the hearing began on July 4th Simpson was represented by a full legal team. This was highly unusual at such an early stage in a case, but Lehane was convinced that, with the State seeming so determined, Simpson's best hope lay in having a powerful defence team from the outset. Lehane himself would instruct, while Séamus Heavey, Henry Barron and Seán Hooper shared the actual courtroom duties. Barron would later become a High Court judge; Hooper, already well known as a formidable Senior Counsel, would enhance his reputation enormously with his ferocious defence of Alan Simpson. But Hooper's expertise did not come cheaply: Simpson would have to hand him £50 in cash (over IR£800 in 2001 prices) every morning before he appeared in court. Though organising that much cash could be a trial in itself, neither Swift nor Simpson would ever doubt that Hooper gave full value for money.

Having been widely reported worldwide, the *Rose Tattoo* case was by now an international phenomenon and on the morning of July 4th the public and press galleries of Dublin District Court were packed in a way any theatre might envy. R. P. Humphries, with Assistant State Solicitor Conway instructing, represented the State. The presiding judge was District Justice Cathal O'Flynn, who would stay with the case till the end. As soon as Humphries began to state the prosecution case it became clear that the goalposts had moved. Perhaps sensitive to the accusations (accepted as obvious fact in Northern Ireland and very widely believed in the South and elsewhere) that the case was inspired by the Catholic Church, the mention of profanity in the charge had been quietly dropped. A number of police officers, Humphries said, would give evidence that they had attended the play. The State would submit that these witnesses' evidence supported the charges: 'namely, that the play was indecent *and no longer profane* but obscene and such that its presentation by Mr Simpson created a breach of the law ...'[7]

The State's case, as became clear from the outset, was to be very simple and relied on convincing the court that *The Rose Tat-*

too itself was obscene. Simpson had demonstrably produced the play and sold tickets for it: if it were obscene then he was *ipso facto* guilty. The interesting thing was how the State meant to prove that the play, which had been made into an Oscar-winning film and was acknowledged around the world as a modern theatrical classic, was in fact a piece of gutter-level pornography. As very quickly became obvious, however, the State did not intend to actually *prove* anything at all. What it meant to do instead was produce a string of police witnesses who would simply *assert*, on the basis of their own interpretation of the play, that *The Rose Tattoo* was obscene, advancing as proof of this fact highly selective and often grossly misrepresented examples of events on-stage. Lehane's recently acquired familiarity with the text became the basis for the point-by-point demolition of the police evidence which ensued.

The first police witness to take the stand, after Inspector Scanlan had briefly described Simpson's arrest, was Detective Sergeant Frank Martin. Martin revealed that he had seen the play on three occasions, attending incognito twice and in uniform on the last night of the run. Simpson and Swift were shocked to hear for the first time that police observers had been among the audience almost from the first night.

In spite of Martin's having seen *The Rose Tattoo* three times, those familiar with the play found it hardly recognisable from his description of it, which concentrated exclusively on anything at all which might lend itself to a sexual interpretation:

> Serafina makes comments on love-making with her husband ... Assumpta mentions that she has some powders and suggests that Serafina ... put [them] in her husband's coffee ... it seemed to be for excitation of her husband ... A prostitute then enters, whose name is Estelle ...[8]

Every removal of a piece of clothing – whether a shoe or a dress and even if made for the purpose of going to bed for the night – was dutifully noted as such. Seemingly unfamiliar with such basic theatrical conventions as the division of a play into different acts,[9] Martin ran the action together in a fashion that left Swift unsure whether to laugh or cry. In Martin's version of the play, people simply came and went:

> At about this time Serafina appears, wearing just a slip and bare-footed ... One of [the] women mentions an incident concerning a girl stripped naked and sent home in a taxi ... Serafina looks up from her sewing and calls the two women "man-crazy things."

After the truck-driver Alvaro turns up – not to mention Rosa's sailor admirer, Jack Hunter – the already-steamy action in Martin's version of *The Rose Tattoo* heats up considerably:

> The lights go out and there is a suggestion that [Alvaro and Serafina] retire together for the night ... Rosa and the sailor enter and they commence love-making. Her dialogue suggests that she wishes to seduce the sailor ... Her actions were very suggestive. She leaned close to him and put her arms around him with a certain amount of abandon. After the sailor goes the daughter enters her house and removes her dress ... [10]

It emerged in cross-examination by Heavey that, on the second of his three visits to the play, Martin had brought his wife along – a fact which, given his lurid account of *The Rose Tattoo*'s contents, roused quite a bit of levity in court.[11] When asked if there was anything in the book that was not in the play Martin referred to a stage direction 'to the effect that [Alvaro] drops a white disc on the floor'. This was a reference to the condom and it is here, with the explicit evidence of the police witnesses, that the last nail in the coffin of that particular myth should hopefully lie: no condom was ever dropped on the stage of the Pike Theatre during any performance of *The Rose Tattoo*. Martin admitted that this particular stage direction had not been adhered to. If it *had* been done, he agreed, it would have been objectionable.

> But it was not carried into the performance? – No. It was a certain portion of a stage direction in the book.

That action was omitted when you saw the play? – Yes, on the
three occasions.

Still Martin maintained that the play as performed had been in
any case indecent, with 'illicit sex [as] the main motif. The only
lawful sex was at the beginning when the widow mentioned her
love-making with her husband.'[12] He had found the play indecent
on his first visit and had not altered his view after subsequent
viewings. In response to a direct question Martin conceded that he
had, in his evidence, concentrated on the parts of the play he had
found objectionable and omitted those that he had not. Heavey
now switched from the play to the topic that would unexpectedly
galvanise the prosecution – the background to the police actions.
He established again that Martin had first purchased tickets on the
day before the play opened. While he didn't follow the matter up,
he obviously found the fact interesting. Simpson and Swift found
it interesting too: it proved conclusively that the police interest
simply could not have resulted from a complaint by anyone who
had actually seen the show. Whatever the real objection to the
play, it could not be to their production as such. It had rankled
from the first that Simpson was denied any knowledge of his actual accuser: at least this basic fact, absolutely fundamental to the
entire legal system of the Western world, would surely have to
emerge in court. But as Simpson and Swift were about to discover,
the State did not want any questions that even appeared to lead in
that direction.

10. Hazy Ideas

It all started innocuously enough: Heavey asked Martin who had actually instructed him to buy tickets for *The Rose Tattoo*. Humphries, the State's barrister, immediately objected. This was a matter, he said, on which the witness must be protected. Heavey seems to have been genuinely astonished at this idea: protected? There was nothing to protect the witness from, he said. He was simply trying to establish Martin's state of mind when he bought the tickets. Justice O'Flynn overruled the objection and Martin said he had acted on verbal instructions from Detective Inspector Scanlan. He had bought the tickets and attended the performances on the Inspector's instructions and doing so had been the full extent of those instructions.

As would soon become evident, the State was unwilling to reveal any information whatsoever about the background to the *Rose Tattoo* case: not the source of the original complaint from the public nor whether there had ever been one. As regards the matter of police orders the state refused to divulge who had issued them or even (somewhat gobsmackingly) what they had been. At this point in the cross-examination, however, the depths of State secretiveness had not yet emerged and Heavey seems simply to have been trying to establish that Martin had gone to the Pike expecting to see a 'dirty' play – that he had formed a prejudice, before setting foot in the theatre, against whatever he might in fact see there. Hearing that buying tickets and attending the play had been the full extent of Martin's instructions, Heavey became at once both solicitous and sceptical:

I wonder whether you really mean that ... Were you told explicitly what to expect at the performance, or were you aware why you were going there? – I was not explicitly told what to expect.

What were you told? – Simply to see the play *The Rose Tattoo* at the Pike Theatre.

I don't suggest for a moment that you are being deliberately evasive: maybe I am not making myself clear to you. Were you told anything about this play that you were being sent to see before you attended the theatre? – I cannot remember any discussion of the play at all.

It seemed frankly incredible that a policeman would simply be given a ticket and told to attend a theatre without being told why – surely he would at least ask the purpose of his visit. But Heavey's attempts to secure an admission that anything like this had happened were stonewalled. Martin, by his own account, was a remarkably incurious human being:

Had you ever been given the price of a theatre ticket and told to go and see the performance in Dublin? – No. This is the first time.

Did you wonder at receiving these instructions the first time? – No. I did not.

Did you enquire what you were supposed to do when you got to the theatre? – I did not ask any questions.

What purpose did you think you were being sent to this performance for? – I thought there might be something objectionable in it. I assumed that.

Did you think the objectionableness had to do with indecency? – I had a hazy idea it would be on the lines of indecency.'

Having admitted this, Martin nonetheless insisted that he had gone to the theatre with 'an open mind'. He had 'hazily' anticipated indecency but at the same time he had not exactly assumed that he'd been sent there to *watch* for indecency. If he happened to see any, of course, it would be his duty to report it. Quite what Martin *did* think he'd been sent to the Pike for seemed to baffle

Heavey, as did the question of why a respectable Detective Sergeant would bring his wife to a play that by then, having already seen it, he was convinced was obscene. But Martin was adamant: he had been instructed to go and he had gone; he had asked no questions and been given no instructions. Not only that, but he and his wife had not discussed the play at all – indeed, the couple seemed well-matched, since she too had asked no questions as to why they were going. This might have been understandable if they were regular theatregoers, but – as Heavey now discovered – they were anything but:

> This much is right, anyway: you thought that there might be something objectionable in the performance before you took Mrs Martin. It was in your mind that there might be something objectionable and your duty was to spot it if there was. – Yes.
>
> Up to that were you anything of a playgoer? – No: I prefer cinema …
>
> How many times would you say you attended straight, legitimate theatre in Dublin? – I might have been a spectator twice over a period of about 20 years.

This admission caused further hilarity among the spectators, but it did help explain why the names of neither play nor author meant anything to Martin:

> Apart from that, did you know who had written it? – I did not; I had never heard of it…
>
> You had never heard of the author before? – No; I don't think so.

Having next established that Martin had written ('typewritten', Martin corrected him) his account of *The Rose Tattoo* only after his third time seeing it – that is, after Simpson's arrest – Heavey turned to the play itself and to Martin's account of it as given in his evidence. In forming his views, Heavey asked, had Martin taken into account the Censorship of Publications Act of 1929? Martin said he had not. Did Martin know that, 'among other

powers in the Act, there was power to prohibit the sale and distribution of a work which, in the opinion of the Censorship of Publications Board, is in its general tendency indecent or obscene?'
Martin said he did.

> Did you know that no order had been made in relationship to the
> book of this play? – I was not aware of that.
>
> Do you know that the book is freely purchasable in book-
> shops in Dublin? – I believe it can be purchased.

Turning finally to Martin's actual evidence, Heavey homed in
on the detective's repeated description of one character – Estelle –
as a prostitute. He asked Martin what made him so identify the
woman, who is nowhere referred to as such: she is in fact a card
dealer. The dialogue and the scenes, Martin answered, suggested it
to him.

> Did you ever, in the course of your official duties, have to deal
> with prostitutes? – No.
>
> Did you hear Estelle referred to as "a blackjack dealer from
> Texas in the Square Roof"[1] – I did; that is correct.
>
> I think blackjack is a card game played for money? – I cannot
> say.[2]
>
> Was there any particular episode that led you to think that
> Estelle was a prostitute? – The scene between Serafina and the
> truck-driver where he drops something from his pocket and to
> which she takes objection. She tells him to go to the Square Roof
> with it. From subsequent dialogue, I assumed that the article was
> a contraceptive.
>
> I understood you to say that no article was dropped in the
> play. – I said the suggestion of an article being dropped. I did not
> see anything dropped.
>
> Is Estelle the character with whom the widow's husband,
> when alive, was supposed to have been unfaithful? – That is cor-
> rect.
>
> And the widow has, a short time before, learned of this infi-
> delity? – I think so.
>
> I put it to you that that could only indicate that, *in the*

widow's view,[3] Estelle was a prostitute? – Yes.

Having forced Martin to correct one serious wrong impression which his evidence had given, Heavey now briefly moved to a second: that unending removal of clothing. Describing Martin's evidence in a 1993 interview, Swift recalled this vividly: 'detective Martin ... was absolutely obsessed with the idea that our production ... contained all sorts of nudity or at the very least indecent exposure. During the performance, if any character took off their coat, jacket, hat, shawl or whatever, detective Martin immediately stressed that so-and-so "removed a garment," so much so that in the end, so many garments were removed, you would almost have thought that the entire cast were absolutely starkers ... It really was the most peculiar evidence but it was also alarming to think that evidence as bad as this could result in Alan's imprisonment.'[4]

Heavey too felt this matter should be clarified, especially in the matter of Serafina's teenage daughter. A few questions sufficed to make Martin concede that 'apart from the removal of her dress and shoes in one scene, the daughter, Rosa, remains fully dressed throughout the play.'

At this point, having corrected some of the worst impressions given by Martin's evidence and started a few hares on the matter of the police instructions, the defence rested. Re-examined by Humphries for the prosecution, Martin still insisted (in spite of the holes Heavey had picked in his version of events) that he 'had given, to the best of his knowledge, a full summary of the play'.

With the conclusion of Martin's evidence the first day's proceedings ended. Alan Simpson was remanded on continuing bail. The court would sit again on the following Monday, July 8th, when Detective Sergeant P.J. Kenny would give evidence. It was in the course of Kenny's cross-examination that the case would become even *more* peculiar, and the State would seem to lose the run of itself entirely and show signs of what Flann O'Brien used to call a case of the headstaggers.

When the court reconvened on Monday morning the gallery was again crowded. Sensational accounts of Martin's evidence had appeared prominently in British and Irish newspapers over the weekend and demand for seats in court was great. Kenny was sworn in and began to give his evidence. He stated that he had gone to the Pike with Detective Sergeant P.J. Farrell on May 14th. Kenny's long account of the play, while less sweaty than Martin's, followed an identical pattern: *The Rose Tattoo* was 'about' sex. The non-condom (as it were) reappeared and Kenny (to further public hilarity) was very clear on the point that the object which did not fall to the floor was definitely a contraceptive: 'That scene conveyed to me', Kenny said, 'that a contraceptive had been dropped, but in fact I saw no object dropped.'

It was also Kenny, on this day, who made probably the most-appreciated comic contribution to the *Rose Tattoo* case from the gallery's point of view. He was referring to Serafina's parrot, a supposed presence on-stage which was, in the Pike production, simply but effectively represented by a half-concealed empty bird-cage and some sound-effects. Reference had been made in the play to the best method of sexing the parrot which, in Kenny's words, '*purported* to be in a cage in the room'. As Swift recalls, the detective's choice of words was almost too much even for the District Justice. It was certainly too much for the spectators: Martin's admission that he had brought his wife to see the play had caused some giggles but Kenny's purporting parrot made the whole courtroom explode into prolonged laughter. When it finally died down Kenny set it off all over again by explaining helpfully that 'It was my opinion that you could not know the sex of a parrot because of the feathers.'

Kenny too had seen the play more than once. He had bought a copy of the text of *The Rose Tattoo* on May 22nd. On May 23rd he'd sworn an information[5] before District Justice Reddin and obtained a warrant for Alan Simpson's arrest, which he had given to Superintendent Weymes. Seán Hooper reserved cross-examination till the next sitting, which would be on the following Thursday (July 11th). It was during that cross-examination that the nonsensical nature of the State's case really began to manifest itself. First Kenny provided the gallery with another good laugh when he revealed that he had bought his copy of *The Rose Tattoo* at Messrs J. Duffy & Co. of Westmoreland Street, a shop synonymous throughout Ireland with the sale of Catholic books and religious paraphernalia. The fact that Alan Simpson was facing prison for producing a play whose non-banned text could be bought from the most famous Catholic bookshop in Ireland seemed to many to underline the absurdity of the entire proceedings.

Precisely as Heavey had done earlier with Martin's evidence, Hooper now began to unpick Kenny's. Hooper, however, was rather less gentle than Heavey, and Kenny was rather less stolid than Martin. Both policemen had referred in their evidence to an incident not performed, only reported, in the play – an occasion when some American Legionaries had (according to them) torn a girl's clothes off and sent her home naked in a taxi. Now Hooper forced Kenny to concede that nowhere in either the text or the Pike production had it been said that the girl was stripped naked – it had simply been his own mistaken impression. Under Hooper's prodding, Kenny was similarly forced to retract or qualify many of the other things he had stated in evidence, in the process – since much of Kenny's evidence basically replicated Martin's – casting doubts on even those aspects of Martin's testimony which had escaped Heavey's assault. Kenny (like Martin) had portrayed the relationships between the two couples in the play – Serafina and Alavaro and Jack Hunter and Rosa – as being dominated by sex. Hooper took him back through his evidence.

> Hooper: Wasn't it plain that Hunter wanted to marry Rosa?
> Witness: I don't think there was any mention of marriage.
> Hooper: Without mentioning the word, wasn't it plain that was what Hunter wanted?

Witness: There was mention that he gave her the little ring on her ear.

Hooper: You said that but you left out one vital thing, 'to put on my finger'.

Witness: When you remind me I can remember that.

By the time Hooper was finished jogging Kenny's memory, the policeman's picture of two rampantly sex-obsessed couples had, under Hooper's relentless probing, turned into a portrait of two loving couples understandably eager to be properly and right-eously married – not quite the same thing, even in 1950s Ireland. Following the pattern established by Heavey, Hooper next turned to the matter of Kenny's instructions. Once again, Kenny's responses pointed to the ridiculous character of the State's case.

Hooper first asked, innocuously enough, whether Kenny had been instructed to attend the Pike. Kenny replied that he had. But when Hooper then asked from whom the instructions had come, the prosecution objected, saying they 'objected to any questions in regard to instructions given to a detective officer'. 'I propose to make an objection', Humphries said, 'but I think it should be based on something the witness says.' Hooper obligingly repeated the question: by whom had Kenny been instructed to go to the play? Kenny said he had received his instructions from Superintendent Weymes. Hooper then stated that he proposed to ask what instructions were given, to which Kenny responded: 'I claim privilege on that.'

This was a definite show-stopper. In recent days the *Rose Tattoo* courtroom had provided moments of laughter and astonishment for the spectators, but now it was the lawyers, or at least the defence lawyers – not to mention the judge – who were astonished. The spectators didn't react to Kenny's claim, for the good reason that most of them didn't know what he was talking about. A claim for privilege was rare, although it was most certainly not an obscure legal technicality – quite the opposite. The 'privilege' involved in such a claim is no small thing: it is the privilege of re-

fusing to answer a direct question under oath and can only be in-
voked in extremely serious matters, where a full answer to the
question posed risks which are – in very special and limited circumstances, such as directly endangering life or perhaps ruining a
major police investigation – against the larger public interest.
'[T]he claim of privilege', Swift notes in *Stage by Stage*, 'was normally used where the revealing of internal communications in the
Secret Service might endanger security.'[6] That Kenny should claim
privilege in a preliminary hearing on a matter such as this seemed
almost beyond incredible. It could not possibly be something he'd
done off his own bat, however frazzled he might be by Hooper's
questioning.

'On whose orders do you claim privilege?' Humphries asked.

'On the orders of my superiors,' Kenny said.

It was official then: as the court would soon discover, everything pertaining to the background of the police actions against
The Rose Tattoo was, in fact if not quite in name, a State secret.[7]

11. Privilege

While the defence team struggled to accept what was happening, Humphries began to cite cases in support of the privilege claim. Hooper's indignation now was very real. He was amazed at the claim, he said. The defence would be hamstrung if it were accepted. In any case only three people had the right to make a claim for privilege – the Garda Commissioner, the Minister for Justice or the Secretary of the Justice Department.[1] If Kenny was – as he said – acting on the instructions of Superintendent Weymes, then the claim was not properly made. Hooper declared himself 'astounded to think that the court might not get all the evidence that the witness had sworn to give. The defendant would not be getting complete justice if the matter were to be kept in the dark.'

District Justice O'Flynn agreed fully with Hooper. '[H]e was satisfied that the question for which privilege was claimed should be answered. He considered that the cases quoted were not to the point and that the question put by Mr Hooper was not intended to elicit save what was strictly germane to the play and its performance.'

Humphries asked for an adjournment so that he might consider the matter further. This was granted and the court adjourned until after lunch. When Humphries came back the situation was hardly ameliorated: the goalposts were moving again, or rather the sworn evidence was. Kenny, in claiming privilege, had said he was acting on the instructions of Superintendent Weymes. Humphries now wished to correct that statement. Asked by O'Flynn if he had any objection, Hooper replied (quite sensibly) that he didn't know what was going to be corrected: 'The claim for privilege, according to the witness, was based on the instructions of Supt. Weymes and he was not the proper person to claim it. What has happened in the interval?'

O'Flynn agreed and refused to allow any correction. Then Humphries played his trump card: 'This matter being of paramount importance to the State', he said, 'I must ask you to state a case for the High Court under Section 83 of the Courts of Justice Act, 1924.'

Hooper had already been annoyed; now he blew a gasket. There was no way that the application should be granted, he said. 'The reality of the present application … was to stop the court from hearing or inquiring into a piece of evidence that was of vital importance.'

In saying this, Hooper had to be fishing: he had no way of knowing the importance or otherwise of the matter. But if you go to great lengths to conceal something, it will naturally seem to people that you have something to conceal; and if you make a great fuss about preventing its discovery, then they will naturally assume that you do not want it found. Hooper smelt a rat. This time, however, O'Flynn did not concur and decided that the point should indeed be referred to the High Court for a decision. In the meantime his own court would continue hearing evidence. The rest of the day was taken up by the evidence of Detective Sergeant Frank Wedick, and there were no further shocks until Wedick's cross-examination began on July 15th, the next day the court sat. Today Hooper knew what he was after and he wasted no time going after it. Had Wedick made a statement about this play before he gave evidence? He had. Had he brought it with him? Wedick believed it was with counsel for the prosecution. Did it relate to what he had seen on the stage and the impression it had made on him? Yes.

At this there was an objection from Humphries. He objected, he said, to any questions being asked about the statement. This seemed plainly preposterous. Hooper said carefully that he was now going to ask for Wedick's statement. Humphries repeated his objection. Hooper pointed out that he was simply asking for the statement 'without details'. Suddenly Wedick, like Kenny before him, claimed privilege. Hooper was now well and truly flabbergasted. Kenny's privilege claim, empty though it had seemed, had at least related to instructions given to him by his superiors. But Wedick's related to his impressions of the play – the very subject he was on the stand to testify about. What could be privileged in that?

Wedick produced a document which he read aloud. The document said he was authorised to claim privilege in the matter of 'any instructions, directions or communications given by or to or between members of the Garda Síochána'.[2] This was quite a claim: the defence was to be denied access to any information at all about the police actions, or their orders, or the source of their orders, or indeed to any internal police communication whatsoever which related to the case. Given that the behaviour of the police had from the first been the most flagrantly odd thing about the whole affair, this would close off one of the defence's most glaringly obvious lines of exploration.

After some semantic arguments about whether Wedick's statement was, as Hooper claimed, a 'statement' (and thus outside the terms of the claim) or as Wedick called it a 'report' (and thus within the terms), O'Flynn decided that they would argue the toss later. First the court heard the evidence of Detective Sergeant Patrick Farrell. Farrell testified that he attended the Pike on May 14th with Sergeant Kenny and went in using two tickets given to them by Superintendent Weymes. In the Pike, Farrell said he 'saw a performance entitled *The Rose Tattoo*', which he proceeded to describe in the by-now standard police manner. After Farrell finished his evidence the lawyers returned to the arguments about police privilege, which – as O'Flynn had already pointed out – seemed to be claimed today on quite a different basis from the previous claim. Humphries cited 'public interest' in support of the privilege claim. Hooper cited the same argument, in terms which sound far more congenial to the modern ear, against it. His utter frustration is clear even from his recorded words:

> If privilege ever did exist; if ever there was a case in which that privilege should be waived in the public interest, this is such a case. I am not seeking to obtain anything that can properly be regarded as confidential communication between a police officer and his superiors. I am simply seeking statements of fact.

This was the nub of the matter: with the prosecution seemingly reliant on the unsupported statements of police witnesses – statements in which cross-examination had already punched substantial holes, forcing retractions in every case – the defence was to be denied access to the most basic facts relating precisely to the most dubious aspect of the entire case. After more argument Humphries again asked, for the second time in two days in court, that a case be stated to the High Court. For the second time O'Flynn acceded to the request. Hooper yielded to the inevitable: given the prosecution's obstructing tactics, the defence case was impossible to conduct as it stood. With this in mind he requested that the entire case be put on hold until the High Court had reached a decision. O'Flynn agreed and set the date of the next sitting for fourteen days after the High Court judgement, whenever and whatever it might be.

With the referral to the High Court, the *Rose Tattoo* case turned the corner that would make it into a marathon affair. Its legal significance also leapt beyond the point where it was about the Pike Theatre or, indeed, any individual case. The issue which went before the High Court was the fundamental one of a defendant's right to have access to information: the Court's decision would establish a legal precedent with implications for every criminal case in Ireland. This was of no consolation at all to the Pike: even nowadays, people in conflict with the Irish State have every reason to worry if the stakes in that conflict are raised. But Simpson and Swift had far more immediate causes for concern. The uncertainty prolonged their current status as pariahs. Worse still, the position of the Pike itself was growing impossible.

From the beginning Lehane had impressed on Simpson and Swift the absolute necessity of avoiding any further controversy. In particular they must be very careful about what plays they staged in Herbert Lane. The vigilantes would most certainly be keeping a very close eye on the Pike now, as indeed would be the State itself; it would damage the defence case immensely if there were even a whiff of controversy – however groundless – connected with another Pike production. Nothing would suit the State better than an excuse to make some further move against the theatre and Simpson and Swift must stage nothing that might offend the sensibilities of even the least rabid lay cleric.

This was easier said than done. Given the often-surreal worldview of the Catholic Right, it was often impossible to anticipate what might offend them. Lehane's injunction was obviously wise but it placed the Pike in an impossible position. The theatre had been established as a place to present challenging dramatic work on the Irish stage. It was precisely by doing so that it had achieved its success. If the sensibilities of religious fundamentalists or an opportunistic State were to dictate what was staged in Herbert Lane then the Pike would no longer be the same theatre. But Simpson and Swift didn't exactly have a lot of choice in the matter: with their mounting legal bills now greatly compounded by the prospect of the High Court appeal (they'd bear costs if they lost), they desperately needed any income the Pike might bring in, whatever plays it staged.

Even here, however, they faced difficulty. Like all the little theatres, the Pike had been perpetually run on a shoestring. It had always depended heavily for its backstage staff on volunteers seeking experience or simply wanting to be associated with the glamour of theatre. Its pool of reliable helpers in everything from the cloakroom to the sale of soft drinks had mainly consisted of nice, young, middle-class Dublin girls keen to be associated with the glamorous theatrical world; but nice middle-class Dublin parents no longer wanted their daughters associated with a theatre stained with scandal. Worse, the possible taint of being associated with the Pike had a terrible effect on both audiences and – particularly – on paying club membership, which the Pike heavily relied on. At its height, membership of the Pike Theatre Club had stood at 3,000; already it was tumbling (by the time the *Rose Tattoo* case ended, it would stand at 300).[3] And staging the sort of work that was guaranteed to offend no one at all would do nothing to rectify that situation.

A combination of these and other factors would, over the coming months, bleed the Pike Theatre white. Worst of all was the knowledge that, with the blackest of ironies, even court-room success would be financially disastrous if the case were prolonged. If Simpson went to trial and were acquitted, he would not be liable to costs. But in a preliminary hearing – which was normally a short, straightforward affair – there was no mechanism by which Simpson might reclaim his costs, whatever the result of the hearing itself. It is only when contemplating the Pike's financial situation that one really begins to understand the bleakness that hangs about Swift's own memories of the next year.[4] For the simple truth was that, whatever might happen in court, the financial situation alone seemed guaranteed to – at best – destroy the Pike's long-cherished plans. Even as early as July 1957, it seemed very possible that it would destroy the Pike itself.

The first casualty of the new reality was the Pike's next scheduled production, Ugo Betti's *Crime on Goat Island*, a play which (like *The Rose Tattoo* itself) Simpson and Swift had longed to stage since seeing it in France in 1953. Betti's British agents had agreed to a London transfer if the play succeeded in Dublin, as Simpson and Swift had been confident it would. Their production had been planned as another vehicle for Anna Manahan – whose performance in *The Rose Tattoo* had, thanks to the English reviews, attracted much serious attention from Britain – along with Dónal Donnelly and Kate Binchy. But these arrangements had been made in that other universe that the Pike had so recently inhabited. If *Crime on Goat Island* were staged now, featuring as it did a man who was conducting simultaneous affairs with several women, the lay clerics of Dublin would have the Pike for breakfast. Production plans were immediately scrapped. Instead, in August, the Pike produced *Stealing the Picture*, a light comedy by Joy Rudd and Carolyn Swift. Swift herself has described the piece as 'a comedy of minimal danger about Irish *mores*'. Reviews were careful and audience numbers on the whole poor. It was a new situation for the Pike; but it was one to which it would have to accustom itself.

Swift and Simpson, of course, were not the only ones involved. Pat Nolan received a severe dressing-down from his employers, Dublin Corporation.[5] Kate Binchy was jostled and heckled on a bus by a woman who recognised her as 'the girl who'd been naked onstage in the Pike Theatre'.[6] Anna Manahan's landlady was approached by concerned neighbours who urged her to get rid of her immoral lodger. Rumours about what had actually gone on in the Pike – the precursors of all the later mythology – were rife. Godfrey Quigley reported to Manahan a story he had heard of how seven men had laced her into a corset on-stage. Swift herself came across a version of the same rumour, only this time it was four men *removing* the corset. It was also Swift who came across a report of a chorus-line of women dressed in corsets.[7] Others spoke of Alan Simpson showing pornographic films on his garage wall.[8]

In the long silence before the High Court sat, the rumours flourished, while media interest, distracted by fresh events, waned. In an effort to keep up publicity and raise funds, Simpson and Swift approached Claud Cockburn with the idea of selling a series of articles to one of the English newspapers. Cockburn put them in touch with his own agents and Swift wrote the first of the proposed series, sending it to London under Simpson's name. But by now there were fresh headlines and six months later the series remained unsold. The agents ruefully reported that the newspapers would only be interested once the case returned to court.

Contributions to the fighting fund continued to come in as before, but they could come nowhere near the amounts already owed. In August Samuel Beckett wrote a sympathetic letter with a cheque. Elia Kazan, Tennessee Williams's close collaborator as a director both on stage and screen, sent fifty dollars. Simpson and Swift would enlist his aid in trying to reassure Williams himself that they had treated his work respectfully, but even Kazan's intercession wouldn't mollify the tetchy Williams, who would remain convinced that the Pike must have traduced his play. Some of those associated with Williams were, like Kazan, more forthcoming: Secker and Warburg, Williams's English publishers, sent a contribution, as did the cast of his play *Camino Real*, then running in London. Local notables also contributed. Lord Longford (perhaps troubled by his conscience) gave five pounds, Lord Kilbracken five guineas. Noel Browne, who had himself fallen so foul of Church *mores*, sent what he could. But still the main potential fundraising tool was the Pike itself and still the Pike was hamstrung by the need to be fantastically careful in its selection of plays. A Ionesco double-bill was put on in October – the Pike, even in adversity, was proud that both plays were again English-language premières – but ran for only 12 performances.

Simpson and Swift were unexpectedly offered a chance to take a Pike revue to England, then on the brink of its own satire boom. They had no material ready for a new revue – it would have been downright insane for them to stage hard-hitting satire in Dublin at that point – but it seemed foolish to let the English opportunity slip. Swift had a little fresh material written and added a selection of the strongest of the existing *Follies* sketches. After the Ionesco double-bill opened she and Simpson went to England to make arrangements for the show, which was to play in Cambridge as well as London. But on October 11th, while they were still in London, an urgent telegram arrived from Con Lehane: the High Court had taken up the case with no warning – the first sitting had already taken place, without them, that very afternoon.

12. Appeals and Alarums

The arguments before the High Court were purely legal and technical and Simpson himself wasn't required to appear. But the fact that his fate was being decided back in Ireland understandably weighed on his and Swift's minds and they hurriedly made their business arrangements in Britain and went home to attend court. The scene in the High Court was very different from that in the District Court. Here there were no witnesses, only lawyers arguing dry legal technicalities to the three High Court judges. There were no cues for even nervous laughter; instead the whole business was solemn, depressing and highly technical. Swift found she could hardly hear the proceedings, never mind follow them.

It is clear from the case District Justice O'Flynn stated to the High Court that he himself was in no doubt that the State's privilege claims were inadmissible. Of Kenny's original claim of privilege and the cases which Humphries had cited in support of it, O'Flynn wrote: 'I considered that the cases ... were not applicable to the claim of privilege ... also ... that the claim of privilege was not properly made nor on proper authority.' He was equally sceptical in Wedick's case: 'I considered that ... the document was not privileged ... also ... that the claim of privilege was not properly made, nor on the directions of the proper authority.' He had stated the case, O'Flynn wrote, only because there were issues at law to be decided. These, specifically, were:

> 1. Is the witness, Detective Sergeant Kenny, privileged in refusing to disclose the instructions he received from Superintendent Weymes?

2. Is the witness, Detective Sergeant Wedick, privileged in refusing to produce his written statement as aforesaid?[1]

This was what the three High Court judges – Cahir Davitt, President of the High Court, and Justices Teeven and Dixon – had to decide. For all that the proceedings were dull, the matter to be decided was a very important one. Humphries had declared that the State, in the person of the Attorney General, did not like revealing *any* inter-police communications in open court. If the State's refusal to produce records in this instance – a refusal that even the presiding judge found dubious – was accepted, it would set a legal precedent for future State prosecutions, permitting the police a lack of oversight amounting to *carte blanche*. That such large issues could be raised by their case seemed almost grotesque to Swift and Simpson and only emphasised their own powerlessness. They had the distinct sense that they were caught up in matters way beyond them.

The deliberations in the High Court lasted for five days. Swift and Simpson, in their separate accounts of the outcome, both use the word 'horror' to describe their reaction to the outcome. One can see why: Justice Davitt, the High Court President, found that the police were not privileged; but Justices Teeven and Dixon, outvoting him, found that they were. Simpson and Swift were not merely back to square one; they were back to square one and, since the verdict had gone against them, liable for the costs of the expensive High Court proceedings – they were financially ruined.

Con Lehane laid out for Simpson his rapidly dwindling options, which by now amounted to a total of precisely two. One was simply to accept the High Court ruling and return to the District Court. This meant the case would continue as it had gone on: with the prosecution seemingly perfectly willing (and, armed with the High Court ruling, now perfectly able) to turn proceedings into an even more complete farce, stopping the defence dead in its tracks whenever an inconvenient question was asked. The other option – an almost insanely risky one at this point – was to appeal the High Court decision to the Supreme Court. If the Supreme Court found for Simpson, the game would once more be afoot; but if the Supreme Court upheld the High Court ruling then Simpson and Swift would bear the costs of the appeal proceedings as well – they would be beyond ruin, facing outright destitution whilst the *Rose Tattoo* case itself would still be at the stage of a preliminary hearing!

That night, at their home on Leeson Street, Simpson and Swift had one of the most important discussions in the whole of the *Rose Tattoo* case – probably one of the most important in their married lives. A few short months before they'd been on top of the world, the darlings of the political and social Establishment; now they were, effectively, already ruined. Whether the case went to trial or not, and whatever the eventual outcome of a trial might be, they were by this stage so much in debt that, as Swift puts it, 'the combined sale of our house, theatre, car and the clothes off our backs looked like being insufficient'.[2] The State seemed committed to having a trial and to doing so no matter what happened in the District Court – the Attorney General had let the defence team know he meant to mount his own prosecution if the District Justice didn't come to the 'right' decision. Now the High Court decision had gone the State's way – Simpson and Swift could either just accept that or they could stake everything on a last throw of the dice in the Supreme Court. There were no other options.

Many things contributed to the decision that Simpson and Swift finally made. Their belief that they had done no wrong was as strong as ever and they also believed that – for the sake of Irish theatre if nothing else – the case must be fought. Given a choice, they would just as soon have seen somebody else fight it; but they hadn't been given that choice. And they were certainly fighters – the mere existence of the Pike itself was proof of that. They had never taken a risk as great as the one that now faced them but in some ways they felt that they no longer even had a choice in the matter. It was, in a way, the very extremity of their position that made up their minds and the heavy-handedness of the State that made them, in turn, stubborn: they were backed into a corner. If they'd been *almost* financially ruined then they might have hugged what little money they had left, in hopes of somehow surviving what lay ahead and starting afresh afterwards. But as things stood they had nothing left to lose.

In the simplest terms, they decided they might as well be hung for a sheep as for a lamb. 'It was', Alan Simpson wrote in 1962, 'really a gambler's decision of Double or Quits.'[3] 'It hardly seemed to matter', Swift wrote more than 20 years later, 'whether we owed thousands of pounds or tens of thousands. We decided to go for broke and appeal to the Supreme Court.'[4] Next day Simpson conveyed the news to Con Lehane. Given his own pugnacity and belief in the importance of the case, it's hard to believe that Lehane wasn't pleased.

After the agonising came the anti-climax: the appeal had to wait until the Supreme Court could deal with it. As it turned out, this would not be until April of the following year, 1958. Determined though Simpson and Swift now were, this was a disheartening blow. The Pike's agony, and its muzzled state, was prolonged. The British *Follies* tour (which had played for a few weeks at the Pike before going to London) was a disappointment. After a sombre Christmas the theatre produced the English-language première of Michel de Ghelderode's *Pantagleize*, but like the Ionesco double-bill it played to half-empty houses and closed after a fortnight.

By the time the Supreme Court hearing arrived, the *Rose Tattoo* case had been joined by a second theatrical furore – the enormous row which broke out over the 1958 Theatre Festival. With the full story behind the *Tattoo* case unknown, but a popular recognition that it could only have arisen through the offending of Catholic sensibilities, one would have thought that the organisers of the 1958 festival would have been extremely careful to avoid anything at all that might give rise to a fresh row. The sight of a daring theatre in the dock could only be a cause for celebration to the zealots, and it is very difficult to avoid the conclusion that there were few things as dangerous in Holy Catholic Ireland as zealotry with the bit between its teeth.

Only months before, Bord Fáilte – who had overall charge of the festival – had assured Robert Briscoe (still chairman of the Tóstal committee) that *Bloomsday* (an adaptation from James Joyce's *Ulysses*), along with *The Drums of Father Ned* (a new O'Casey play) and works by Beckett, 'should be the basis of the 1958 programme'. This was because '[I]n the opinion of the board, the *Bloomsday* and O'Casey productions would be likely to have the greatest effect towards inducing people to visit Ireland for the festival'[5] – that is to say, they would attract the most tourists. With this seemingly settled, someone asked Archbishop McQuaid to sanction a votive Mass blessing the Festival, as he had done before. But because of the inclusion of 'anti-Catholic' writers – especially Joyce – McQuaid declined. What followed was a hugely complicated comedy of errors typical of the times, with double- and triple-dealing, misunderstandings, secret plots, massive integrity, utter spinelessness and – as so very often in the controversies of the era – Dr McQuaid standing innocently by as his lay allies, particularly his close associates in the Knights of St Columbanus, exerted both public and covert pressure on the Theatre Festival committee.

While the documents relating to the matter in his archives make it clear that McQuaid's original involvement was not deliberate on his part (the ultimate author of the conflict may be seen as the person who decided – off his own bat, it would seem – to ask the Archbishop to sanction a Mass for a programme that included work by the Irish Church's *bête noire*, Joyce) it is also clear that, once involved, the Archbishop fought effectively, ruthlessly and secretively, using third parties to exert pressure on officialdom while maintaining a public pose of haughty rectitude. The end result was that both *Bloomsday* and the O'Casey play – so recently seen by its sponsors as the basis of the whole Festival – were taken off the programme, the former entirely through the committee's (and Bord Fáilte's) funk but the latter (it must be admitted) at least in part because O'Casey himself was a contrary old git – as he had, of course, earned every right to be. Beckett, outraged by the whole affair and by the insult to his mentor, Joyce, not only removed his own work from the programme but placed a blanket ban on any of his plays being performed in the Irish Republic – a ban which was particularly galling to the Pike, which had hoped to use its friendly relationship with him to help its fading fortunes.

In the welter of insult and injury, accusations, counter-allegations and counter-counter-allegations, the entire Theatre Festival collapsed. Perhaps the best comment on the whole affair was that made by Hilton Edwards, who'd been scheduled to produce the Joyce play and whose long-standing contempt for the everyday hypocrisies of Irish officialdom was glacial both in its size and its temperature: 'What this really means', Edwards said, 'is that that there is, as there always has been, a rigid censorship of plays and everything else ... everyone will feel very smug and very pure here and they will be wrong as usual.'[6]

The whole affair had taken place against the background of the Hierarchy's great Campaign against Evil Literature, an enormous drive against a foul tide of depraved material – including paperbacks and horror comics – which took up much of the first part of that year.[7] This campaign, aimed at forcing the Government to extend and strengthen Ireland's already-notorious censorship of printed matter, involved the use of the full bag of tricks of both the clerical and lay Catholic Establishments. Between that, the *Rose Tattoo* affair and now the Tóstal row, many seemed to see a sort of giant Church conspiracy in operation and there was very genuine paranoia and fear in the air in arts circles. At a meeting called by angry members of Actor's Equity on April 27th, following the scrapping of the Theatre Festival, Alan Simpson made by far the most uncompromising and pugnacious of the recorded contributions. 'Whatever plans are made for future festivals', he told the meeting, 'no compromise must be made on the freedom of the theatre, which was won during the early battles between the Abbey Theatre and the Castle Authorities. We must continue to fight for the Festival and on no account compromise our principles.'[8]

While this might seem to fly in the face of Lehane's advice about keeping a low profile, perhaps Simpson felt the die was already cast: though the judgement had not yet been given, the Supreme Court hearing in his own case had concluded the previous day. The Court had spent four days considering the matter and on May 9th – three days short of the anniversary of *The Rose Tattoo*'s first night and (though this would not be known for more than 40 years) a year to the day since the Irish Department of Justice had first had *The Rose Tattoo* drawn to its attention – delivered its verdict. While it was, from the Pike's view, a bit of a parson's egg, the judgement contained a great deal of very good news. But it also contained elements of the sort that left mere laymen scratching their heads.

First of all the Supreme Court found that, as the defence had insisted all along, District Justice O'Flynn had been wrong to state a case to the High Court. Therefore the High Court's decision that O'Flynn had been *right* to refer the case was struck out. In the matter of costs for the High Court hearings, the Supreme Court ruled that – since the case should never have been stated in the first place – these would no longer be borne by the Pike but would revert to the State. Furthermore, costs in the present Supreme Court hearing would be split, with the defence paying for only one of the five days that the court had sat and the State paying for the other four. The Pike was still cripplingly in debt and Simpson still faced the possibility of trial and prison; but the huge costs of the higher court hearings had been almost entirely removed and the law had come down firmly, on this point at least, on the side of Alan Simpson.

Unfortunately for the Pike, these were not the only matters dealt with in the ruling and it is here that the Supreme Court judgement left the layman's mind behind. The Court found that the High Court's ruling in *favour* of the prosecution on the privilege issue still stood – even though the case should never have gone to the High Court in the first place. '[A]lthough the District Justice had ruled that the police were not entitled to claim privilege', the Supreme Court found, 'the High Court had ruled otherwise. This established a precedent by a higher authority which the law would now have to follow.' For the moment, at least, the implications of this were lost in the tide of relief that surged over Simpson, Swift and their supporters. Four of the five Supreme Court judges had supported the ruling, with only Cearbhall Ó Dálaigh, the future President, dissenting. Simpson himself would later describe the Supreme Court judges' decision as 'a cunning judgement worthy of King Solomon and the Baby'.[9] It was all of that.

The *Rose Tattoo* case returned to the District Court on June 3rd, where the parade of police witnesses resumed. There was, however, a notable difference in the atmosphere of the court – or rather in the prosecution's attitude. Humphries and his colleagues were now far less prickly and belligerent and their main aim seemed to be to have the case over and done with. Though the prosecution duly introduced the rest of its evidence, they struck Simpson and Swift as merely going through the motions. Perhaps it was simply confidence: the Supreme Court decision had tied the defence's hands on the issue which had seemed most to exercise the prosecution – questions relating to the policemen's instructions. Deprived of the power to investigate these, the defence was limited to picking holes in the actual police evidence. This, however, Hooper made a point of doing. Inspector Ward, the policeman who'd first called to the Pike, described the events of that fine May evening, now just over twelve months before. As Ward recalled it, he'd gone to Herbert Lane and 'told Captain Simpson that if the play was not immediately taken off or expurgated to the point where all objectionable passages and situations were removed, he and his colleagues would be arrested'.[10]

The defence, naturally, fastened on Ward's depiction of this as a reasonable request. Under cross-examination the Inspector did admit that he 'had not given Capt. Simpson or any of his co-directors or officials of the theatre any particulars of the passages or situations required to be removed.' Given the heavy-handedness of the actual police behaviour, no attempt by them to portray themselves as the voice of sweet reason could be allowed to go un-challenged.

At the end of an anti-climactic day the case was adjourned for a further 48 hours and on Thursday, June 5th, on what was proba-bly the most anti-climactic day of all, the prosecution finished presenting its case. The case itself seemed tired. Cathal O'Flynn deferred his judgement, which he said he would deliver on the following Monday. Of all the periods of suspense for the Pike, that weekend was possibly the most agonising of all. Asked now about those three miserable days, Carolyn Swift cannot recall a single thing that she or Simpson did or said. It was simply a blank period of waiting to hear what the fate of Simpson – and, by ex-tension, of his family and his theatre – was going to be. After all of their efforts, the matter was finally out of their hands: their whole future depended entirely on Cathal O'Flynn. Simpson and Swift were still certain of their own (and the play's) innocence, but after the last 13 months they were no longer so certain that, in 1950s Ireland, that would make any difference.

13. Endgame

The greater part of District Justice Cathal O'Flynn's judgement, delivered on June 8th 1958, gave no real clue as to what its final conclusions would be. More than half of the 90-minute judgement was taken up with matters of definition and with emphasising the importance of the case, which O'Flynn was at pains to stress. This lengthy preamble was a conscious attempt to lay down the most solid possible foundation for what he was about to say. To Simpson and Swift, though, as they sat in court and tried desperately to glean hints of what was coming, it was a torment.

There were, in retrospect, a few moments in the judgement's early stages when some indication of O'Flynn's views did seem to seep into his words. Perhaps the most telling of these was when he spoke of his own responsibility in the case, noting that his basic job, in determining whether or not to send the case for trial, was to decide whether a jury might reasonably be expected to convict the accused on the basis of the evidence the prosecution had produced. In his clarification of what exactly he meant by 'a jury', however, the bland legal tone of the judgement's early part seems briefly to slip and a strong, genuine distaste for extremists of all stripes to show through.

> The word jury does not connote twelve self-righteous bigots, or twelve hypocrites, or twelve humbugs, or twelve hysterics, or twelve amorists, or twelve debauched *roués*, or twelve dedicated thespians, or twelve lubricists, or twelve ritualistic liberals who have made up a martyrdom of authors or playwrights who have suffered from enforcement of the laws of obscenity. 'A jury repre-

sents a cross-section of the community and has a special aptitude for reflecting the views of the average person.'[1]

O'Flynn was obviously well aware of the larger issues which, beyond the courtroom, had attached themselves to the case and which for many people already overshadowed all questions of Alan Simpson's innocence or guilt. He explicitly rejected any idea that he himself was there to pass judgement on those larger issues and specifically on any question of the artistic merit (or otherwise) of *The Rose Tattoo* itself. His duty was (as he would say later in the judgement) 'to find if the evidence establishes a *prima facie* case … Is the play a filthy play? – That is the question. Not is it a great work of art in the tradition of Euripides, Aeschylus, Sophocles, Shakespeare? Not is it a play written by the half-educated for the half-witted? What is wrong with contemporary writing? I am not concerned with these questions; I am not obliged to deal with them.'

He cited the statement made by the prosecution itself at the outset of the case: that its evidence would show 'that the presentation of [*The Rose Tattoo*] was concerned with sex, that its overall presentation was lustful and in that way the presentation of the play was a breach of the law and was against the society of which we are all members'.[2] All that O'Flynn had to decide was whether the prosecution case had in fact shown these things in a manner that stood a chance of convincing a jury. If it had, then he was justified in committing Alan Simpson for trial – in 'giving informations', as it is technically known. If the prosecution had failed – if O'Flynn deemed that its case as presented did not stand a chance of convincing a 'cross-section of the community' that Simpson was guilty of committing an offence – then he could not commit Simpson for trial: he would 'refuse informations'.

The full text of O'Flynn's landmark judgement may be found in volume XCIII of the *Irish Law Reports*. Much of the earlier part – up to the point at which O'Flynn turned from general matters to the court proceedings themselves – makes for earnest and unexciting reading. But from that point on, and though O'Flynn was particularly careful about offending the sensibilities of the police witnesses, there could be increasingly little doubt about either his feelings or his conclusions.

'I must approach the evidence calmly and reasonably,' the District Justice began. 'Let there be no confusion or rash judgement of the facts.' He had, he said:

> had before me police witnesses, Detective Garda Martin, Detective Sergeant Kenny, Detective Sergeant Wedick, Detective Sergeant Farrell, Inspector Ward and Detective Superintendent Weymes. I have had over several years many opportunities to assess the qualities of these members of our police. I can say with assurance and without reservation that they are of the highest calibre, most efficient and men of unimpeachable probity. They have been witnesses before me on many occasions in different cases, many of them most serious crimes ... I have pleasure in stating that their high standing would do honour to any police force and that the community which they serve is indeed fortunate to have them as police officers.

Swift, listening to this panegyric, felt her heart sink. But if O'Flynn's fulsome praise of the police witnesses might seem to bode ill for the accused, it was also the sort of statement that could be turned on its head by a well-placed 'but'. And this is what Cathal O'Flynn now proceeded to do: not just to find against the prosecution case but, in effect, to demonstrate that it was so incoherent as hardly to amount to a case at all.

'I am not unmindful', he said of the admirable police witnesses, 'that as police officers they are in this Court in exactly the same position, as witnesses, as any other witness and the same test applies to them ... The credibility of any witness depends upon: (1) his knowledge of the facts he testifies; (2) his disinterestedness; (3) his integrity; (4) his veracity; (5) his being bound to speak the truth under oath ...'

The witnesses had, of course, been ordered to dodge the fifth item on this list, but O'Flynn chose to ignore this: 'It is the first of these requirements that I wish to dwell on. How credible are the witnesses by reason of their knowledge of the facts they respectively testify? Although a witness is … a man of integrity and veracity and has a sense of the moral obligation of the oath he has taken, still the degree of credit to be given to his testimony depends upon his real knowledge of the facts he testifies.'

The witnesses' obvious ignorance of theatre was a point that from the first had simultaneously appalled and amused Swift. O'Flynn seemed not only to have picked up on the point but also to have identified it as crucial. It was the first real indication that Simpson might have cause for hope. But more such indications were now to come:

> 'I now come to the actual evidence of the police witnesses who attended this play', O'Flynn said, 'and I shall deal with certain aspects of their evidence.
>
> 'First is detective Garda Martin … He states: "He very seldom went to theatres, only twice in the last 20 years. There was nothing imported into the play that is not in the book, that the general impression was that the play was indecent. *The only legitimate or lawful sex was at the beginning of the play when the widow mentioned her love-making with her husband. That if a certain portion of a stage direction in the book had been carried into the play it would have been objectionable, but it was not carried into the play*"[3] and therefore it was not objectionable.'

O'Flynn juxtaposed these statements, given in direct evidence, with what the prosecution itself had said:

> Counsel, if I understood him correctly … said that this play was obscene because of undue dwelling on matrimony and sex in matrimony. He also submitted that because of the legislation in this country against contraceptives, the incident [referred to by Detective Garda Martin] was another instance of indecency or obscenity. But there is the evidence of the prosecution from Detective

Garda Martin and I shall repeat it:

> *'The only legitimate or lawful sex was at the beginning of the play*
> *when the widow mentioned her love-making with her husband. That*
> *if a certain portion of a stage direction in the book had been carried*
> *into the play it would have been objectionable, but it was not carried*
> *into the play'* – and therefore it was not objectionable. [4]

Copious sexual activity within marriage was both licit and illicit and a condom which was never dropped was proof of the non-dropper's immorality: the prosecution's contention, in other words, was blatantly at odds with the evidence of its own witness. Hitting his stride now, O'Flynn went through the witnesses one by one. Detective Sergeant Kenny, he noted:

> had to correct himself under cross-examination as to the incident of the naked girl sent home in a taxi when it is palpably apparent that this was a completely erroneous mis-statement of an important fact. He said that 'Alvaro was making advances to Serafina gradually.' ... It is clear from his evidence under cross-examination that Alvaro wanted to marry Serafina. The witness was inferring that Alvaro's motive was fornication, but again under cross-examination he concedes that marriage was the motive.

Having quoted lines of Alvaro's which Kenny had cited, O'Flynn let something like a flash of temper show:

> 'I do not consider it reasonable', he said, 'for anyone to infer the motive of fornication from these words, if the English language is an intelligible means of expression. And yet Detective Sergeant Kenny goes on to say in the next sentence of his evidence: "I think his designs were not as honourable as the fact that he desired to marry her."
>
> 'I can well understand that counsel for the defence had some reasons for endeavouring to pursue his cross-examination ... with a view to ascertaining the instructions given to the police witnesses in this case ... [5]
>
> 'But all of this is as a result of cross-examination and it again

exemplifies what an important duty devolves on defence counsel … This particular cross-examination clearly demonstrates … the danger of misconception by a witness and of his mistaken reasons for believing the fact to be as he has stated. At that stage defence counsel decided it would be useless to cross-examine further'.

This decision had, of course, been made because of the prosecution's obstructiveness, as O'Flynn clearly recognised. Measured though his words were, they seem to contain a deep frustration, not only with the incoherence of the prosecution's case but also with the entire manner in which the case had been conducted. Speaking of Wedick's evidence – which had, O'Flynn noted, neither suggested that the play was indecent nor 'point[ed] out any part of it which he consider[ed] could come within such description'[6] – the judge's anger with the prosecution tactics became plain: '[Wedick] was not asked what conclusion he arrived at, though I could see no objection why he could not be so asked. This is not a matter for expert witnesses, it is for reasonable men to say what they think about what they see and hear.'

This was a rare intrusion of common sense into the *Rose Tattoo* courtroom and O'Flynn continued in an even more common-sensical vein:

> The police are not Philistines on the one hand nor literati on the other. If a police officer can tell me today in a case of driving while drunk that he observed certain matters about an accused, certain actions which he made and certain words which he spoke, what appearance the accused had and from all of which he considered the man was drunk, I cannot see why the police officers in this case could not have stated their conclusions about this play.

He had, however, as it happened seen one good reason why the prosecution might not want them to do so: '[O]f course, if they did they would have been cross-examined.' O'Flynn suspected, in other words, that the prosecution had feared cross-examination, which – as he had just noted – had played a vital role in establishing the actual facts. This in turn implied that the prosecution had not wanted the real facts to emerge: a highly irregular attitude to take in a court of law, whose entire function (at least in theory) is precisely the establishment of fact.

O'Flynn was content to imply this point rather than state or pursue it but his remarks suggested a genuine sense of outrage on the part of the legal system. The picture drawn of the prosecution in the judgement is an appalling one. According to O'Flynn, the State had hardly bothered to make its case coherent and that case had consisted of little more than a mass of often contradictory opinions and statements which cross-examination had consistently shown to be untrue. In the face of this the prosecution had, in O'Flynn's obvious opinion, preferred to dodge cross-examination and obstruct both the defence and the court. District Justice O'Flynn clearly did not see this as showing respect for the court or the law.

'I have had several dissimilar versions of this play from [the police witnesses]', O'Flynn said, 'and the matter is then left there and I am asked on that evidence to put an accused man on trial on a criminal charge.' His feelings about that request were by now clear. Cathal O'Flynn took his legal responsibilities seriously; it is clear that he did not feel the same had been true of the prosecution.

Nor did O'Flynn's dissatisfaction stop with events in the courtroom. He was also obviously unhappy with the arrest process itself, as Inspector Ward had outlined it. The accused had been told to make changes in the play but had been given no idea of what changes were required. Having obtained legal advice ('as every citizen is entitled to do', O'Flynn pointedly added) the accused had continued to produce performances of the play. What did the police do then? Did they summons the accused, as might have been expected? No: they behaved completely abnormally – '[A] warrant of arrest ... was obtained against a citizen of this country who has a fixed place of abode and ties in the jurisdiction and is an army officer by occupation.' And then the judge got to the nub of the matter – the reason for this highly unusual act: 'I can only infer that by arresting the accused the object would be achieved of closing down the play. But, surely, if that was the object, nothing could be more devastating than to restrain the production before even a hearing is held. It smacks to me of the frontier principle – "Shoot first and talk after."'

Having raised this particularly sensitive matter – having, in effect, verged on accusing the police, or those who issued their orders, of playing fast and loose with the law – O'Flynn (perhaps wisely) backed away from it ('I do not dwell on any further particulars of the evidence') but reminded his listeners of what he himself had been expected to do on the basis of evidence he had just comprehensively rubbished and State behaviour which he obviously found highly suspect:

> A person convicted of any of these charges can be sentenced to an unlimited period of imprisonment, that means that he can be sentenced to life imprisonment. Short of the capital offences, that is the greatest sentence that can be inflicted for any crime known to the law of this country and consequently these are very serious crimes. The legal position as to proofs is that the burden of proof in this criminal case, as in all criminal cases, rests on the prosecution from start to finish. The more serious the crime, the stricter the proof.

The implication, again, was clear: the prosecution had brought Alan Simpson before Cathal O'Flynn on very serious charges, which it was their absolute duty to prove; instead they had served up a sorry farrago of dubious evidence, on the basis of which dog's dinner of a prosecution case they had asked O'Flynn to commit Simpson for trial. One suspects that, as much as anything else, Cathal O'Flynn was professionally and personally offended at what even now seems little better than an insult both to the law and himself.

And what of the play itself – the scandalous, lustful, immoral and pornographic *Rose Tattoo*? 'It appears', O'Flynn said, 'that the book of this play ... is freely on sale in this city. I must take judicial notice of the Censorship of Publications Acts, 1929 and 1946, which statutes make provision for the prohibition of the sale and distribution of unwholesome literature and for that purpose provide for the establishment of the censorship of books and periodical publications ... The evidence in this case indicated that the book of this play, *The Rose Tattoo* by Tennessee Williams, has not infringed the provisions of that statute.'

He had, he said, found only a single previous case involving an accusation of an indecent performance – a hoary British one, in which two men had kept a booth on Epsom Downs for the purpose of giving an indecent exhibition during Epsom Races.[7] 'The play, *The Rose Tattoo* and the circumstances of the performance are not in the same category. This was a play produced during An Tóstal, our National Festival. The play was part of a National Theatre Festival during An Tóstal.'

The reiteration of this simple fact, which the prosecution had seen fit to ignore as an irrelevance, seems – like much of O'Flynn's summing up – like a voice from a sane world breaking in on a Mad Hatter's tea party. It had been patently obvious to all but the most unbalanced observers that the State prosecution in the *Rose Tattoo* case was in the position of the Emperor in 'The Emperor's New Clothes'; it had been left to Cathal O'Flynn to play the part of the little boy and declare that his Majesty was stark naked. O'Flynn now offered his own summary of the play, one which, with its further simple sanity and humanity, was a million miles away from the grotesque travesties offered previously in the same court:

> It appears that while there is a theme relating to sexual behaviour between men and women in the play, there are also many other themes in it. The mother is very concerned with the preservation of the virginity of her daughter; she despises modern women who at the age of thirty discontinue the use of the conjugal double bed and have recourse to a single bed; she glories in what might be re-

garded by some as excessive conjugal relations; she despises the use of contraceptives; finding after his death that her deceased husband had not been faithful to her, she is crushed; she despairs once in her religious faith and she has one lapse from the path of virtue. The secret of the Sacred Tribunal of Penance is portrayed as being utterly and absolutely inviolable.

What is the over-all effect of the play? I think that it is one of sadness, that this humble woman, a woman of great sexual appetite who is widowed by sudden disaster to her husband, lapses once from the path of virtue.

Does the play as described in the evidence tend to corrupt and deprave? Does it lead to certain lascivious thoughts and lustful desires which will affect character and action? Is the play a cloak for something sinister … ?

If my brief synopsis of the play is correct, can anyone reasonably say that the accused, Alan Simpson, was exploiting a filthy business and showing a complete disregard for the primary requirements of decency?

Did the accused, Alan Simpson, intend to deprave and corrupt other persons?

The judge's own answer to these questions was by now entirely clear. Before stating it, however, he repeated the details of Simpson's ordeal:

The accused has been visited by the police, warned by them, arrested, detained and charged. He has appeared in this Court on six actual days of hearing and has made another seven appearances on remand for mention. His case has been brought to the High Court and, feeling aggrieved, he went on his appeal to the Supreme Court and he has come back here for two further days of hearing and again today for decision. Altogether this must be quite an ordeal … [I]t is not my province to suggest how matters of this kind are best regulated, but I cannot fail to remark that the position of the accused in this entire matter must have been less than satisfactory.

With that massive understatement, the substance of the marathon judgement finally arrived. Cathal O'Flynn had not gone into the mysteries of why Alan Simpson's arrest had ever happened or what on earth the State had *thought* it was doing; but then that was not his job and in that Ireland these were the sort of questions which it was better for even a judge to avoid. What O'Flynn had done, however, was far more important to Simpson: he had comprehensively rubbished both the State's case and the manner in which it had, from the first, been conducted. He now directly addressed Alan Simpson himself for the first and last time:

> You, Alan Simpson, are in a position here today that is noteworthy for two reasons: –
>
> 1. You are the first person as far as I am aware to stand accused in the dock of this Courthouse on the charge of showing a performance of a play alleged to be indecent and obscene and profane;
> 2. You are also the first citizen in this country in my experience of many thousands of criminal cases to stand in the dock of this Courthouse in a preliminary investigation and to find your case brought to the High Court and then, by your appeal, to the Supreme Court.
>
> As a result of your efforts to vindicate your position as an innocent man, we can be assured for the future in the process of holding a preliminary investigation, that to use a phrase of the theatre, 'the show must go on' and without any interlude for the litigation of Case Stated.
>
> In applying what I consider to be the correct legal test of obscenity to the charges; in carefully reviewing the evidence adduced by the prosecution in support of those charges and in exercising my discretion judicially and taking into account the evidence tendered on behalf of the Attorney General, I am of the opinion that no jury weighing the probabilities of this case might reasonably convict. I am of the opinion that no jury would *or ought to*[8] convict.
>
> I am not satisfied that the evidence in this case is sufficient to justify me in committing you for trial. Consequently, I find a *prima facie* case has not been made out. I refuse informations and I discharge you.

Little short of a year after it had publicly begun, the *Rose Tattoo* case, judicially at least, was over and Alan Simpson was a free man.

14. Aftermath

Many contemporary observers simply took it for granted that the *Rose Tattoo* case was an abuse of power by the State. And while speaking in such terms could be downright dangerous for anyone in 1950s Ireland, it seems that District Justice Cathal O'Flynn was quite clear in his mind about the implications of the State's actions and found them unacceptable. What is far more indicative of the realities of life in 1950s Ireland, however, is not O'Flynn's judgement but the response to it.

Such a damning indictment of a high-profile State prosecution case would nowadays cause a sensation. There are few more telling illustrations of how different that other Ireland was than what actually ensued from O'Flynn's judgement in 1958: nothing at all (at least officially). Coverage of the judgement, while wide, was for the most part curt. In Ireland itself only the *Evening Mail* and the *Irish Times* reported O'Flynn's comments at any length, even dwelling on the more scathing parts; but neither newspaper made any comment on either the content or implications of O'Flynn's words. While British newspapers also reported Simpson's release, for them the matter no longer rated the extensive coverage that the lurid police accounts of goings-on at the Pike had once brought. 'ROSE TATTOO GETS A CLEAN BILL' reported the *Evening News*. 'TENNESSEE WILLIAMS PLAY NOT PROFANE'.[1] The *Daily Mail* contented itself with a laconic 'ROSE TATTOO CASE FAILS' over a three-sentence note of Simpson's discharge.[2] The *Daily Express* was hardly more forthcoming: '"TATTOO" MAN IS CLEARED' said the headline, while the report itself was perhaps twice as long as the *Mail*'s.[3] The scathing implications of the summing up were not referred to. None of the British papers noted much beyond the mere fact that Simpson had been cleared: it was left to the *Times* and the *Daily Telegraph* to cite details of the actual judgement. In Ireland, however, the sheer breadth of O'Flynn's condemnation of the case was simply not widely publicised,[4] and the rumour (which began to spread immediately) that Simpson had somehow got off on a technicality found many willing believers.

The deafening silence is no reflection on the intelligence of Irish journalists or newspaper editors. Irish journalists in 1958 were just as curious as they are now; but neither they nor their editors were stupid. The State, by the very weight of its expensive actions, had shown how seriously it took the matter, while the case itself had for many reeked from the first of the tacit involvement of the Catholic Church. As with so very many issues then, these facts were more than enough to guarantee silence. The pillars of Irish society were as vindictive as they were powerful and the *Evening Mail* and *Irish Times* were, even by dint of simply publicly recording some of O'Flynn's more pungent remarks, sticking their necks out.[5]

The questions that would nowadays follow in the Dáil were likewise completely absent. When Simpson tried to arrange for the matter to be raised in the Senate he was advised against persisting even by sympathisers. Simpson, however, still had the threat of pursuit from Aindreas Ó Caoimh, the Attorney General, hanging over his head, not to mention his desperate financial situation. He felt that any public awareness of the real state of affairs would at least warn Ó Caoimh off. William Bedell Stanford, Senator for University College, Dublin, had considered putting forward a motion in the Seanad deploring the financial situation in which Simpson had been left but had decided against going ahead with it. 'On the whole', he wrote to Simpson, 'I think it would do more harm than good, now that you have been so triumphantly vindicated. My original intention ... was to show that public opinion supported you. If we did rub salt in the wounds of the Department of Justice now, there is, I'm afraid, some danger that they might introduce legislation for censorship of the theatre.'[6]

Simpson didn't agree. 'A question would act as a deterrent to the Attorney General from indicting me in the Central Criminal Court,' he wrote to Stanford, 'an action which he has power to carry out and which he threatened to do if the District Justice refused informations.'[7]

Stanford (correctly as it turned out) was sure that the Government would now be distancing itself from even the memory of the case. He felt that pursuing the matter might simply rouse the State's vindictiveness and that it might act against Simpson precisely in order to have further discussion quashed: 'It seems to me that the prospect of a debate in the Senate might be the last straw which would make the Dept of Justice instruct [the] A[ttorney] G[eneral] to take further action; by doing so they could prevent discussion in the Senate again, as the matter would be *sub judice* once more.'[8] He left the final decision to Simpson, who asked him to go ahead. But when Stanford duly attempted to raise the matter in the Senate, on June 25th, he didn't get very far. The *Cathaoirleach* ruled the question out of order before it was even put:

> I have received notice from Senator Stanford that ... he proposes to raise the following matter:
>
> That in view of the hardship and financial loss sustained by members of the Pike Theatre Club, Dublin, as a result of the legal action of the Minister for Justice in connection with the production of the play entitled *The Rose Tattoo*, the Minister should take steps to compensate them and ensure that injudicious proceedings of this kind will not be instituted in future ...
>
> I have ruled that this is a matter not suitable for discussion ... on the following grounds:
>
> (1) That the institution of proceedings of this kind is not a matter for which a Minister of State is responsible,[9] and

(2) that, in any event, it would appear that legislation would be required to give effect to the Senator's proposal.

Stanford, stung, asked whether this ruling meant that when an innocent man was imprisoned and left in debt, 'and when the State is brought into considerable ridicule by this injudicious action, that there is no machinery under Standing Orders ... for bringing the responsible member of the government before the Seanad to defend his action?'

This, of course, was precisely what it meant: 'responsibility' was a word as unwelcome in Irish State circles then as it has often seemed since. The Cathaoirleach refused even to discuss the issue with Stanford and merely repeated his ruling. When Senator Owen Sheehy-Skeffington, veteran of countless civil-liberties debates, demanded to know whether 'we understand that no action of the Attorney General can be discussed in this House at all?' the Chairman simply ended the 'debate': 'I cannot go into any action of the Attorney General in this matter. I have given my ruling and the matter must rest on that.'[10]

And that, so far as Official Ireland was concerned, was that: after all that delirium of the brave and the not-so-brave, this brief exchange represents the only meaningful reference to the *Rose Tattoo* judgement in any official debate since 1958.[11] From the State's point of view the affair was not simply ended: it was effectively consigned to what the writer William Burroughs used to called the 'It-never-happened Department'. As for the Pike Theatre, it limped along for another year and a half and even had some successes,[12] but nothing on the scale to which it had been accustomed before May 1957. It was, to all intents and purposes, finished. Its finances, its club membership, its audience-base, its reputation and its integrity had been destroyed and in the popular mind it remained a 'dirty' theatre. The taint of rumour hung like a shroud over the Pike just as debt hung over its owners: in the Spring of 1958 even a double-bill of Behan adaptations – theatrical world premières, at a time when Behan was at the height of his fame – had failed to fill the theatre.[13] In the end Simpson's legal bills would amount to some £2,600 – more than IR£42,000 in modern terms – though Lehane and Heavey refused all payment for the services which, as O'Flynn had made plain and both Simpson and Swift were certain, effectively saved Alan Simpson from the State. The Irish and British defence funds, and a third fund launched in America, gradually brought in some money, but nothing like enough. In November 1959 the Pike applied to the Arts Council for two grants and two subsidies. In today's terms the itemised submission seems pathetic. The grants were for £175 (IR£2,850) to clear the theatre's overdraft and £140, twelve shillings and threepence (IR£2,295) to cover losses incurred in staging the world première of Dominic Behan's *Posterity Be Damned*. The subsidies were for a guarantee against loss of £75 (IR£1,225) for the première of J.B. McGowan's *God's Child* and £125 (IR£2,040) for the première of James McKenna's *The Scatterin'*.[14]

'The Pike has been run at a loss for over two years,' Simpson wrote in the accompanying letter. 'This loss has been borne out of personal income.' Previous losses had been subsidised by profits from the ever-popular *Follies* shows but these had been abandoned: neither Simpson nor Swift had much energy left and somehow it was hard for them to find much cause for laughter in Official Ireland any more. 'The financial position of the Pike has now become so critical', Simpson's letter concludes, 'that we will be forced to close unless we get some assistance.'[15]

They would get none. The Arts Council Secretary, Mervyn Wall,[16] wrote back querying Simpson's figures and stressing the need for detailed and audited accounts. Wall was not unsympathetic, simply powerless: 'I have to point out in general that the funds at the Council's disposal are public monies voted by Dáil Éireann and as such subject to audit and scrutiny by the Comptroller and Auditor General. For this reason the Council cannot make anything in the nature of a general grant, however worthy the object, but in respect of every payment by the Council it must be shown where exactly the money has gone.'[17]

There were worthier destinations for taxpayers' money – such as, one supposes, defending the public from pornographers. The ongoing strains of the situation would contribute greatly to the eventual disintegration of Simpson and Swift's marriage. She has herself written all that she wishes to record of the circumstances,[18] but the enormous drain resulting from the entire *Rose Tattoo* affair was undoubtedly (at the very least) a major factor in their parting. It had killed their theatre and its seemingly endless repercussions (they were still paying Simpson's legal costs years later) simply drained the life from their marriage. By 1960 both of them were at the end of their tether both personally and professionally. In October 1960 Simpson brought the Pike's production of *The Scatterin'* to London; Swift stayed in Dublin with their daughters. Simpson did not return. Their marriage ended. The Pike stood empty or was rented out to companies. In March 1964 Swift finally sold it. It was bought by an engineering company, which used it as a warehouse. Less than an hour after she signed the deeds, Swift heard the news that Brendan Behan was dead. It seemed, she has written, like the end of an era. It was.

The story of the *Rose Tattoo* case did not die. In fact, over time, it grew. And since not one single fact ever emerged about its many peculiarities, the growth could feed only on rumour and myth, which it duly did. The Ruritanian behaviour of the State throughout the case and the occasionally hilarious contents of the police 'evidence', meant that the case was sometimes portrayed as a sort of jolly sideshow in the more serious sociological war that the history of Ireland in the 1950s frequently resembled and, as more about its secrets are revealed, looks more and more like having genuinely been. Even many of the most basic of the facts about Alan Simpson's ordeal recorded in these pages became lost in the stories which, while distorted, were in all fairness far more amusing than much of the truth. Even Simpson and Swift, on the soundtrack of a 1979 RTÉ television programme raking over the matter, can be heard occasionally laughing about particular aspects of the case and the mythology. They had, one supposes, had to learn.

PART TWO

BACKTRACKING

'If action is taken, as recommended, there is bound to be *some* criticism and, perhaps, widespread newspaper publicity …'
Department of Justice memo, May 1957

15. Papers

Between 1958 and the present, the Irish State (so far as can be ascertained) made not one direct comment on the *Rose Tattoo* case. The partial release of the State papers at the dawn of the current millennium marked the first State action taken on the matter since 1958. Certain things about the case were, however, regarded as so obvious that they became accepted as fact even among those with some actual knowledge of it. Such 'facts' included among their number the assertion that the case was begun by the League of Decency, the allegation that it was begun on the orders of Archbishop McQuaid and the 'contention' (based presumably on their known role as McQuaid's men and their hyperactivity during the period) that the Knights of Columbanus had a hand in the matter. Amidst the welter of speculation there was one consistent trend: the certainty that the case's origins lay in the murky, conspiratorial and occasionally addled world of what we must refer to as the Catholic Right.[1]

While this seemed pluperfectly obvious – where else, after all, could a 1950s Irish censorship matter have its origins? – it was not a conclusion based on any direct evidence. But the *Rose Tattoo* case was the first in an unprecedented string of controversies involving the less artistically moribund elements of Irish theatre. The two most celebrated of these – the 1958 Theatre Festival débâcle and the 1959 cancellation of J.P. Donleavy's *The Ginger Man* – clearly involved Dr McQuaid and his Knights to some degree, though the exact nature and extent of their involvement was confused by the screen of obfuscation, denial and third-party involvement which both parties habitually employed.

Still the media reports on the State papers released in January 2000 stated clearly that the State had acted against Alan Simpson simply from *fear* of a public statement by McQuaid: a story which might have made sense in the 1930s but in the late 1950s seemed, to say the least, highly unlikely. For his part, Dr McQuaid was not given to making public statements about plays or, for the most part, anything else – he was a natural intriguer, who much preferred to get his way behind the scenes. And, given the evidence available of numerous private disagreements and even clashes between McQuaid and de Valera, why would Dev behave so uncharacteristically in this particular instance? If a de Valera Government *had* jumped at the Archbishop's dictation in the 1950s, no one would have been more surprised than the Archbishop himself, who would immediately have suspected an ulterior motive. And yet the newspapers had stated that it was there in black and white in the released papers.

Carolyn Swift and I spent the better part of a day with the released papers in January 2000 and had photocopies made of almost all of them. They are an odd assortment of papers and are clearly sifted from a much bigger dossier. Whether the rest of this dossier remains on some dust-laden Government shelf, or the remaining papers from it have been lost over the years, is unknowable. All of the released papers originate in either the Department of Justice or the Attorney General's office. Interestingly there are no released documents from the office of the Taoiseach, Eamon de Valera. Quite apart from Florrie O'Riordan's claim of de Valera's involvement, it is simply inconceivable that the Justice Department could have acted as it did without at least his permission. In all, perhaps two dozen *Rose Tattoo* documents were released, ranging from brief covering notes (sometimes notes once attached to larger files which are themselves now missing from the file) to detailed minutes and Garda statements. Between them the documents do shed a good deal of light on the history of the case's inception and are of undoubted historical significance. But a close examination suggests that the nature of this significance – what exactly it is that the papers signify – must be in some doubt.

The majority of the released papers relate to the period before the *Rose Tattoo* court case began – indeed, most date from before even Simpson's arrest – and most of the later documents (although enormously suggestive when subjected to detailed analysis) are in themselves curiously inconclusive.

The central characters in the released papers are Oscar Traynor (Minister for Justice), Aindreas Ó Caoimh (the Attorney General), P.P. O'Donoghue (a senior figure in the Attorney General's Office) and Peter Berry (of the Department of Justice).[2] Elements of the Knights of Columbanus, who had their own reasons for detesting Traynor's Justice Ministry, would later hold that, during his tenure as Minister, the Justice Department was in reality being run by its Secretary, Thomas J. Coyne.[3] But, with the exception of one late document, Coyne's name is notably absent from, at least, the released *Rose Tattoo* papers. Given his position and his influence (we shall see later how central he was to the Department) this in itself is quite remarkable and it may well be that his name figures far more prominently in the full file. Of the papers so far released, however, more or less all of the major documents were drawn up by, or at the behest of, Berry and O'Donoghue, on the orders of, or for the attention of, Traynor or Ó Caoimh. Almost all of the following details are taken from those papers.

The papers reveal that from the Irish Government's point of view the *Rose Tattoo* case began on May 9th 1957.[4] On that date Seán Brady, a Fianna Fáil TD for Dún Laoghaire, called to the Department of Justice. Brady was not a Minister, but he was, in Fianna Fáil terms, something much more important than any mere Cabinet member: Brady was an *Alte Kampfer* of the highest order, a man who had stood by de Valera through thick and thin since long before Fianna Fáil even existed. His Republican and Party credentials were almost stupefying in their thoroughness:

he'd joined the Volunteers at their inaugural meeting in 1913, worked with Seán MacDiarmada before the Rising, been courier to Seán MacBride *during* the Rising, a member of the Republican garrison of the Hammam Hotel under Oscar Traynor at the outbreak of the Civil War and had been imprisoned by the Free State in 1922. He was a founder member of Fianna Fáil and a neighbour (in Blackrock) of the de Valeras[5] – a man, in other words, whose Fianna Fáil credentials were almost as impeccable as those of his old comrade and Civil War commander, Oscar Traynor, Minister for Justice. In the old men's club which the top echelons of Fianna Fáil had by then become, Seán Brady was a man, first and foremost, to whom Oscar Traynor would *listen*.

What Traynor listened to on May 9th was a series of extraordinary assertions. There are two overlapping State accounts of what exactly Brady said, one a letter dating from later that day, the other an undated memo apparently written sometime between May 20th and 22nd. The May 9th version, as related in Peter Berry's initial letter of the same day to P.P. O'Donoghue in the Attorney General's Office, seems (on the face of it) straightforward enough:

> I am directed by the Minister for Justice to state that he has been approached by a member of Dáil Éireann with reference to the intention … of the management of the Pike Theatre, Herbert Lane, to produce, next week, the Tennessee Williams play *The Rose Tattoo*. The Deputy stated that the play was unquestionably indecent and that its production had been prohibited in several American cities and, he thought, in France or in places in France. The Minister is anxious to know what steps are open to him in this matter.[6]

The letter requests the Attorney General's views of two options the Minister is considering. The first (which has obviously been examined in some detail already) is that, since the Pike (like all other theatre clubs) is operating without a licence, it could simply be ordered to close. If this were done then the existing law (which dated from 1786) allowed for an automatic fine of £300 for each performance (of anything at all) given by the offending theatre thereafter. The second possibility mentioned (almost as an after-thought) is prosecution for producing an indecent play. There is nothing in the letter to indicate that the Minister is acting on any-thing beyond Seán Brady's statement that the play is indecent, nor is there any indication that Brady's assertions have been checked with any statutory body.

The second, fuller account of Brady's visit is much more in-triguing. This appears in a crucial seven-point memo (unsigned as well as undated) which is far and away the most revealing of the released papers. This account actually names Brady as well as add-ing some fascinating detail of what he had in fact said on May 9th:

> Before the play was put on, Mr Seán Brady, T.D., called to the Department and stated that the play was indecent, that he was aware that His Grace the Archbishop had 'called for the script' and that he (the Archbishop) was aware of Mr Brady's representa-tions to the Department. *As a result of this,*[7] we asked the Attorney General in writing whether, if the play were thought to be inde-cent, a prosecution could be brought, seeing that the theatre is run, ostensibly at any rate, as a club. The Attorney General said, 'yes' – a prosecution could be brought.

The questions raised by this second account might fill a book all on their own, as would the rest of this memo's contents. But before examining the memo in detail let us first examine the May 9th reaction to Brady's visit. After Brady leaves, Peter Berry im-mediately writes his letter to the Attorney General's office. Re-markably, by the time Berry writes, he has already investigated the Pike's circumstances and is in a position to detail its legal status, making use of information that Simpson had given the Gardaí in Dún Laoghaire in 1955.[8] The Attorney General's Office deals with the matter on the same day and responds by instigating Garda surveillance of the Pike – or so at least it seems for, while there is no released documentary evidence of this last, Seán Brady (obviously informed of developments) could already (still on May 9th) report to third parties 'that the Attorney General has directed Gardaí Action against the play'.[9]

This is an incredibly swift response for a government department anywhere, never mind an Irish one in the 1950s: it indicates that the matter is being treated as a high priority. But why? Brady says that the play is 'indecent', that Archbishop McQuaid has called for the script and that the Archbishop knows Brady is approaching Traynor. 'As a result of this' (according to the crucial seven-point memo) the Department of Justice gets a move on. As a result of the play's alleged indecency? This seems entirely unlikely: as we would discover, the Department was used to receiving allegations of indecency against plays, books and much else, not least thanks to campaigns organised by various bodies of lay clerics attempting to influence Departmental actions. Even the involvement of a party stalwart such as Brady would hardly inspire such hyperactivity. Clearly what galvanised the Department of Justice (and what Peter Berry neglected to mention in his initial communication) was the notion that Archbishop McQuaid had taken an interest in the matter and was even aware of Brady's visit. The Departmental alacrity was not due to Brady's party seniority: it was done as a result of the supposed interest of McQuaid.

And what of this interest and of Brady's statement that the play had been banned 'in several American cities and ... in France or in places in France'? Had McQuaid really 'called for the script'? Did he know of Brady's visit to Traynor? If so, how had Brady come to possess this information? What had drawn *The Rose Tattoo* to his attention at all? The press reports in January 2000 did not ask these questions. They should have, because while there is no reason to suppose that Seán Brady was anything but sincere in what he told the Minister, it seems equally certain that all of these claims were completely untrue. Subsequent official attempts to locate a place where *The Rose Tattoo* was banned failed,[10] and such evidence as exists would suggest that Dr McQuaid did not learn of

Brady's May visit to Traynor until June, a month after it occurred.[11] As for *The Rose Tattoo*, it seems the name meant nothing to the Archbishop until he read the newspaper accounts of Simpson's arrest. In short it would seem that somebody somewhere was taking a few liberties with the facts; and since these falsehoods (inadvertent or otherwise) seem to have set the entire *Rose Tattoo* case in motion, their source is important.

Did the Attorney General immediately instigate some form of Garda action, as Brady would claim later on May 9th? None of the released papers say. What *is* in the released files is a brief drawn up by P.P. O'Donoghue for his boss, Aindreas Ó Caoimh, in response to Berry's initial query. This points out that while Theatre Clubs did in fact operate technically outside the law, the law itself dated from 1786 and 'there has never been a proceeding for a contravention of the Act … certainly in the last thirty years' and '[t]he penal provisions of the statute are somewhat archaic and it would require care to fit it into present day procedure.'[12] O'Donoghue also pointed out that the Pike was by no means alone in operating as it did: it would be difficult to pursue one particular theatre club for an offence which all of them broke daily. This whole strategy was, in other words, a bit dodgy and would lead to too many complications.

On the matter of pursuing the Pike for obscenity, however, the Attorney General's Office reached a different conclusion. There did seem some room for action here, if action should be deemed absolutely necessary. 'It is a misdemeanour at common law', he wrote, 'to have an indecent exhibition.' Admittedly the law here was also ancient and obscure and the case O'Donoghue cites involved 'two prisoners [who] held on Epsom Downs a booth for the purpose of showing an indecent exhibition, that they invited all persons who came within reach of their solicitations to come in and see it and that those who paid went in and did see what was grossly indecent.'[13]

Across the bottom of the reply is scrawled a terse 'I agree' from

Ó Caoimh. Some sort of precedent – though one obviously dating from another era – had been found. But this is the most that one can say, because at this point the *released* files (apart from the police reports on the play) go silent and so remain for a further ten to twelve days – a near-fortnight during which *The Rose Tattoo* opened, triumphed and drew its tremendous reviews. The silence is mysterious because the first Garda surveillance took place as early as May 14th, two days after the play opened. It is also, from a researcher's point of view, a most unfortunate silence; because if the involvement of Brady and the supposed interest of McQuaid explain the speed with which the Department checked its options, they do not explain why, when the silence ends, the matter has suddenly become so important as to demand immediate action.

16. The Seven-point Memo

The silence is broken by the unsigned memo containing the second account of Brady's visit.[1] This document is the single-most remarkable paper among those released, a cold-bloodedly political analysis that summarises events so far, lays out options for action and estimates the potential consequences involved. Its author is the person who first suggests taking a specific course of action against the Pike and, while it is anonymous, still the memo is obviously the work of a very experienced civil servant.[2]

Whoever its author, the document gives a truer indication of Government thinking than anything which emerged previously, in court or elsewhere. The memo is addressed to the Minister for Justice, Oscar Traynor, and consists of seven numbered points. The first of these notes simply that reports 'by three policemen who attended the current production of ... *The Rose Tattoo*' are attached. The second says that, on the basis of these reports, 'I think there is no doubt that the play is indecent and that, too, is the view of Mr O'Donoghue of the Attorney General's Office.'[3] The third paragraph, quoted above, elaborates on Brady's original visit and on the reasons for the Department of Justice's approach to the Attorney-General. This is the first truly fascinating point of the seven, although the rest of the document is at least as remarkable. Italics throughout are the present writer's:

> 4. It now appears from advertisements in the Press that the play is being transferred from the Pike Theatre to the Gate Theatre at the end of this week, where, in the ordinary course it would be shown to a much wider audience than the 70 odd persons who

can be accommodated nightly in the Pike. *This makes the question of the continuance of the play much more important.*[4]

5. Our recommendation, which is supported by the Attorney General's Office, is that a uniformed Inspector should –

a) approach the management of the Pike Theatre forthwith and tell them that if the play is not immediately either taken off or expurgated to the point where all objectionable passages and situations are removed, they will be prosecuted and,

b) approach the management of the Gate and tell them that if the play is put on with the objectionable passages and situations included, they will be prosecuted and that the matter will be noted for the information of the Attorney General when their application for Letters Patent for the Theatre comes before him in due course. (The application for Letters Patent are [sic] held up at present while the Theatre is undergoing repairs).

6. In making this recommendation, we have in mind the fact not only that the play as produced is, in our opinion, indecent but that if there is delay in taking action *you may be faced with a demand – possibly a demand made in public – from any one or more of several sources, including the Archbishop,*[5] for action and that you would then be put in the position of having either to take no action – though the play is believed to be indecent – or to give the impression to the public that you acted only at the dictation of the Archbishop or of somebody else.

7. If action is taken, there is bound to be some criticism and indeed, [*here the word* 'perhaps' *is added in ink]* widespread newspaper publicity and it may be noted in that connection that the production is stated in the programme to be 'guaranteed' (i.e. presumably financially) by the Dublin Tóstal Council. This, however, is the lesser of two evils and a difficulty which, we think, must be faced.[6]

This document offers the only real glimpse into what was really going on in the Justice Department, yet it is profoundly puzzling. Most of the other released papers can be read as relatively innocuous illustrations of State agencies going about their various businesses, but the seven-point memo is a revealing example of the

actual thinking at work – the single such example among the released papers. The document twice states the Department's opinion that *The Rose Tattoo* is indecent: but this 'indecency' does not
seem to weigh particularly heavily on the writer *per se*. His main
cause for concern is not *The Rose Tattoo* at all but the attention it
has supposedly drawn from Archbishop McQuaid and certain
'others'. Specifically, the problem is that there is a danger of the
Archbishop (and the mysterious others) using the play as a stick
with which to beat the Government. What is on the memo-
writer's mind is not the decency or indecency of *The Rose Tattoo*;
his concern is to forestall action by the Archbishop and the 'others'.

Somewhere during the silent period, the Pike Theatre has become a problem which may cause serious difficulties for the Minister; but again the problem lies not with the 'indecent' nature of
The Rose Tattoo itself (which has been playing to tiny audiences
and has in any case almost concluded its run) but with the announcement that it is to transfer to the Gate, where it will be seen
by much larger audiences. It is specifically this which makes the
matter 'much more important', because it is deemed to make public statements by McQuaid and the 'others' more likely. Continued inaction seems set to draw the (possibly public) wrath of Dr
McQuaid and the unnamed (but seemingly just as dangerous)
'others'. But there is a clear realisation that to take action may also
draw public criticism, possibly even 'widespread newspaper
publicity'. Both are regrettable, but there is no question which is
worse: stopping the play is recommended; the possible bad
publicity that may result is 'the lesser of two evils'.

The possibility that the Pike might resist an attempt to close
the play does not seem to have occurred to the memo-writer for an
instant. If the situation is serious enough to call for Government
intervention, still it is regarded as easy enough to solve. The preferred form of action is the tried and tested 'quiet word': a uniformed Garda Inspector should simply tell the Pike to alter the

play, close its run or be prosecuted. It is revealing that no mention is made of exactly what passages in *The Rose Tattoo* the Pike was supposed to alter – revealing but hardly surprising, since there is no indication that anyone in the Department had ever seen the text[7] or knew anything about the play beyond the sensational versions supplied by the Garda observers. This explains why Simpson and Swift's initial demand to have the 'objectionable' passages identified left Inspector Ward at a loss – indeed, it also explains the police's failure to indicate the same thing in response to Con Lehane's written request: nobody had given a moment's thought to the matter of actual changes, since (as O'Flynn would note a year later) the intent was never to alter the play but to stop it in its tracks.

It is also notable that the writer of the memo seems entirely unaware of the attention the production had been drawing both nationally and internationally. Obviously the inhabitants of the Department had little interest in theatre. And it is in this light that the reference to newspaper publicity in the seventh point must be read. The writer expected the 'quiet word' to do the job and if he anticipated any demurral from either theatre then it was from the Gate – Lord Longford is the one for whom a threat greater than simple prosecution has to be found. Longford, after all, was *somebody* – he was a Lord and proprietor of a large city-centre theatre. In the political world in which we are now moving, Simpson and Swift were nobodies and the Pike a glorified garage up a back lane. When the writer refers to the potential for negative publicity, he clearly has no concept of the worldwide coverage the case would eventually receive; but then he is not anticipating a 'case' as such at all. The Attorney General has indeed agreed that there is – after a fashion – some sort of precedent on which a prosecution might be based; but there can be no guarantee that any such prosecution would succeed. Clearly no one in the Department of Justice, at this stage, expected the matter to ever come to court and talk of prosecution was basically intended as little more than a bluff. The negative publicity referred to in the memo's seventh point is publicity that would result from the play's being quashed.

What of Lord Longford, the man for whom a threat had been thought necessary? There is no evidence that he was ever actually visited by the police, but equally there is no evidence that he was not. The visit to the Pike took place precisely as suggested, right down to the detail of using a uniformed Inspector. It seems reasonable to assume, therefore, that a similarly uniformed inspector, as also recommended, may have called on Edward Longford and told him what was here suggested: that, should the *Rose Tattoo* transfer proceed, his gargantuan efforts to raise funds for the Gate refurbishment would all be for naught; that the government itself would ensure the destruction of the theatre which Longford had personally kept going for almost three decades, leaving his life's work in ruins. Given this it is conceivable that Longford's apparent jollity in the face of Simpson's trouble, which so incensed Simpson at the time, was born of a need to put a brave face on an impossible situation. It must at the very least be strongly suspected that an Irish Government presented Longford with a choice that seems little (if at all) short of blackmail: cancel the *Rose Tattoo* transfer, or else lose the Gate.[8]

The rest of the released documents, while they do contain fascinating material, pale into insignificance compared to the seven-point memo. The file contains records of some of the State's belated attempts to find evidence (beyond the police accounts) of the play's 'indecency': the transcript of a telephone message from the poet Val Iremonger, by then in the Irish Embassy in London, and a reply from the London Metropolitan Police to an Irish Garda query. Iremonger had obviously been asked to check the play's status with the British censors and reported that while *The Rose Tattoo* had never been produced in Britain it would be given a licence if some minor cuts were made.[9] This news was duplicated by the letter from the Met.[10]

Of the remaining documents one of the most useful (certainly from a researcher's point of view) is the only one signed by Thomas Coyne, the Secretary of the Department of Justice. Its usefulness lies in the fact that it seems to reveal one aspect of the case which has always fascinated commentators as being in reality a red herring. This is the matter of the State's determined resistance to questions about the police orders – the point on which the Garda witnesses made their claims of privilege. The question of what exactly these orders were has intrigued commentators ever since and the State's willingness to fight tooth and nail against having to disclose that information has for decades suggested to many – including Carolyn Swift – that the orders had some special significance. It may very well be that this is the case – the orders themselves are not among the released papers – but the memo suggests that there is quite a different reason for the State's resistance, namely Oscar Traynor's (and the Irish State's) genuine secretiveness about such things.

Coyne's memo is addressed to P.P. O'Donoghue at the Attorney General's Office and was written at the end of May 1958, in the wake of the Supreme Court judgement. While it tells us little about the *Rose Tattoo* case it does reveal much about the mindset at work in the Department of Justice at the time. Coyne writes to convey the Minister's great reluctance to produce the police orders in court. The memo makes it clear, however, that Traynor's reluctance is not specific to this case but is a matter of general principle – the Minister feels that producing the orders would 'create a very bad precedent'.

There is no reason to think Traynor's stated feelings were anything other than genuine: given the almost obsessively secretive nature of political power in Ireland, they make perfect sense. And equally we must bear in mind the political situation at the time – in July 1957, when the issue of the police orders was a live one in Dublin District Court, the Government was in the middle of launching its fight against the IRA. Internment was being introduced and the security situation was a fraught one. Situations were likely to arise where the public revelation of police orders might genuinely place individual Gardaí in physical danger. As such the production of such orders in the present case would quite literally set a precedent that might later, in very different circumstances, rebound with lethal effect on individual police officers. It would have been irresponsible of Traynor as Minister not to think of this. At any rate Coyne writes that the Minister believes the Gardaí should be instructed to refuse to produce their instructions, even if the District Justice ordered them to do so. In passing, such a scenario might have raised fascinating Constitutional issues but it also suggests that the State's reasons for withholding the police orders may not have been wholly mendacious.

Another item of some interest in this document lies outside the actual text in a crabbed note by the Attorney General which, illegible in the photocopied document, finally became (just about) readable in a magnified computer scan. 'Discussed with Minister & Taoiseach', the initialled note says of the matter, '& decision taken.'[11] Ó Caoimh avoids recording the nature of the 'decision taken' but, given the view of the participants, it can hardly be in much doubt. This note of a single meeting (of which no other record seems to exist) is the only documentary evidence even indirectly confirming Florrie O'Riordan's report to Alan Simpson that the Government pursuit of him had been authorised by the Taoiseach. Nevertheless Ó Caoimh's note does underline the seriousness of the issues raised by the case and the level at which they were discussed.

And that – together with a few more scraps and largely unrevealing bits and pieces – is that: the full extent of the State papers released and (on internal evidence alone) nothing like the complete file. While almost all the released documents throw light on various aspects of the *Rose Tattoo* case – and on the nature of State thinking at the time[12] – the seven-point memo is by far the most illuminating, marking as it does the actual point at which the State decided to take action against the Pike. After the release of these files most media comment fixed on this memo as yielding the final 'explanation' of the *Rose Tattoo* affair. It seemed a confirmation of what 'everyone' had always 'known': that (put baldly) McQuaid had barked and the State had jumped – The Church Done It (Yet Again).

In fact the memo proves nothing of the kind and its seeming fear of McQuaid is, at least on the face of it, frankly baffling. No late 1950s Irish Government – least of all a de Valera one – would act on anything as insubstantial as a second-hand account of a bishop's interest in any matter, even when the bishop in question was John Charles McQuaid. Anyone aware of the behind-the-scenes haggling that went on over various issues between de Valera and the Hierarchy – and specifically between de Valera and McQuaid – would know immediately that there was something very wrong about this picture. It might tally with the image of the era now popular, but in terms of the actual history of the relationships involved it simply made no sense. Worse again, it actually threw up more questions than it answered. Yet as the media reports in 2000 pointed out, the only direct evidence so far available permitted of no other conclusion than McQuaid's involvement.

In an attempt to begin reconciling these contradictions we identified three important questions deriving from the released file. The questions are these:

- There is no indication that Seán Brady had any special interest in either theatre or censorship. What drew the Pike's *Rose Tattoo* production to his attention? In other words where did Brady hear of the play's supposed history and the Archbishop's supposed interest in it?
- Was this interest real? Dr McQuaid's methods were long-established and consistent. He was a fixer, not a brawler: he shunned public interference in controversies, preferring covert action, ideally through third parties. On more pressing issues, he acted in concert with the other members of

the Hierarchy, through the Knights of Columbanus or even through direct personal intervention with senior politicians. In an era when complaints against theatre performances were common, there is no record of McQuaid's ever having made any kind of approach – through any of these channels – to Government on the matter. Still less had he made any public pronouncement on it. Nor had Seán Brady suggested that this was what McQuaid meant to do in the present case. Why on earth did the Department of Justice take seriously the notion that, on this one occasion, he might immediately speak out without at least contacting them? Or had he contacted them already?

- Who were these mysterious 'other sources' who might also make a public statement condemning the Minister for inaction – a statement which could, it seemed, be as dangerous as one from dreaded McQuaid, yet at whose dictation the Minister could, at the same time, not publicly seem to be acting?

Considering these questions, it seemed clear that if the State's public behaviour throughout the *Rose Tattoo* case had been baffling, its private stance – at least as indicated by the papers chosen for release – was no less so. The papers took the story to a previously unknown level, but they failed to provide a satisfactory answer to the original question of why the Pike had been targeted. The questions indicated that there was still another level of the story, one that the released file did not even refer to, never mind explain. Reaching that level seemed to offer the only hope of getting to the bottom of the matter; and the only way of reaching that level seemed to be through the abstracted questions themselves: if these could be answered, then the answers might at least point towards a *plausible* cause for the *Rose Tattoo* action – something which these papers, *pace* the media coverage, simply did not provide. The result might not be the ultimate 'real' story of the case, but it would at least be far more 'real' than the discredited one advanced in court in 1957 or the deeply implausible one suggested by these papers.

The rest of this book will do neither more nor less than give the results of our attempts to answer these three questions, in the hope that the answers may help to do something that the release of the State papers signally fails to do: give a credible picture of what exactly lay behind the Government's actions against a small Dublin theatre.

17. Paydirt?

After Swift and I had received photocopies of the released papers and had time to study our separate sets in more detail at home, we were constantly on the phone to each other noting fresh lacunae and inconsistencies, speculating on what might be contained in the missing documents and above all trying to decide where to look for further information.

The supposed involvement of Archbishop McQuaid at least made the last decision a straightforward one: the Archbishop's papers were now open to examination by researchers and they were the obvious next port of call. It was, at the same time, a daunting prospect: while we were certain by now that the story the State papers seemed to tell was at best a very partial one, we still had no very clear idea of what exactly we were looking for. And one of the most frequently remarked-on aspects of the McQuaid papers was the sheer size of the archive – over 700 large cartons of papers, on ever conceivable subject, amassed over the 30-odd years of McQuaid's reign as Archbishop. Looking for a needle in a hay-stack sounded simple by comparison.

The most obvious thing that would carry the story forward – or, more accurately, backward – was something that explained Seán Brady's references to McQuaid during his May 9th meeting with Oscar Traynor or that would at least establish a connection of some kind between the archbishop and the politician. From what we could discover about Brady he was no religious zealot, but his information about McQuaid – inaccurate though it even then seemed likely to be – had to come from somewhere.

Often as I listened to Swift on the phone I had to think of
Maureen Simpson's description of her mother's state less than a
month before. There was certainly no sign of tiredness about Swift
now – she had the bit well and truly between her teeth. The actual
physical examination of the released State papers – which included, of course, material that Alan Simpson's lawyers had fought
hard and unsuccessfully in court to see, including Wedick's statement – had positively galvanised her. At first hesitant when the file
was placed before her in the reading area of the National Archives,
she'd quickly become absorbed by the decades-old documents, re-
reading and cross-checking them tirelessly for several hours. The
gaps in the story they told and the references to other documents
missing from the file seemed both to frustrate and to spur her on.
There was certainly no talk of weariness from her now: if anything
she seemed downright impatient to just get stuck in to the
McQuaid papers. Having so recently been worried by Maureen's
description of her mother's inertia, I now found myself starting to
fret about what I'd begun to feel was her over-optimism. As we
parked her car outside the Dublin Diocesan Archives on the
morning of our first visit, I felt obliged to caution her against expecting too much.

'Carolyn', I said, 'you must know we're not going to find any
smoking guns in this place: we're not going to come across any
pieces of paper that say *"Dear Archbishop McQuaid, I done it,
signed XYZ."*'

These were fateful words. Later that same day I would be compelled to eat them. But at the time they were made they seemed
only sensible.

Although we were particularly alert for any mention of Seán
Brady, TD, this first foray into the McQuaid papers would really
be little more sophisticated than a gigantic trawl through the most
likely-seeming files, taking into account all the various 'solutions'
to the *Rose Tattoo* mystery suggested down the years. We'd already
made arrangements with the archivist, David Sheehy, to examine a

selection of dossiers from the relevant period – those on general censorship, on the theatre and any dealing with the various Catholic organisations whose names speculation had linked with the case down the years. This reduced the total number of files but not their individual size: some were very large indeed. The file on the Knights of Columbanus in particular was huge, but then McQuaid was well known to have had an especially close relationship with the Knights, who had on occasion acted as his spiritual shock troops in the war against sin. It was only reasonable to expect that a large body of correspondence would result from such an intimate and lengthy association.

The file on the theatre was, naturally, Swift's first port of call, but it was disappointing. Though there was quite a bit of material on the collapse of the second Theatre Festival in 1958, there was hardly a mention of the Pike and only one stark reference by McQuaid himself to *The Rose Tattoo*: responding to a letter from a Father Tuohy about the 1958 Festival, McQuaid ended by opining that '*The Rose Tattoo* ought to have been a lesson to the Tóstal.'[1] At first this seemed potentially meaningful: a lesson in what? Did the phrase imply, as it could be taken to, that McQuaid knew more than he had pretended about the matter? But of itself the phrase meant nothing.[2]

In recent years much obloquy has been heaped on the memory of Dr McQuaid, such that one might almost think that he was personally responsible for every abuse, lay and clerical, practised in Ireland in his time. Indeed, there were many who held this view even during his years as Archbishop. Such simplicities are, of course, inane; but like most such two-dimensional characterisations, they have a grain of truth in them that makes them difficult for his defenders to fully explode. Dr McQuaid's papers, however, are another matter. Gobsmacking above all in their sheer *completeness,* the McQuaid papers, with their mixture of high politics, low intrigue, Church business, newspaper clippings and plain letters from ordinary folk at home and abroad, form one of the most complete pictures in existence of life in Ireland during the middle of the twentieth century. Above all they are an invaluable insight into the mechanics of how Ireland was actually run in an era which, whatever one may think of it, was in many ways largely a creation of McQuaid, his old friend de Valera and the often-fractious interplay between them.

The incredible richness of the Archbishop's papers can in itself present problems for any but the most dedicated researcher. The McQuaid papers contain so much compelling material that it can be very difficult to keep one's mind fixed on what one is actually looking for. Time and again on that first morning I found myself following some unknown controversy, or marvelling at the hypocrisy of some public figure as revealed in a private letter to the Archbishop, instead of looking for any references to the Pike Theatre. Swift, naturally, was far more single-minded. Apart from anything else she'd lived through these years and many of the long-buried controversies that came as shocks to me were to her very old news. So it is unsurprising that it was she who first struck paydirt – though it was paydirt of a most peculiar kind, for which we had not been looking at all. And it broadened our search a great deal, making us certain that there really was, among all these ancient papers, a great deal more to be found.

What Swift located, perhaps an hour into our search, was a brief sequence of communications sent to Father Christopher Mangan, McQuaid's secretary, by a man named Joseph J. Cooney, not in the summer of 1957 but almost a full year before. The communications were short and to the point, but what they both said and implied came as a complete surprise. The first brief letter, dated May 25th 1956, bewailed – in a manner that would become familiar to us from letters both in the McQuaid papers and the National Archives – the depraved state of theatre in Dublin. As proof Mr Cooney attached two newspaper advertisements from that evening's *Press* and *Herald*. Both were for the same play and theatre. The play was Jean Paul Sartre's *The Respectable Prostitute* and the theatre was the Pike. Between the two advertisements, however, there was a significant difference. The ad which most horrified Cooney was in the *Evening Press* and read as follows:

'PIKE – 8pm: *The Respectable Prostitute*, *A Phoenix Too Frequent*. Booking and M'ship, Brown Thomas (77829) business hours. Booking Monday only. Phone 67069. Last 3 weeks.'

The advertisement for the same theatre in the *Herald* was slightly but significantly different:

'PIKE – 8pm: A Play by Jean Paul Sartre and *A Phoenix Too Frequent*. Booking and M'ship, Brown Thomas (77829) business hours. Booking Monday only. Phone 67069, Last 3 weeks.'

'What do you think of this?' Cooney asked Fr Mangan rhetorically.[3]

Three days later Cooney wrote again to Father Mangan, to report happily that the 'literary' work of the foreigner, Sartre, was now the subject of a court case in Belfast. He thoughtfully enclosed a cutting from that evening's *Herald*, which described how 'Mr J.H. Campbell, the Belfast Resident Magistrate, today ordered to be destroyed as obscene a large number of magazines, a number of medical books and a novel by Jean-Paul Sartre, the French writer.'[4]

As regards *The Respectable Prostitute*, Cooney had his own ideas about what might be done. The play, he wrote, had six nights to go. It might not be permitted to continue: Superintendent Gill, at Dublin Castle, would (Mr Cooney was sure) have it called off on receipt of a phone call from Father Mangan. Absolute confidence, he assured Mangan, would be observed.[5] Less than a week later Cooney wrote yet again, stirred by a further ad from the *Herald*, which he helpfully attached with stamp-paper:

'PIKE – 8pm – A Play by Sartre and *A Phoenix Too Frequent* … Owing to enormous demand, retained next week only.'[6]

Cooney expressed amazement that a respectable firm such as Brown Thomas's (he understood, he said in amazement, that the heads of the firm were Catholics) should be the booking agency for such a play. But he then went on to make the fascinating claim that 'Superintendent Gill's' Special Branch were actually going to see the production.[7] It seemed that Mr Cooney, or someone, had made a complaint to the police and Cooney at least believed that they intended to check the play out.[8]

As we would later discover, the Archbishop (to whose attention Mangan obviously drew the Cooney reports) seems to have re-acted to Cooney's news in a typically roundabout fashion by hav-ing the Knights of Columbanus send someone to the Pike and report back on the play. On June 11th the investigating Knight submitted his terse report, which was forwarded to McQuaid. The well-trained Knight had seen through the literary pretence of the piece and described his visit to the Pike in words which might have served as a summary of the later police evidence in the *Rose Tattoo* case: 'A mixed capacity audience of perhaps sixty people applauded the most filthy and immoral performance it has ever been my lot to attend. Need I say more?'[9]

There is no indication that McQuaid pursued the matter any further, probably because the play had in any case reached the end of its run.[10] As for Joseph J. Cooney, his reaction was one of bitter disappointment that the police had failed to take any action against the theatre. Almost exactly a year later, in June 1957, he recalled that disappointment in another letter to Mangan: all that was done about *The Respectable Prostitute*, he reminded Mangan, was that the Special Branch had visited it and said it was a bad play.[11] The police, as ever, simply did not appear to appreciate the vital importance of the matter and the official channels of com-plaint had failed. Mr Cooney seems to have learned a lesson from this. He had gone the official route and nothing had happened: if such an occasion arose again, he would try another way.

18. The Plot Thickens

The job of fully sorting the McQuaid papers into a final coherent and readily accessible form is one which will possibly take decades; ironically, part of the difficulty stems from precisely those things which make the collection so valuable as a true-to-life portrait of its age – its enormous size and the sheer range (both in subject and in origin) of its contents. The documents we consulted had been divided up for insertion into those named files to which they seemed most clearly to belong. Thus any papers clearly relating to the activities of the Knights of Columbanus were in the Knights of Columbanus file, anything relating primarily to censorship in the censorship file and so on. But in cases such as ours turned out to be, where researchers are attempting to follow a multi-faceted story through a variety of areas, such clear-cut divisions do not really apply. As it was, our basic initial ignorance about what we were looking for turned out to be a godsend: it was precisely in trawling through a variety of files that we uncovered, one by one, the scraps of seemingly unrelated paper which permitted us, after a surprisingly short time, to piece together the background to Seán Brady's visit to Oscar Traynor on May 9th 1957.

I say 'we', but again it was Swift who located the next and most important piece in the jigsaw – a piece that bore an uncanny resemblance to what I had explicitly warned her that we would not find. To be sure, it did not say '*Dear Archbishop McQuaid, I done it, signed XYZ.*' But that was only because the writer wasn't called XYZ: in every other particular, it said almost exactly that. What Swift in fact found, in a file labelled 'Censorship', was the first of a series of documents that seemed in a way to sum up much of what we would, from our research in these archives and elsewhere, learn about that whole remarkable era. The author of these was, again, Joseph J. Cooney. The first Swift found was written on June 1st 1957, almost two weeks after Alan Simpson's arrest and was prefaced by a brief note to McQuaid (presumably from his secretary) which read: 'Your Grace might be interested to read attached communication I received.'

The communication in question was a one-page letter with a single-page attachment, the first of two such items in the file sent by Cooney to Mangan that month. At first, after all the years of wondering, Swift simply could not believe what she was reading as she scanned the page:

'Rev. and dear Father,' the letter began, 'exactly, this date 12 months ago, I drew your attention to the production of a play, "The Respectable Prostitute" at the "Pike" theatre (?)[1] all that was done about it; the Garda Special branch visited it and to say "It is a bad play."'

'Now, as you must know, the same theatre (?) has again transgressed with "The Rose Tattoo" by Tennessee Williams. But in this case the action taken, is different – a higher level.

'On the accompanying sheet, are the details …'

The details? Swift didn't trust herself to read the foolscap attachment alone. She called me over and we went through it together. It was headed simply '*The Rose Tattoo*, Pike Theatre' and though the two sides of closely written foolscap mentioned other matters still it was the first half-page or so that we read again and again:

> Prior to the opening performance there was reason to believe the play was an immoral one.
>
> Efforts were made to get an interview with some important Deputy at Leinster House.
>
> Through the instrumentality of a Mrs Byrne, Ormond Road, Rathgar, an appointment was made with Mr Seán Brady T.D.

(Dun Laoghaire-Rathdown Area) for a Mr F. O'Farrell[2] and myself.

In advance of the arranged date of interview we furnished him with the *Rose Tattoo* script.

On the 9th May we met Mr Brady, to be informed the script was very bad and that the Attorney General has directed Gardai Action against the play. Hence, the arrest and court case (adjourned to 4th July).

Meantime, I have received a letter from Mr Brady asking me to call again to Leinster House.

The purpose of this call, was to ascertain if I can get more details for the purpose of strengthening the case for prosecution. (a) Was *The Rose Tattoo* ever prohibited in England, or elsewhere? (b) Is the Author – Tennessee Williams – one of repute – etc.

In regard to these querys [sic], I have written to 'The Public Morality Council', London, for verification.

If you, dear Father, feel disposed to add anything, that would be useful and relevant, I would be grateful – In confidence.[3]

Cooney's report (it is difficult to think of it in other terms) went on to discuss the 'most disgusting' *Look Back in Anger* at the Olympia. Stunned by what we'd already found we almost missed a final reference to the subject of *The Rose Tattoo:*

After the hearing of the *Rose Tattoo* case in court, Miss Binchy (actress) did not appear on last two shows. It is accountable to her father being a Circuit Court Judge. Still, she was adamant in continuing on with the show, until an almost hysterical attitude enveloped her mother, so in deference to her, the domestic trouble subsided.[4]

Next, the play was to go over to the 'Gate' but here complaints inundated Lord Longford,[5] plus the Gardai, that his Lordship cancelled the contract. We now await 5th July. At present the forces in defence of the play are being mobilised – at home and across channel [sic].

It will be a major case. I am convinced the producer will not get the verdict. For the script damns him.

After that the report turned to the Irish Censorship Board, where Cooney was worried about the 'activities' of liberal agents who'd been planted on the Board by the Irish Association of Civil Liberties. But neither Swift nor I paid much attention to these closing paragraphs. Here was a claim that seemed perfectly credible. The letter was addressed to Mangan, but there could be no doubt that its contents were meant ultimately for McQuaid. Cooney was proud of the blow he and O'Farrell had struck for morality and wanted his Archbishop to know about it. There could be no question of this being a tissue of lies – not to John Charles McQuaid. Then too, Cooney simply *knew* too much to be anything other than genuine: Brady's name had never been breathed in connection with the case until a few weeks before we sat and read Cooney's 43-year-old words. The dates, too, matched: Cooney and O'Farrell had seemingly met Brady some time after his visit to the Justice Department on May 9th. He could already tell them that the Attorney General meant to have police action taken (though this cannot have referred to anything beyond observation). And the two men had been to Leinster House again, some time before June 1st, and had been asked to find evidence of the play's – and presumably the playwright's – obscenity. This tied in well with the evidence in the released papers of the State's search for such evidence.

The date of Cooney's letter, and the whole tone of its contents, seemed a final nail in the coffin for the myth of McQuaid's personal responsibility for the *Rose Tattoo* case: Cooney clearly believed that what he was telling McQuaid would be news to the Archbishop. And it seemed even more clear that he and O'Farrell had been acting off their own bat, stung into their unusual action by the way in which the Gardaí had proved useless the year before. But who *was* Joseph J. Cooney – and had this report to Mangan been the only one of its kind? A further search through the same files turned up several items. The next in chronological order was a document almost contemporary with the first. It was dated June

22nd and again it consisted of a one-page letter and an attached report.[6]

This second letter was actually headed *The Rose Tattoo* and advised Mangan/McQuaid of the actions Cooney had taken in fulfilment of Brady's request to find evidence against Simpson. He had written to the Public Morality Council in London querying the status of both the Williams play and *Look Back in Anger* and – while he was at it – asking the Secretary of that organisation to investigate 'a series of publications – six in all – by the "Camera Studies Club" London ... These are booklets ... containing absolutely nude female film stars' photos.' The replies to all three queries could, the letter said, be found 'on the accompanying sheet'. Though the members of the Public Morality Council were clearly not Tennessee Williams enthusiasts, the relative neutrality of the response from their Secretary, George Tomlinson, cannot have cheered the team trying to prosecute Alan Simpson if they saw it:

> *The Rose Tattoo*
>
> We have no very high opinion of the plays of Tennessee Williams. Generally, they deal with sordid and unsavoury themes but there are some who think they have some degree of merit. I have not seen the play you mention, *The Rose Tattoo*, but I did see the <u>film</u> of the same title ... the film was not objectionable.[7]

Cooney did not comment on the Society's response, though later in his report (which mainly concerns the nude models and 'awful' books) he noted that 'The film *Rose Tattoo* was listed as "morally objectionable in part for all" by the Legion of Decency, America.'

This second letter, though confirming that the search for evidence against Simpson had used unofficial as well as official channels, told us little beyond that. What *did* extend our knowledge was another Cooney document, a two-page foolscap note advocating theatre censorship and headed *Items of Interest*. If the note ever had an accompanying letter, it has been lost or misplaced. From internal evidence it was written in early 1958, in the middle of the furore over the second Dublin Theatre Festival. It is a call for theatre censorship in Ireland and reads in part as though originally intended for publication, perhaps in the correspondence column of a newspaper. The note begins by praising the existing censorship of films and especially of literature ('More needed today, than when first enacted. It is the greatest legislation in our times') before decrying the lack of an existing theatre censorship, an absence which requires much thought ('Men and women whom can think – Wanted!'). It then lists five plays 'that are immoral, indecent or profane'

(a) *Rose Tattoo* by Tennessee Williams

(b) *Time and Again* by the Lunts

(c) *Street-car Named Desire* by Tennessee Williams

(d) *The Respectable Prostitute* by Jean Sartre

(e) *Tea and Sympathy* by Robert Anderson (American Production)

This was where matters developed again: speaking of these foul plays, Cooney notes that 'Having advanced knowledge of the presentations: (a), (d) and (e), the "Irish League of Decency" promptly moved. Hence the present (protracted) law case.'

Here was a fine how-d'you-do indeed. The Irish League of Decency was the group that had sent the letter to Brendan Smith during the *Rose Tattoo* rehearsals. We knew little or nothing about the organisation, but it had certainly consisted of more than two members. Yet Cooney had previously spoken of himself and O'Farrell as though they had acted alone. With the discovery of Cooney's claims to responsibility it had seemed, briefly, that we'd actually reached the end of our investigation in record time. As with the State papers earlier, and in a way we would become all too familiar with over the next year and more, the riddle of *The Rose Tattoo* had seemed just about to divulge its solution, only to grow even more confusing and elusive. The only thing for it, at that stage, seemed to be to find out more about the Irish League of Decency. Fortunately we were in possibly the best place in Dublin to do so: for sitting right on the table beside us was a file containing Dr McQuaid's own papers on that very organisation.

Looking back on it later, this seemed like another turning point in our search. For in opening that slim, harmless-looking file on the table we were opening a door into the ante-room of another world, a world at once familiar and very, very strange. It was the world of Catholic vigilantism in the 1950s and beyond that anteroom lay much that was weird and wonderful. There too lay a world of genuine power, a profoundly political place where Church and State vied for control of Ireland's future and where the dreams of inclusive idealists, whether in Galilee or the GPO, seemed every bit as distant and remote as those of idealists in Herbert Lane.

19. Concerned Citizens

The search for the story of the Irish League of Decency was our own introduction to a fact noted above: essential though it was to introduce some kind of classification system into the McQuaid papers, the very process of so doing could create difficulties for anyone wishing to follow an individual case. Dr McQuaid was at the centre of an enormous intelligence-gathering web which there is every indication that he set out quite deliberately to create. Much of the information he received was actively sought out, most notably through the Knights of Columbanus, whose successive Supreme Knights during the 1950s kept the Archbishop informed of developments on a huge range of fronts and from any number of sometimes unsettling places. Membership of the Knights at this time was determinedly exclusive and the organisation's members were highly placed in every conceivable Irish institution although their affiliations to the order were often unacknowledged. The contents of many Knightly documents in the McQuaid papers make it plain that some of these individuals – including some within Government Departments – were, on occasion at least, engaged in what can really only be called espionage on the Order's and on the Archbishop's behalf.[1]

More of Dr McQuaid's information came through the vast clerical network of 1950s Ireland, especially from the informal group of well-placed clerics who, for one reason or another, were favoured by the Archbishop and – not least because of his patronage – found themselves in positions which gave them access to precisely the sort of information Dr McQuaid required.[2] The

Archbishop was also alerted to many matters by unsolicited letters and notes from ordinary members of the public – such as the original 1956 letter from Joseph J. Cooney which led to the Knights checking out the Pike. Nor was there anything very unusual in this treatment of Cooney's report. While some of the letters McQuaid received from members of the public were plainly more of a nuisance than anything else, many were followed up and this could mean involving people and institutions whose documents, because of the Diocesan Archives' classification system, are to be found in dossiers quite separate from the originals.

For example the file on the Irish League of Decency itself, while it told us much that was interesting, gave us little or no insight into the League's condition in 1957 or how Cooney could claim at one and the same time that Simpson's arrest had been the result of work both by individuals and by the League. What the League of Decency file did offer was some insight into the organisation's origins and nature, as well as into McQuaid's habitual methods. The organisation was founded in 1955 and immediately after its launch the League's Secretary, C. O'Sullivan, wrote to the Archbishop seeking official approval and requesting the appointment of a chaplain to the League, whose 'main purpose will be to combat the following':

(a) Immodest post-cards and improper Book-covers
(b) Indecent fashions in clothes and the advertisement of same
(c) Glamourising Religious pictures and statuery [*sic*]
(d) Immodest cartoon stripes [*sic*] in newspapers and periodicals.
(e) Advertisements that display immodest pictures[3]

However it may strike the modern eye, there was nothing on the list itself that would have been regarded as odd at the time – McQuaid himself took a special interest in 'immodest' ads and whatever 'glamourising' religious pictures may have meant, the Archbishop deeply loathed modernism in religious art and seems to have found naturalism little short of sacrilegious.[4] But Dr

McQuaid was nothing if not cagey and his immediate reaction was to have O'Sullivan checked out ... by having someone *else* check him out, via his local parish priest – a classic McQuaid manoeuvre. In the response, as in just about every other reference to O'Sullivan in the McQuaid papers, came a suggestion that O'Sullivan was a man who, though a 'good' Catholic, was regarded as at least a trifle 'off' – 'Fr McKenna says that Mr O'Sullivan does tend to be extreme in his views on most subjects. If that is so his League of Decency, excellent in itself, might easily run [?] into imprudent measures, unless there are restraining influences.'[5]

This note of caution – often far less muted – is found in almost every reference to O'Sullivan in the McQuaid archives.[6] He was a man whose zealousness appears to have inspired reservations in all who had dealings with him, even within the League of Decency itself. He seems to have been prone to exaggeration and had pretensions of grandeur: even the name of his organisation – modelled on the immensely powerful American Church organisation, the Legion of Decency – seems in keeping with these suggestions. Dr McQuaid noted on the letter responding to his own initial query that he saw no sense in giving approval to the request for a chaplain 'in view of the danger of imprudent action'. As he had done earlier with Maria Duce, the Archbishop kept the League at arms' length while maintaining an interest in its activities, refusing to appoint a chaplain to it but granting permission for the League's members to report their activities to him.

This was about all one could learn from the League file itself and it left us none the wiser about the League situation in 1957. Again it was Swift who located the document which solved that particular riddle. It had been catalogued in the Knights of Columbanus file and was yet another remarkable letter,[7] originating from a Mrs Byrne of Rathgar, the woman through whose 'instrumentality' Cooney and O'Farrell had first been put in touch with Seán Brady. The letter dated from 1958 but gave a picture of the state of affairs in the League in 1956–57 which both explained our latest puzzle and, in the light of the impression the League file itself gave of O'Sullivan, was entirely credible.

According to Mrs Byrne, the League of Decency was already in disarray within a year of its formation, due largely to what was seen as the excesses of its president. O'Sullivan saw filth everywhere – as was of course common in some Catholic circles at the time; however, even within his own organisation he was clearly regarded as what would nowadays be called a control freak, while his public zealotry was an embarrassment to more refined members such as Mrs Byrne, who had joined the League at its formation. The letter gives a retrospectively semi-comic picture of O'Sullivan's working methods in (from the scanty internal evidence) 1956 or '57. At a League Committee meeting, the Secretary had been instructed to write a letter of complaint to the Superintendent of the Gardaí about a particular shop which (presumably) was selling material the League found indecent. Mrs Byrne, even then wary of O'Sullivan's extremism, insisted that the letter be drafted there and then by the entire Committee, which was done; but at the next meeting she was horrified to learn that O'Sullivan had scrapped the Committee version and instead written and sent a letter of his own, informing the unfortunate policeman in the name of the Blessed Virgin that 'Mary' called him as one of Her 'soldiers' to come to Her aid in preserving Her from violations of Her virginity.[8] The names of all the League's Officers – including Mrs Byrne – had been signed to this missive and, though Mrs Byrne protested, the letter was already sent.[9]

Having described O'Sullivan as an egoist who was impossible to control, Mrs Byrne's own letter goes on to outline what seems, in the context, a natural series of developments. O'Sullivan's outrageous and embarrassing behaviour alienated many of the League's original members, who had joined it in good faith – most of the 'good people', as the letter says, fell away or resigned, but O'Sullivan kept gathering new people more in tune with his own views. Those who 'fell away', however, had not lost interest in fighting the good fight and some became what might be called semi-detached League members, undertaking similar work off their own bat or in tandem with League activities. Cooney and O'Farrell were, according to the letter, two such semi-detached League members:

> When *The Rose Tattoo* was banned it was two ex-members who worked on that case – two splendid men who used their own money to buy doubtful books etc. and sent them to Seán Brady to pass on to the Minister so as to side-track the Censorship Board, which was in a state of siege at the time. When O'Sullivan found that Mr O'Farrell and Mr Cooney were doing this he would not co-operate but went to Charlie Haughey T.D. with his story thereby cutting across the work we were doing undercover. As Haughey is not the person I would approach on such matters [sic].[10]

Mrs Byrne's letter seemed to fill in all of the gaps in our story, at least those about Brady's sources. We had a clear line now from Joseph J. Cooney's outrage at the 1956 newspaper advertisements right up to Seán Brady's visit to Oscar Traynor on May 9th 1957. A certain imprecision of language in Mrs Byrne's letter meant we couldn't be certain that *The Rose Tattoo* was the only item brought to Brady's attention by Cooney and O'Farrell, but for our purposes this was hardly relevant: on this matter, at least, Brady had acted. The source of Brady's statements about *The Rose Tattoo*'s having been banned remained a mystery, but given the League's general penchant for exaggeration it might well have derived from 'information' provided by Cooney and O'Farrell. Like Brady's statement that McQuaid knew of his visit to the Department it appeared, whatever its source, to be demonstrably false. Which left us with …

As we realised, once the euphoria of our discoveries wore off, it actually left us with very little. We had succeeded in tracking down the original complaint about *The Rose Tattoo*: a complaint made through extraordinary channels, before the Pike production ever opened, by someone who was by no standards an ordinary member of the public. This at least gave Swift a feeling of vindication on one matter: the idea that their *production* had been somehow at fault – that the Pike had, as Tennessee Williams insisted on believing, traduced the play – was once and for all demolished. The basic decisions about the play's obscenity had been taken, sight unseen, before their production even opened, not simply by the State but by the original complainant. And the question of whether some sectarian organisation had been responsible for the assault on the Pike had, in a sort of way, been answered: as seemed so often the case in the Ireland of the time, the answer to that question was both 'yes' and 'no'. Certain ex-members of the League had set the machinery in motion, but they'd had nothing to do with the actual prosecution. Nor was there any indication at all that those *bêtes noires* of liberal thought at the time, the Knights of Columbanus, had had any hand in the matter. And the assertion that the Catholic Church (in the person of McQuaid) had been behind the whole thing also seemed definitively demolished.

The more we thought about it, though, the less our discoveries added up to an *explanation*. If anything, in fact, they only deepened the mystery. The papers we'd found in the McQuaid archives seemed to prove beyond reasonable doubt that Dr McQuaid was innocent of involvement in this censorship case at least. Yet the released State papers were even more unequivocal in what *they* indicated: that the Government had decided to act against the Pike in 1957 precisely from fear of a statement – particularly a public statement – from McQuaid (and the unnamed but dangerous other 'sources') about the play. It was far more than a mere matter of Departmental ignorance: the two things seemed impossible to reconcile. This was a man the Department and the Fianna Fáil Government then in power knew very well indeed: the same John Charles McQuaid who had never shown any particular interest in theatrical censorship, who (whatever he might do behind the scenes) eschewed making personal public statements and had made no direct ones on matters of far greater importance to him. When he wanted something from Government, he made sure that Government knew about it and if it was important enough he thought nothing of calling on the Taoiseach himself – as he had done in 1953, when he brought some 'indecent' books bought in Dublin to the Taoiseach's office, to show de Valera how badly the censorship system needed beefing up.

Both the Government and the civil service, after almost 20 years, knew exactly what to expect from the Archbishop; more importantly, since he was a man of very consistent behaviour, they also knew what *not* to expect of him. Except, apparently, on this one occasion. In late May 1957, when the seven-point memo was written, the senior civil servant who wrote it took very seriously the idea that McQuaid might bypass the Department and make some form of negative public statement, reflecting badly on the Minister, unless the State took some action against the Pike. That civil servant – someone senior enough to recommend action to Traynor – took the possibility so seriously that he recommended the taking of such action immediately, despite the fact that this might in itself draw negative public comment from other quarters.

This made no sense for all that it was stated in black and white in the State papers. On the very simplest level, if the Department thought that McQuaid had some objection to the play then what was to stop someone there from simply phoning Archbishop's Palace in Drumcondra and clearing the matter up? For that matter, were they not curious as to why McQuaid himself had not contacted the Department if he was so exercised? Was there some existing frostiness between the Department and the Archbishop at the time – some disagreement that led the men in Justice to think McQuaid might welcome an opportunity to castigate the Minister? Or, to put this in terms more in keeping with McQuaid's normal methods, did the Department think that Dr McQuaid might find it in some way *useful* to castigate the Minister right then … as a means (since this too would be unexceptionable) of applying pressure on some related matter?

It was an intriguing thought. In terms of Church–State relations, which by the later 1950s were seriously skewed, it would even make sense – which nothing else did at this point. But if this did all relate to some Church–State clash, it would need to be a pretty big one to explain the facts; and surely any disagreement of the requisite proportions at that time would be well known. It was not, at any rate, well known to us. In that decade of notorious episodes involving the Church and its allies, the only well-known one going on at the requisite time was the shameful Fethard-on-sea boycott,[11] an event on which the State had acted and spoken relatively honourably, albeit only when the situation in Wexford proved impossible to ignore any longer. Nor is there any indication that McQuaid regarded the Fethard boycott as anything but what it was – a public relations disaster for the Church.

We'd found more jigsaw pieces in the archives of both Church and State, but even combined with the pieces we had they refused to make a coherent picture. It had always been generally assumed that discovering the original source of the *Rose Tattoo* complaint – the 'who' of the matter – would do much to explain the 'why' of the case. We had tacitly assumed as much ourselves. But now we knew the 'who' of it in far greater detail than we could have imagined even a few weeks before, the 'why' remained as elusive as ever. As had been the case since its beginning, the *Rose Tattoo* affair seemed to point to another quite different story about some other matter entirely. The central riddle of the case remained, though its form had changed: the question was no longer one of who had complained about the play – we knew that now, for what little it was worth; the question instead had become one of what the Department Of Justice had really been afraid of.

20. Another Country

The idea that the roots of the *Rose Tattoo* case might have something to do with a *conflict* between Church and State was completely at odds with the usually accepted interpretation. It was especially novel to Carolyn Swift, who'd spent 40-odd years thinking that if the Catholic Church played any part at all in the matter then it must have been as an instigator. In the strict sense at least, the Cooney letters seemed to show this wasn't true. The idea seemed worth investigating, if only so that we could discount it. Certainly we could think of nothing else that would explain the oddities in the Department's thinking and expectations. We had no idea what any such Church–State disagreement might have been about, but certainly the idea of a Church–State disagreement itself was perfectly feasible, especially towards the end of the 1950s, when the State was (however reluctantly) inching towards accepting the long-avoided idea of opening Irish society.

The very thought of any such attempt was almost literally anathema to the Irish Hierarchy, whose enormously powerful position in Ireland was ultimately dependent on the Republic's having the kind of closed society engineered since the 1930s. But by the late 1950s the Irish Republic was widely regarded abroad – and increasingly at home – as a failed social and economic entity. The most glaringly visible failure – the one which forced itself on ordinary people's attention every day of their lives – was the economic one. During the war the country's poverty could always be excused by pointing to the undeniable blessings of peace and even in the immediate aftermath of war the desolation of the former

European belligerents was obvious. But the economies of other North European nations had rallied rapidly and in all of them economic recovery had gone hand-in-hand with massive political and social reforms – in health-care, in education, in every conceivable aspect of general public welfare – which threw the appalling condition of Ireland's social institutions into ever-greater relief.

It was not simply that Ireland lacked the money for such schemes: most lay in areas where the State had long ago found it for one reason or another expedient to cede effective control to the Church. The Church guarded this control with a ferocity no Irish government dared face – as was amply demonstrated by the fate of Noel Browne's Mother and Child Scheme. In many ways the Republic had what amounted to two governments, one secular and one clerical, with the clerical rulers not simply running a separate fiefdom but claiming – and exercising – an influence on the secular in policy areas normally regarded as the business of the State, while utterly denying any form of reciprocal oversight. In that parallel Ireland which was the Church's realm, the State's function was mainly limited to providing funding; otherwise its writ, by and large, did not run. Given the intransigence shown by the Church in these areas and the fact that its preferred social model was quite literally medieval, this division of control was an almost sure-fire recipe for social stasis at a time of rapid change elsewhere.

In the 1950s Ireland's inertia and poverty reached their nadir. The early fifties were marked by growing political instability and even a cursory glance through the newspapers of the time gives a sensation of the growing public frustration and anger. In 1950 there were shipping, bus and train strikes and, with the Government's borrowing of £15m to fund development schemes, the national debt reached £52 for every man, woman and child in Ireland, at a time when the maximum salary of a teacher was £500 per annum. In 1951 and 1952 there were bank strikes, the first of which forced larger businesses to fly in cash to pay their employees.[1] In the single year between 1954 and 1955, Ireland's balance of payments deficit rose from £5.5m to £35.6m.[2] The end of the war had seen Establishment panic at the imagined prospect of a flood of redundant Irish workers returning from war-work in British factories; but even by 1950 it was emigration that threatened to destroy Ireland and destroy it frighteningly quickly – even official emigration figures (thought by many modern authorities to be underestimates) suggest that almost half a million people (nearly 15 per cent of the population) left Ireland in the course of the decade. Meanwhile the 1952 census revealed, among other things, that female emigration had increased by almost 50 per cent since the mid-thirties. By 1954 the decline in national birth rates had led some of the contributors to John A. O'Brien's book, *The Vanishing Irish*, to conclude that the Irish race would simply die out – a combination of emigration, economic stagnation and three decades of anti-sex hysteria (though this is curiously ignored in the book) having reduced the nation almost to the point where it was not replacing the dead with new children, while a huge proportion of those who were born were, like Irish beef, being raised for export. And even with the youngest and most restless leaving, social unrest mounted throughout the period, with unemployment marches in Dublin frequently degenerating into clashes with police.

As the 1950s progressed, the State had increasingly found itself caught between the rock of growing public demand for change and the hard place both of its own reluctance and of Church intransigence, the latter bolstered by influential sections of the laity which had benefited greatly from Church hegemony.[3] The history of the 1950s in Ireland is littered with clashes not simply between Church and State (some of them only now gradually being revealed) but between the Church, the lay auxiliaries through which it often operated in civil society and growing sections of that society itself. The mere certainty of Church disapproval may have been enough to keep some matters completely out of political discourse, but it could no longer stifle all debate in broader society.

Though social and political pressure kept all but the most flagrant abuses out of the news, still the history of post-war Ireland is increasingly littered with a roll-call of incidents which were essentially outcroppings of deeper and often hidden political and sociological struggles, struggles which were, fundamentally, about two things: who was to control the country and what rights and freedoms the individual was to have in it.

While the list of such incidents could be protracted almost indefinitely, its more prominent items would include such one-time burning issues as the Mother and Child affair, the Yugoslav football match, the Papal Nuncio Affair, the Meath Hospital scandal, the Fethard Boycott, the Clonlara assault case … and, of course, the *Rose Tattoo* case itself. All of these incidents seemed to feature ugly aspects of Catholic power, sectarianism or arrogance at one level or another and the controversy and even hysteria surrounding each served both to underline and to exacerbate the febrile social and political climate of the times.

Looking for evidence of a Church–State disagreement in such a period was at once a straightforward matter and, paradoxically, a fool's errand. There were any number of areas to look in and any number of sometimes unlikely sounding matters, great and small, which might have given rise to a squabble. But at the same time, contact between the two pillars of society was often conducted in a tortuous way, with neither side actually saying what it meant – at least in recorded form. Each institution scrutinised public statements by leading figures in the other, alert for hidden meanings and coded references to matters other than those supposedly being talked about. Church pressure was often applied through laymen, particularly the Knights of Columbanus whose quasi-secret membership and habitual use of third parties – including TDs and other organisations with less easily identifiable affiliations – allowed them to provide still further layers of disguise and deniability. Thus even arguments that on the surface appeared straightforwardly political not infrequently masked deeper struggles.[4]

The idea that the Department of Justice might suspect McQuaid's 'interest' in *The Rose Tattoo* to be a ploy masking an attack on some other front would fit in very well with such shenanigans. Such an approach by the Archbishop would – unlike just about any other interpretation of his supposed intentions – have seemed almost unexceptional ... *if* there were a pre-existing dispute or if the Department had reason to expect one. Swift (who had after all lived through those times) could think of no public issue from the requisite period – though this proved nothing, since one of the few ground-rules observed by both Church and State in their rows seems to have been that such undignified squabbles were best kept from public view. In fact letting it be known that they meant to go public with their own version of events was, precisely, a tactic the Hierarchy had employed only a few years before, during the stupefyingly complex negotiations over de Valera's Mother and Infant Scheme.[5] And certainly the whole tenor of the seven-point memo suggested that the Department (at least by the time the memo was written) was almost *waiting* for trouble from McQuaid. It was as though *The Rose Tattoo* would provide the Archbishop with not so much a *reason* for a public statement as an *excuse* for one.

And yet, by May 1957, there hardly seemed *time* for the Fianna Fáil government to have fallen out with the Church: the Party had been back in power for barely two months – hardly long enough for what amounted to a complete breakdown of communications with the Archdiocese of Dublin. Fianna Fáil had been returned to power almost by default, for want of any alternative, when the second Inter-Party Government collapsed internally in the face of the IRA Border Campaign that had begun the previous December. The Border Campaign is now seen as pretty much the last gasp of the IRA of the period; but at the time, when the Irish State itself was regarded by many as teetering on the verge of collapse, it was taken very seriously indeed. De Valera had returned to office determined to crush the campaign and evidence of the

seriousness of the intent was seen by many in the decision to replace Fianna Fáil's long-time man in the Justice Department,
Gerry Boland, with Oscar Traynor, a man whose Republican credentials made those of even Seán Brady seem almost weak by
comparison. Boland (it is said) was regarded as being somewhat
'soft' on the Northern issue and only someone with Traynor's
cast-iron Republican credentials could hope to get away with employing the type of ruthless measures – including internment –
that de Valera planned to use against the IRA.

In an attempt to narrow the field of possibilities for our phantom row we re-examined the released papers and in particular the
seven-point memo. 'If there is any delay in taking action', the
memo tells Traynor, 'you may be faced with a demand – possibly
a demand made in public – from any one of several sources, including the Archbishop, for action.' What would the political effect of such a demand be on the Minister's and the Government's
image? The only conceivable answer to that, as far as we could see,
would be to portray the Department of Justice as being soft on
censorship – a great crime indeed in the eyes of the Church and
the Catholic Right, who placed enormous importance on the
whole censorship issue. Had the frequent worries of many in 1957
been correct then? Had there actually been some kind of concerted
attempt by the Church and its allies to pressurise the State into
introducing censorship of the theatre as well as of everything else?
And had the State been resisting that pressure?

Given the lingering secrecy about the history of Church–State
relations in Ireland, it is almost impossible to give a definitive 'yes'
or 'no' to such questions. Nonetheless every available fact suggested that the idea could be dismissed outright. Certainly the
League of Decency kept a watchful and appalled eye on the Dublin theatre, as did the Knights of Columbanus (which established a
special committee for the purpose in 1951) and several other
fringe organisations. Certainly letters to newspapers (and the Department of Justice) about the sinful nature of many plays per-

formed in Dublin were not uncommon and we found numbers of letters in the McQuaid papers from ordinary members of the public – some of them Protestant – driven to express their outrage at performances they had innocently witnessed.[6] We had even found one in the State's *Rose Tattoo* file, though not a complaint about the Pike: it was a stray letter from Mr O'Sullivan, Secretary of the League of Decency, denouncing the notorious Globe Theatre production of *I Am a Camera*.[7]

Since co-ordinating 'spontaneous' campaigns of 'independent' complaints seems to have been another common tactic of the Knights, there was a probability that many of the 'unrelated' letters to the newspapers and the Department were (as they most certainly were in the matter of book censorship) nothing of the kind. But we found no evidence in Dr McQuaid's files to suggest that an *organised* campaign for theatre censorship existed. And if it had done so then one could be almost certain that the evidence would be there, since far more potentially embarrassing documents can be found in the files. Without access to the McQuaid papers it might have been possible to believe in a secret conspiracy to secure the introduction of stage censorship – secret conspiracies seem to have been a perfectly normal way of doing business in Ireland at the time. But the lack of even a shred of evidence for it in the McQuaid archives seemed proof that this particular conspiracy had not existed. Dr McQuaid's own censorship hobbyhorse was well known and it was *printed* material: books, magazines, periodicals, comics, Sunday supplements and even newspaper advertisements. Whether on moral or theological grounds, whether it was adult literature, children's Bible stories, trashy paperbacks, movie magazines or English newspapers, print censorship remained an abiding interest of the archbishop's for the more than three decades of his reign.[8] He himself kept a collection of especially objectionable material; he preached sermons on the subject; he repeatedly enjoined the Knights of Columbanus to pay strict and constant attention to it; he contacted Ministers and civil servants about it … and on at least that one occasion even paid a personal call on the Taoiseach, his old friend de Valera, to show him some depraved volumes freely available in Dublin.

If Dr McQuaid were ever to have a row with any Government about censorship, then every single thing known about the man would suggest that the row would be about *print* censorship, not censorship in the theatre. And indeed he – or rather the Catholic Hierarchy, for the whole Hierarchy was involved – would have precisely such a row, beginning at the end of that same year, during the Campaign Against Evil Literature. An attempt to portray the Government as being soft on censorship would have made perfect sense as a propaganda tactic then, and indirect attempts to do exactly that formed a basic part of the campaign. But in May 1957 the Campaign Against Evil Literature still lay some seven and a half months in the future. Nonetheless the matter might be worth looking into from our perspective.

Our latest reading of the State papers did seem to provide one possible hint, if not about the nature of our theoretical row then about its timing. Re-reading the flurry of documents which resulted on May 9th from Brady's visit to Oscar Traynor, one was struck by the nature of the only State action clearly decided on that day: to set police to watch performances of *The Rose Tattoo*. Even when we first read the papers this had seemed like no more than a precaution and though the reports of these policemen were later referred to in court, several of those reports were not written until immediately before Simpson's arrest – an indication that the matter had not been deemed terribly important on their initial visits.

By now, however, we had come across other references to policemen attending plays. Joseph J. Cooney had reported that the Gardaí had sent men to see *The Respectable Prostitute* in the Pike the year before; O'Sullivan of the League of Decency had also been told that the police had been to see *I Am a Camera*, that it had been disgraceful but that, since it had now finished its run, there was little that could be done about it – precisely what Cooney had been told about the Sartre play. Two examples were not enough to establish a pattern, but it certainly seemed that sending police to observe a complained-of play was relatively ordinary practice, if only so that the complainant could honestly be assured that something had been done. This reinforced the impression that the action taken by the Department of Justice on May 9th was – though conducted speedily and at a senior level (as befitted the fact that the matter had the interest of an Archbishop) – little more than a normal precaution. The really unprecedented thing was the complete change that had taken place in the Departmental attitude approximately twelve days later by the time the seven-point memo was written – twelve days for which not a single document had been released by the State.

It looked as though something had happened during those twelve days; something had happened or the Department had learned of something happening. Something that made the level-headed men in the Department of Justice believe that Archbishop McQuaid might well break with his habits and issue some statement that reflected badly on the Minister, backed up by similar statements from someone else, whether the political Opposition or McQuaid's Knightly allies. What we were looking for, therefore, was something that the Department of Justice would have learned about between May 9th and perhaps May 21st. The only logical candidate for subject matter seemed censorship – not the chimera of theatre censorship, but the very real print (not, as seems nowadays generally assumed, simply literary) censorship. It was McQuaid's hobbyhorse; it was the Justice Department's responsibility. Within a year of Brady's visit to Traynor, the Minister would find himself under siege on this very subject. What exactly had all *that* been about? The Irish censorship system was, for much of the twentieth century, a by-word for extremism: what exactly had the Hierarchy wanted from the Campaign Against Evil Literature? There seemed only one way to find out.

'We have to find out what was going on in the Censorship Board in May 1957,' I said to Swift when we next spoke on the phone.

'But what has that got to do with anything?' she asked.

'I don't know. Probably nothing. But do you have any better ideas?'

As I'd expected, she did not. If I'd sometimes felt frustrated by the dead ends, as I watched the months tick by, I knew that Swift's frustration must be ten times greater. This, after all, was her story we were investigating: these things had actually happened to her. All she really wanted was an explanation; but after a four-decade wait and almost six further months of digging beneath the surface of the supposed solution, she felt no closer to the truth.

'All right, then,' she said. 'But if there's anything in it then you know that it's probably withheld in a secret State file somewhere.'

As it happened, the first hint that we were at least sniffing in the right direction came from no very secret place. It came, instead, from a parenthetical reference in a book in the National Library of Ireland. The book was Michael Adams' groundbreaking – but often maddeningly careful – *Censorship: The Irish Experience*, published in 1968 but still the only dedicated history of the once enormously controversial field of Irish print censorship. The book was no longer in print, nor to be found in any of the public libraries we checked; so we'd gone to the National Library in search of a copy.

The reference we found in the book was, very simply, to a date: May 8th 1957. That was what first caught my own attention. It was on the evening of May 8th that a bitter disagreement boiled over at a meeting of the Irish Censorship Board, the body charged with deciding what the Irish people might legitimately read, whether in the form of books, newspapers or periodicals. The striking thing about this date to anyone researching the *Rose Tattoo* case is, of course, that it is the day before Seán Brady's visit to Oscar Traynor. The Censorship Board was a voluntary body composed of men with full-time jobs: it seemed only common sense to assume that their meeting had taken place in the evening. Given the number of things that had taken place in the Department of Justice after Brady's visit on May 9th, we had already concluded that Brady's visit took place at a reasonably early hour. So the two events had taken place far less than a day apart. It proved nothing, but it was certainly enough to get our attention. Reading a little more about the Censorship Board row, though, even in Adams's brief account, made the hair on the back of one's neck begin to stir. Because the row, even on the basis of Adam's short account of it, obviously had features which slotted precisely into the criteria for our phantom crisis: it involved print censorship and therefore would have been of great interest to McQuaid; it had resulted from actions taken by the previous Government and so had had time to fester before Fianna Fáil even took office; it had led – since the resulting resignations from the Board were commonly held to be a prelude to the Campaign Against Evil Literature – to an enormous Church–State row. And, exactly as our hypothesis required, it was unlikely that, early on May 9th, the Government had yet learned about the acrimonious meeting of the night before. By May 21st , however, they certainly knew all about it.

To anyone who had spent time with the McQuaid papers, the description of the Censorship Board row in Adams's book had another immediately striking feature. For the names of some of those who resigned from the Board in 1957, though we were seeing them here for the first time in this context, were already very familiar to us from the McQuaid archives: they belonged to very close allies of the Archbishop's indeed. What on *earth* had such individuals been doing on the Irish Censorship Board during its most controversial period?

The story briefly told in Adams's book was obviously only the tip of an iceberg and that iceberg looked, even at that point, as though it might be a very big one. Adams's account had loose and

The tiny stage of the Pike Theatre, 18a Herbert Lane, in 1953. Even including standing-room, the little theatre could never hold more than perhaps 65 patrons at a time.

Brendan Behan (centre) and Alan Simpson (in dark suit, left) with members of the cast before the world première of *The Quare Fellow*.

Derrick Michelson

The finale of *Further Follies*: (l-r) Pauline Bewick, Alan Barry, Deirdre McSharry, Milo O'Shea, Rosamond Stevens, T.P. McKenna and May Ollis.

Samuel Beckett's favourite photograph from the production of *Waiting for Godot*; Dermot Kelly as Vladimir "looking at the boot as if it were an early 17th century skull".

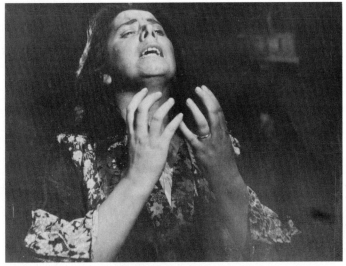

Anna Manahan as Serafina in *The Rose Tattoo*. Harold Hobson, writing in *The Sunday Times*, called her career-making performance 'a *tour de force* of sustained intensity'.

Anna Manahan (kneeling) and Gearóid Ó Lochlainn as the priest in a production shot from *The Rose Tattoo*.

Swift and Aidan Maguire attempt to follow Simpson into the Pike box office, where Special Branch detectives had physically dragged Simpson. The police slammed the door on Maguire's wrist, injuring him.

Simpson is led from the box office to a waiting unmarked police car . . .

... and driven away to the Bridewell Prison.

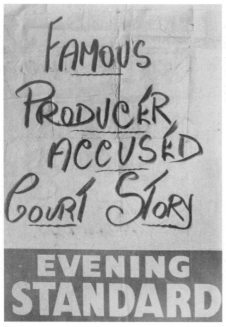

FAMOUS
PRODUCER
ACCUSED
Court Story

EVENING
STANDARD

The Dublin newspaper headlines next day were only a foretaste of the publicity the case would receive.

A victorious Pike group surrounds Simpson after his first court appearance. Their optimism was not well-founded – the case would drag on for over a year.

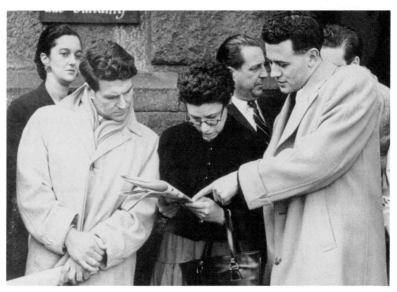

Swift studies the early newspaper reports.

Pornographers? Carolyn Swift and Alan Simpson embrace outside Dublin District Court.

Minister: (Oscar Theatre.)

Production of "The Rose Tattoo" at the Pike Theatre
_____

1.   Attached are three police reports (tabbed "A", "B" and "C") by three policemen who attended the current production of the Tennessee Williams play "The Rose Tattoo" at the Pike Theatre.

2.   On the basis of the police reports, I think there is no doubt that the play is indecent, and that, too, is the view of Mr. O'Donoghue of the Attorney General's Office.

3.   Before the play was put on, Mr. Seán Brady, T.D., called to the Department and stated that the play was indecent, that he was aware that His Grace the Archbishop had "called for the script" and that he (the Archbishop) was aware of Mr. Brady's representations to the Department.   As a result of this, we asked the Attorney General in writing whether, if the play were thought to be indecent, a prosecution could be brought, seeing that the theatre is run, ostensibly at any rate, as a club.   The Attorney General said, "yes" - that a prosecution could be brought.

4.   It now appears from advertisements in the Press that the play is being transferred from the Pike Theatre to the Gate Theatre at the end of this week, where, in the ordinary course it would be shown to a much wider audience than the 70 odd persons who can be accommodated nightly in the Pike.   This makes the question of the continuance of the play much more important.

5.   Our recommendation, which is supported by the Attorney General's Office, is that a uniformed Inspector should -

(a)   approach the management of the Pike Theatre forthwith and tell them that if the play is not immediately either taken off or expurgated to the point where all objectionable passages and situations are removed, they will be prosecuted, and

(b)   approach the management of the Gate and tell them that if the play is put on with the objectionable passages and situations included, they will be prosecuted and that the matter will be noted for the information of the Attorney General when their application for Letters Patent for the Theatre comes before him in due course.   (The application for Letters Patent are held up at present while the Theatre is undergoing repairs).

6.   In making this recommendation, we have in mind the fact not only that the play as produced is, in our opinion, indecent but that if there is any delay in taking action you may be faced with a demand - possibly a demand made in public - from any one or more of several sources, including the Archbishop, for action, and that you would then be put in the position of having either to take no action - though the play is believed to be indecent - or to give the impression to the public that you acted only at the dictation of the Archbishop or of somebody else.

7.   If action is taken, as recommended, there is bound to be some criticism, and indeed, widespread newspaper publicity, and it may be noted in that connection that the production is stated in the programme to be "guaranteed" (i.e. presumably financially) by the Dublin Tostal Council.   This, however, is the lesser of two evils and a difficulty which, we think, must be faced.

The 'seven-point memo' – an anonymous Department of Justice document, released over four decades after the *Rose Tattoo* case ended, whose oddities and internal contradictions fuelled the authors' hunt for the real story behind the case.

extremely suggestive threads, some of whose relevance might not have been clear to Adams himself. Loose threads and unanswered questions are common in the public versions of many incidents in 1950s Ireland – the *Rose Tattoo* affair, as we have seen, was largely composed of them. The story told in the second part of the present book is derived, frankly, from tugging on some of the loose threads in the story of the Censorship Board row. When the threads were pulled, the story that emerged was very weird and wonderful indeed. The information available to Michael Adams when he wrote of the dispute was limited and it is clear from his own account that he wasn't permitted to use in his narrative much of the material to which he was allowed access. The account given here – more than 30 years after Adams wrote – comes largely from sources that became available only in the late 1990s. Even so the story was constructed, jigsaw-like, from references in scores of documents in both the McQuaid and National Archives. It is a big story, which took more than a year to tease out – not least because much of the central State documentation is still withheld, but also because it seems to show some of the highest and mightiest in 1950s Ireland engaged in quite astonishing webs of deceit. Even now many details of the story remain uncertain; but the pattern is clear.

As the following story unfolded, with its welter of secrecy and hidden manoeuvring, we watched each new development with a kind of horrified fascination; as each layer seemed to lead only to another one beneath, we often wondered if we would ever reach firm ground again at all. But there was never any question of letting the matter lie, because with each passing month we also had the growing conviction that, in spite of these complexities, this search was related to our original one. For though the interpretation that began to suggest itself was completely at odds with *anything* we had expected, and even though it relegated the assault on the Pike from a major deliberate attack on civil liberties to a botched attempt at a quick political fix, still we soon became completely convinced that in the story we were discovering here lay precisely what we had set out to find: the twisted and decidedly unhealthy roots of the *Rose Tattoo* case.

PART THREE

THE CENSORSHIP BOARD CRISIS

'In politics in Ireland, we sometimes live in the world of the bizarre'
Professor Dermot Keogh, UCC,
in the RTÉ television series 'Seven Ages'

21. A Bloodless Coup

The Irish censorship of the printed word, while its frequently embarrassing details are now largely forgotten, was in its time an enormously contentious issue on which debate was largely characterised (on all sides) by vituperation, rancour, black mistrust and on at least one occasion the threat of physical violence in the Irish Senate. The main part of our own story takes place in the 1950s, but in order to make it comprehensible it is first necessary to backtrack somewhat and give a brief sketch of censorship history.

The only full book on the subject, Adams's *Censorship: The Irish Experience*, dates from 1968 and is a notably stilted work that gives the impression of having been written under some constraint. While it does give a great deal of information, much of that information seems at times almost deliberately obscured,[1] and the text requires very careful reading. This lack of a plain and really coherent history of the censorship system is unfortunate from the point of view of entertainment as well as education, since the story is at once remarkably sinister and often outrageously – if rarely intentionally – funny. Very little of it, however, was funny at the time and it was certainly not regarded as such by anyone involved.

The introduction of the Censorship of Publications Act in 1929 followed a long campaign by Catholic groups to exert pressure on the Free State Government. The campaign moved into overdrive with the involvement of the Hierarchy in the mid-twenties. Central to its success was the work of the Irish Vigilance

Association (originally founded by the Dominicans but soon boasting the heavy involvement of the Knights of Columbanus, then recently arrived in Dublin from the North)[2] and the Catholic Truth Society of Ireland (set up by the Hierarchy and also featuring high-level Knightly involvement). As with many things in Ireland then, animosity towards England played as great a part in the campaign as anything else and the primary focus of complaint was not books at all but the English 'yellow' press – the 1920s equivalent of today's tabloids.

The Government, buying time, set up a committee to look into the matter and, when the committee's report was delivered in 1927, did nothing about it until pressurised by a further public campaign which included some startlingly direct actions – armed men held up trains carrying parcels of suspect newspapers and burned the parcels.[3] Moves to frame legislation followed. What look (from the vantage point of the 21st century) very like attempts to smuggle usefully ambiguous wording into the Act were largely spotted and foiled by those who feared that the entire Act was a Trojan Horse for Catholic Church control of the flow of information. A particular bone of contention was a clause permitting the Minister to 'recognise for the purpose of this Act any group or association of persons' to act as what Adams calls 'the source or sifting-ground of complaints'.[4] This clause, which had not featured in the Committee report but mysteriously appeared in the original Bill, was widely seen as a blatant but secretly engineered attempt to hand control of censorship over to Catholic vigilante groups. This was regarded as a step too far and all mention of such groups was specifically voted out of the legislation: if there had to be censorship then it would at least, the Dáil decided, be closed to sectarian abuse.

Even the modified Act drew fire from critics of the stature of Shaw, Yeats,[5] Gogarty and AE.[6] Since the legislation as passed did include a specific ban on the dissemination of information on birth-control, it could be termed sectarian; but on the whole it would not be the Act itself so much as the manner of its enforcement which would cause controversy. The Censorship of Publications Act established a five-man Censorship of Publications Board under the auspices of the Department of Justice. In the event of the members disagreeing on any particular item, board decisions would be reached on a qualified majority voting basis: for a book, newspaper or periodical to be banned, a minimum of four votes in favour of a ban were required. Thus if two members of the Board voted against a ban, it could not be imposed. Membership of the Board was voluntary, with a permanent post of Secretary, and there was to be a guarantee of minority representation in that one place was to be filled by a Protestant.

From the beginning there was criticism of some of the Censorship Board's decisions, but the first real controversy only came in 1937 with the resignation from the Board of the novelist Lynn Doyle. Since Doyle was a known opponent of the Censorship, his resignation was less surprising than his appointment to the Board in the first place – an appointment which was described by the Minister of the day, P.J. Ruttledge, as 'something of an experiment', and which appalled the four existing members, who refused even to attend Board meetings with Doyle.[7] In the event the experiment lasted for little more than a month before the novelist resigned. Doyle himself wrote to Ruttledge explaining his resignation, citing as the main reason the Board's practice of banning books solely on the basis of 'objectionable' passages marked by the complainant rather than on the book as a whole – a practice which many saw as against both the letter and the spirit of the 1929 legislation.

To the Catholic Right, predictably enough, the main complaint against the Censorship Board was that it wasn't strict enough and in 1937 the influential Catholic Truth Society presented a report to the Government which suggested 'improvements' to remedy the Censorship Act's 'failings'. But opposition to the Board's practices was gradually growing too and it was also growing more difficult to ignore. Until the end of the Thirties one of the very few forums for public criticism of the regime was the editorial and letters pages of the *Irish Times*, but with the advent of *The Bell* in 1940 and the platform the magazine provided for Seán Ó Faoláin's incisive articles against the practices of the Censorship Board, a genuinely new era in protest arrived.

O'Faoláin and other mid-twentieth century critics of the Irish censorship regime – men such as Yeats, Ó Faoláin, Frank O'Connor and Peadar O'Donnell – are frequently nowadays mistakenly referred to (often approvingly) as having campaigned 'against censorship'. This is an entirely misleading description and was in fact a charge frequently levelled against them by their opponents. All of the above – and, without exception, all those who fought against the rigours of Irish censorship in the middle decades of the 20th century – fully accepted the need for some kind of censorship mechanism. What they fought against was the *abuse* of censorship – specifically, the extreme (and, as was repeatedly suggested, actually illegal) manner in which successive Irish Censorship Boards carried out the terms of the 1929 Act. To understand the outrage felt in some quarters at the Board's decisions, one need do little more than glance at even a casual list of some of the authors banned between 1930 and 1945: Beckett, Boccaccio, Austin Clarke, Coward, Daphne du Maurier, Faulkner, Freud, Stella Gibbons (for *Cold Comfort Farm*), Gogarty, Gorki, Graves, Graham Greene, Hemingway, Huxley, Isherwood, Joyce,[8] Kavanagh, Maura Laverty, Thomas Mann, Maugham, Malcolm Muggeridge, O'Casey, Frank O'Connor, Seán Ó Faoláin, Liam O'Flaherty, Proust, Shaw, Steinbeck and Wells. It may be noted that, apart from anything else (and there are already several Nobel Prize winners here) the list includes just about every major Irish writer of the period; it should also be noted that all these authors' works were banned as being in their 'general tendency' indecent or obscene, which is to say that they were placed on precisely the same plane as the most blatant pornography.

Opposition to the Censorship Board's practices and calls for its reform grew stronger throughout the early Forties and by the middle of the decade a highly reluctant Fianna Fáil government felt obliged to at least make a gesture in this direction, though the prime intent seems to have been to wash Government hands once and for all of involvement in an increasingly contentious matter in which the State had little real interest. As all Irish governments well knew, any attempt at genuine reforms would be met with a storm of protest from the pro-censorship lobby; yet when Minister for Justice Gerald Boland eventually introduced a supposedly re-forming Bill in the autumn of 1945, it was greeted with a silence from the proponents of censorship which Michael Adams, obvi-ously mystified, calls 'uncanny'.[9] In truth it was anything *but* un-canny: it has emerged that the censorship lobby had, almost liter-ally, written much of the Bill themselves.

William Magennis, Chairman of the Censorship Board, had had a private conference with Boland as far back as mid-May.[10] Magennis was a remarkable figure – tooth-grindingly overbearing and viperishly malicious, he was the single most controversial member of the Censorship Board in its original (pre-1946) incar-nation and had been heavily involved in pro-censorship agitation since the 1910s. Like many major figures in the field, Magennis was a prominent member of the Knights of Columbanus. Indeed, the Knights' own official historian largely credits the Order's ef-forts – and the (not always open) presence of its members among Dáil deputies and Senators of all political parties – with the suc-cessful passing of the original 1929 Act, with which Magennis himself had been closely involved.[11] Magennis's relationship with Dr McQuaid was particularly close and his current approach to the Minister was co-ordinated with the Archbishop, who oversaw the entire proceedings that followed.[12]

What Magennis wanted from Gerald Boland was nothing less than control of any proposed reforms. With an ease which took even Magennis by surprise, this is essentially what he got. Boland can have had little doubt that Magennis was acting on McQuaid's behalf, nor could he have any doubt about the good Professor's own views. Magennis was (to put it mildly) not overly sympathetic to progressive tendencies in the arts, a fact which was publicly acknowledged – when the government had proposed putting him on the board of the Abbey, Yeats had said that he would rather close the theatre. Only two years before visiting Boland the good Professor (whom Frank O'Connor summed up as 'a windbag with a nasty streak of malice') had been the most prominent speaker in the incredibly rancorous Seanad debate on the banning of Eric Cross's luminous hymn to the real Ireland, *The Tailor and Ansty*,[13] a debate which Frank O'Connor later likened to a 'long, slow swim through a sewage bed'.[14] The tenor of Magennis's own contribution to the debate may be gauged by the reference (in the course of four and a half hours of speaking) to the eponymous Tailor as 'sex-obsessed' and his elderly wife as a 'moron'.

William Magennis seems the least likely figure imaginable to propose any censorship reforms but then reform was not his actual aim. What he offered the Minister instead was a scheme that would have the appearance of reform while in fact leaving the situation more or less as it was. Boland had been considering scrapping the Board entirely and replacing it with a single, full-time, government-appointed censor, as was already the case with film censorship. Magennis persuaded him to drop this idea and institute instead an Appeals Board (though without the retrospective power to remove bans already imposed by the Censorship Board, as Boland at first intended). The great attraction of the Appeals Board idea for Boland (as Magennis reported to McQuaid the day after the meeting)[15] was that it would remove responsibility for appeals from the Justice Ministry altogether and thus keep censorship debates out of the Dáil and Seanad. There would be no repeat of the *Tailor and Ansty* debate.[16]

Boland's eagerness to take Magennis's proposals on board took even the Professor himself by surprise. Magennis went so far as to write up the scheme in the form of an actual draft Act (to make it, he explained to McQuaid, easier for the politicians to understand) but sent it to the Archbishop for vetting before submitting it to the Minister. The Bill as later enacted was, with some changes, substantially based on Magennis's draft. It passed legislative scrutiny with a minimum of fuss. In the Senate, Magennis actually had the brass neck to speak *against* the new Bill – though what he was objecting to were the elements in it that differed from his original draft. The Professor's more robust side emerged during the Bill's second reading, when he took violent exception to a suggestion by Senator Kingsmill Moore, who felt it only fair that one member of the new Appeals Board should be nominated by the Irish Academy of Letters. Out of 34 members of the Academy, Magennis thundered, fully nine had had books banned, while the organisation's Secretary was Lennox Robinson! 'Is Ireland to be Irish', he demanded, 'or is it to be subjugated again by a foreign printing press by means of a spiritual defeat?' The point actually under debate had been a motion proposed by a Senator Douglas, but '[e]ventually it became so clear that [Magennis] and Kingsmill Moore were liable to come to blows that Senator Douglas felt obliged to withdraw his motion.'[17] 'One gets the impression', Adams writes, 'that Professor Magennis was interested in appeal only as a sort of "advertisement for the sale of *appearance* of justice".'[18] Indeed. And one also gets the impression that, in this at least, Magennis was at one with Boland.

In the end the Bill passed easily enough, with harmony and good fellowship restored: even Professor Magennis (as well he might) congratulated the Minister on it and the Minister in turn congratulated the House. In spite of Magennis's carping, he had carried out a remarkable coup. 'Boland', as McQuaid's biographer John Cooney bluntly puts it, 'had handed over ministerial responsibility to … bodies effectively under McQuaid's hidden rule.' Speaking to Michael Adams 20 years later, Boland would disclaim all memory of ever having seen Magennis's draft Bill, even though the Professor had openly referred to it in his Seanad speech during the debates. In 1966 the former Minister could only recall some 'proposals' from the good Professor;[19] 20 years earlier, however, Boland cannot have failed to understand the implications of his actions or to know that the Archbishop of Dublin was a sleeping partner in Magennis's approach. By then, less than four years after his accession to the Archbishopric, McQuaid's closeness to the Knights was well known – it would certainly be well-known to Boland, since he was himself a member of the Order.

In 1947 the Archbishop, by then himself a Knight, would charge the Order with a special task dear to his own heart. Identifying the 'flood-tides of obscenity' which had occurred elsewhere as – quite apart from anything else – 'signs that Communism was on the upsurge', he begged them in an address to 'help to stem the tide of bad literature … It is so easy to criticise; so hard to build up. Therefore let you be constructive.'[20]

By the time McQuaid gave this address his friend Magennis was dead. Whether the Minister for Justice was among the audience is not known. But it is in the wake of McQuaid's injunction that the story of the Knights, the Minister and the Censorship Board begins to get particularly interesting, as the events began which would culminate in the great bust-up of 1957.

22. Being Constructive

In the years after 1946 the censorship issue faded into the background of politics as the Fianna Fáil financial scandals, the rise (and fall) of Clann na Poblachta, the declaration of the Republic, the Mother and Child controversy, the seemingly endless escalation in emigration and the miserable poverty of the country took precedence in the public mind. Censorship had not, however, gone away. Instead Irish censorship now entered what Michael Adams terms its 'distinct second stage'. If the 1945 'reforms' really had been tantamount to a silent coup, one would expect to find some sign of this in the actual performance of the Board. And indeed, as time went on, this 'distinct second stage' of censorship might best be termed its truly Pathological Period, particularly after the appointment of a new Board in 1951.

Many events relating to the Censorship Board in this period are still obscure. This is partly because the institution of the Appeals process had the desired effect of removing discussion of censorship issues from the Dáil. A more serious cause, however, was laxness in publishing the annual Reports which, under the new legislation, both the Censorship and Appeals Boards were obliged to produce. There were complaints from the start about the Censorship Board's delays in producing its reports,[1] though (as Adams demonstrates) much of the publishing delay was due to Ministerial disinterest.[2] This absence leaves many questions unanswered but does not obscure the oddity of the Board's behaviour during these years nor make it any less glaringly suspect.

The first Censorship Board to operate under the new legislation consisted of four existing members – Magennis (as Chairman), Father Deery, Professor Shields and Professor Wigham – and C.J. Joyce, a newcomer. This Board, however, never actually sat, as (within days of his appointment) Magennis suddenly died.[3] Father Deery succeeded Magennis as Chairman, reviving the practice from the Board's inception whereby its Chairman had been a Catholic priest. Deery was replaced on the Board itself by J.J. Pigott, Professor of Education at St Patrick's Training College. It is with Pigott's entrance, in April 1946, that the history of the Censorship Board begins to become truly fascinating. Pigott's position in such an important post at the teacher training college marks him out immediately in that era as McQuaid's man.[4] As such, it seems superfluous to say that he was also a Knight of Columbanus.[5] Pigott would serve loyally on the Board for over a decade, including the years of its most patently ludicrous excesses. He would become Chairman – the second layman after Magennis to do so – on Father Deery's resignation in 1956 and would leave the Board, reluctantly, during the crisis of 1957.

The Board that finally settled down in April 1946 remained unchanged until the resignation of Professor Wigham in February 1949. There is no indication that there was anything acrimonious or untoward about Wigham's resignation, but the same cannot be said for the departure of Dr J.D. Smyth, his successor as the Board's token Protestant. Smyth, a Trinity lecturer, resigned in disgust after less than six months, publicly complaining to the Minister for Justice that the Board had its own (unwritten) internal rule dictating that, in judging a book, 'moral'[6] considerations must in every case outweigh such matters as literary merit or authorial intention. The Board's permanent Secretary, Brian MacMahon – an inveterate writer of often vituperative letters to the Press in the Board's name[7] – denied these charges in a letter to the *Irish Times*.[8]

The aftermath of Smyth's departure seems indicative of the actual situation on the Board. For whatever reason, Smyth's replacement – District Justice T.G. O'Sullivan – was a Catholic. Although Protestants in Holy Catholic Ireland had by and large learned to keep their heads well down, it seems that the faculty of Trinity (whence Protestant Board members were mainly drawn) had finally concluded that the presence on the Board of a single Protestant was really no more than a fig-leaf designed to legitimise the otherwise sectarian basis of Board decisions. Certainly Paul Blanshard, in *The Irish and Catholic Power*, would claim that 'since Smyth's resignation the Government has been unable to find any Protestant professor of Trinity College to co-operate in such proceedings.'[9]

There can there be no doubt that many powerful elements in Irish Catholicism will have seen the advent of a Protestant-free Censorship Board as a very welcome event. The degree to which Catholic thought in Ireland at the time included a fantastic belief in a Protestant conspiracy to work towards power in the Irish State in the 1950s is nowadays (for fairly obvious reasons) downplayed, but various clerics and others made both private and public reference to it – and to their own supposed counter-campaign.[10] Whether the presence of a single Protestant on the Censorship Board in the coming years would have made any difference is doubtful; but there can be no doubt that Smyth's departure marked the point at which the Censorship Board entirely lost the run of itself. Indeed it seems terribly fitting that one of the first books banned after Smyth's resignation was George Orwell's *1984*.

'After 1949', Adams reports blandly, 'the number of bannings steadily increased.'[11] This is one way of putting the case, but it hardly begins to describe the actuality. The first Board of the 'new' dispensation was due to be replaced in 1951. In its final full year – 1950 – the number of bans imposed was fully two and a half times greater than in the previous year. Over the following two years, due to deaths and (uncontentious) resignations, membership of the Board fluctuated a little, but the upward trend continued. A Dr Breathnach had replaced the departing Professor Shields in

1950 and Breathnach, though confirmed as a member of the new 1951 Board, died in June and was replaced by Christopher J. O'Reilly, another member of the staff of St Patrick's College. In 1952 the board was joined by Dermot J. O'Flynn, a Dublin businessman. Board membership thereupon stabilised as follows: Father Joseph Deery (chairman), Pigott, O'Reilly, O'Flynn and Joyce. This version of the Board would remain, as Adams puts it, 'remarkably stable' until 1956 and it is with this version that definite identification of what was going on finally becomes possible.

Of the members of the newly stable board, the affiliations of Mr. Joyce are not known. The new Chairman, Fr Joseph Deery, was – like all priestly members of the Censorship Board – a McQuaid nominee, put in place at the same time as Magennis's approach to Boland.[12] While a less combative figure than Magennis, Deery held views on censorship which were every bit as extreme as the late Professor's.[13] As is clear from correspondence in the McQuaid archives, Deery would also keep McQuaid informed of developments on the Board and of what he learned of opposition to it.[14]

As it happens, Fr Deery's input here was probably superfluous: whether Deery was a member of the Knights of Columbanus is not known, but J.J. Pigott certainly was. The other two members of the Board were, if anything, even more interesting: Christopher J. O'Reilly, in the same year that he joined the Censorship Board, assumed the office of Supreme Knight – the head of the entire Order. Meanwhile, by the time of the Board crisis in 1957, Dermot J. O'Flynn would be Provincial Grand Knight for Leinster and he would himself become Supreme Knight in 1960. These were, in other words, people with the most prominent positions imaginable in the secretive organisation which McQuaid had specifically charged with imposing Irish Catholic standards on reading material available in Ireland. Both (as their voluminous correspondence in the McQuaid archives makes perfectly clear) took his instructions very much to heart. And they, with their allies, held the controlling votes on a panel which (at least on paper) had a non-sectarian remit to govern the legal availability of printed information and literature for the Irish State – and from which the involvement of such dedicated, agenda-driven groups as they represented had been specifically and deliberately excluded by the Dáil in the framing of the original 1929 legislation, a stipulation untouched in the revised Act of 1945.

It took us an incredible amount of work and time to piece together even this much of the real situation on the Censorship Board at the time we were most interested in. Often as we researched this material Swift seemed to wonder what exactly we were now pursuing, so far had we come from the supposed object of our research. At the same time she was fascinated by this story itself and it was a fascination I met with again and again when I mentioned various aspects of our discoveries to friends who had lived through those times. 'In those days you took it for granted that various fixes were in,' as one man said to me. 'It was just a fact of life. But I never thought I'd live to see it spelled out like this.' Still it seemed a long way from *The Rose Tattoo*; but as each fresh fact emerged from our combing of books and documents, both Swift and I felt certain that all of this was leading *somewhere* … that it was leading, in fact – although we'd no real idea how – towards Herbert Lane, in May 1957.

The presence of three Knights, at least two of whom were informants of McQuaid's, on a Board (chaired by another informant) charged with regulating a subject on which the Archbishop had already told their Order to take firm Catholic action might of course be entirely a coincidence. The further fact that all three were appointed by Boland, a Minister for Justice who belonged to the same Order, might be equally coincidental. The fact that two of the three were appointed to the Board at the first available opportunity after the Order (with the Archbishop's approval and encouragement) made the 'wholesale clean-up of evil literature' its principal task[15] may also be a matter of happenstance. Even the fact that the brakes really came off the Board's banning activities in the same year (1950) that the Order undertook this task may be accidental, as may be the facts that the Board's hyperactivity continued in the face of all calls for sanity, provoking the most concentrated opposition it had ever faced and, eventually, forcing governmental action from not one but two successive (and mutually loathing) Irish governments. But if all of these things were coincidences, still there can be no denying that it was an extremely *odd* series of coincidences.

In 1953, having achieved complete if covert control of the State's censorship mechanisms, the Knights of Columbanus instituted an extraordinary nationwide campaign among their branches to hunt down 'questionable' publications. One of the main elements of this campaign was to funnel all such material, when found, to none other than the Irish Censorship Board. The meticulous detail in which the campaign was planned is shown by an extract from a report from the Order's Publications Committee. The extract accompanied a note sent by the Knights' Supreme Secretary in September 1953 to the provincial Grand Knights (who included, of course, Censorship Board member Dermot J O'Flynn) conveying the wish of the Supreme Knight (Censorship Board member Christopher J. O'Reilly) that they put the recommended measures into immediate operation. Knightly Councils throughout the length and breadth of Ireland were instructed, as a high priority, to establish a 'carefully chosen and permanent Sub-Committee' whose duties were carefully laid out: the members must

a) Act as readers of books and periodicals

b) Invite suitable persons inside or outside the Order to report on objectionable books ...

c) Submit books and/or periodicals direct to the Censorship Board ...[16]

d) Keep an up-to-date List of Prohibited Publications ...[17]

e) Maintain records of work done

f) Keep watchful eye on the material displayed at local newspapers and booksellers[18]

g) Obtain representation on Library Committees ... and press for the establishment of such Committees where they do not exist ...[19]

h) Avail of local and daily Press correspondence in support of the campaign ...

i) Organise Lectures, Debates, etc., with a view to raising the standard of literary taste ...[20]

j) Endeavour to *influence* newsagents and booksellers to exercise care in selecting the books and periodicals they supply[21]

k) Arrange where possible for questions in Dáil Éireann by local TDs re number of prosecutions under the Censorship Act ...

l) Furnish regular reports on the work to their Council and through the Council Secretary to the Provincial Council of their area ...[22]

It should be noted that these quite extraordinary mechanisms of surveillance and control were not a part of the later Campaign Against Evil Literature but were being put in place at a time when Irish Censorship, already long regarded as both notorious and ridiculous both at home and abroad for its severity and rank philistinism, was felt by many to have finally gone stark raving mad. The numbers illustrate this: between 1930 and 1945 the Censorship Board had banned a total of 1,841 books, an average of very slightly more than 115 per year.[23] Following the supposed 'reform' of the system, the yearly figure had begun to creep upwards – still only 116 bans in 1946, but 164 in the following year, 181 in 1948, slipping to 166 in 1949 but making up for it with a brave leap to 410 in 1950. Thereafter the numbers simply went crazy – 539 in 1951, 640 in 1952, 766 in the very year of the report, 1953 and, in 1954 – their vintage year – 1,034.[24]

To put it another way the Board, between 1950 and 1954, banned almost twice the entire number of books banned by the first incarnation of the Censorship Board between 1930 and 1945, with almost one third of this total being banned in the single year of 1954. Having in effect privatised Irish Censorship, it seems that the Knights of Columbanus were now setting out to industrialise it. In 1955 the Censorship Board, perhaps a little winded by its exertions, banned less than 500 books.[25] But the damage had been done: in its five years of existence the present Board had, based on the pre-1945 average, banned almost 30 years' worth of books. Such excess would have been noted at the worst of times; in the changing Ireland of the 1950s it met with opposition which was not simply loud but also organised. It also roused increasing newspaper comment both at home and – always a sensitive matter for Irish governments – abroad, where (even more maddeningly for Irish authority) it was generally treated as a matter for laughter and an indication of how primitive the Irish Republic was. In the face of the evidence, it was very difficult for even an Irish Government to deny that something very unusual was indeed going on (although officially of course an Irish Government would do precisely that). In the end it would be the intransigence of the Board itself which would be its undoing. In the meantime it had committed a grave sin against the prime directive of all Irish Governments: the whole matter of the Censorship Board, which Fianna Fáil thought it had kicked into touch by the institution of the Appeals Board, once again threatened to become a live and embarrassing political issue.

23. A Low Ebb

The undoing of the Knights of Columbanus's hidden control of the Irish Censorship system would come about through an unprecedented – and possibly unrepeatable – combination of circumstances and would happen in an Ireland where, in spite of appearances to the contrary, much had changed since 1945. Although those who uttered articulate dissent with the status quo were still few and were subjected to a very great deal of vituperation by their opponents, it is impossible to research the period without noting the seemingly unstoppable growth, on every level of society, of a tidal swell of dissatisfaction with the country as it stood. The weak link in the Church–State relationship was the State itself, or rather the political parties that composed its various governments. Their vulnerable point was the simple fact that, as those who put themselves forward as candidates for the job of running the country, they were liable to be held responsible by the electorate for its failings. If it was the Church's perceived power over the electorate which ultimately gave it a stranglehold on successive Irish governments, it was growing public dissatisfaction which would force the same governments to increasingly take steps that risked bringing the State into conflict with the Church.

The Irish Hierarchy's solution to the increasingly critical condition of Ireland in the 1950s was (almost predictably) to ban, censor and control even more. This was the period when the postwar crusade against the changing world truly got underway, with a special emphasis on the Arts, which threatened to import all sort of nonsensical ideas about how people might or might not think and behave. It was the golden era of the Catholic lay vigilante: 1951 was the year when it was felt to be too dangerous for Sartre's name to appear on posters for *Huis clos* in Dublin and of the demonstrations of Maria Duce's Catholic Cinema and Theatre Patron's Association against Orson Welles at the Gate. The Knights of Columbanus, with McQuaid's approval, set up their own Theatre Censorship Committee to join their surveillance of the cinema and of course printed matter.[1]

In 1952 came the outrageous campaign against the writer Hubert Butler following the so-called 'Papal Nuncio affair', when Butler unwittingly offended that dignitary at a meeting of the International Affairs Association.[2] In 1954 came the publication of Paul Blanshard's hard-hitting *The Irish and Catholic Power*, the first really detailed exposé of modern Ireland in practice rather than theory. In Ireland its publication was of course greeted with fury, though even the Censorship Board could find no excuse to ban it.[3] June of that year also saw the burying of another case involving cruelty in the Industrial Schools, this time in Artane.[4] 1955 saw the founding of the League of Decency, whose letters of complaint about 'obscene' publications and theatrical productions would quickly become a nuisance to the police and the Department of Justice alike.[5] The same year also saw mini-riots outside the Gaiety over the production of Seán O'Casey's *The Bishop's Bonfire*. In 1956 the Irish practice of basically *selling* 'illegitimate' babies for adoption by foreign (mainly American) Catholics was finally exposed by British newspapers. Throughout the period, until their destruction by McQuaid, Maria Duce commonly held well-attended street meetings at which semi-fascistic sentiments were freely expressed and loudly applauded.

But it was not simply the Right which mobilised in these years and indeed the intensity of the Church-instigated campaigns against modernity were in themselves partly a response to an unprecedented rise in opposition. In October 1955, the large public turnout for an Ireland v. Yugoslavia soccer game, in the teeth of a ferocious boycott campaign led by McQuaid and the Knights of Columbanus, included many whose interest in soccer was at best minimal. Their attendance was always acknowledged as being largely a direct response to the Church-led campaign. Furthermore, for the Church and its allies the large crowds at the match simply confirmed what they had already realised: that opposition to their domination of Irish society was not simply growing, but growing more daring.[6] Such public flouting of the Archbishop's will would have been unthinkable even a few years before. The mere fact that over 20,000 people had ignored the call to boycott the match was politically meaningless however. In dealing with a State that could be every bit as authoritarian as the Church, only sustained and organised action could hope to be effective. It was to provide precisely such action, and to keep an eye on Church, State and the unhealthy links between them, that the Irish Civil Liberty Association had been founded in Dublin in 1948.

Though its mere title was enough to put it high on Dr McQuaid's blacklist, the Civil Liberty Association was never a populist movement – mere membership was regarded as a black mark by the Church, though from the first the Association's primary focus was on State rather than Church abuses. The Civil Liberty Association's first public meeting was held in the Royal Hibernian Hotel in 1947, with an attendance numbering a mere 65.[7] The attitude of at least part of the gathering may be gauged from two rejected motions from the floor – that the Hierarchy should have five seats on the Committee and that the Association should immediately declare itself anti-communist.[8] Listing among its members such rare articulate defenders of civil rights in the era as Owen Sheehy Skeffington, Christopher ('Christo') Gore-Grimes, Seán Ó Faoláin and even disillusioned former Dev hagiographer Dorothy Macardle,[9] the Association would in time become a thorn in the side of the Catholic Right. Non-stop schemers themselves, those on the Right saw conspiracies everywhere and would eventually decide that an Association plot was behind the 1956 events on the Censorship Board. In its early days, however, the Association seemed as powerless as it was badly needed and, while its original aim was to concentrate on State abuses of civil rights, its attentions must perforce have taken in Catholic extremism in a country where the interrelatedness of Church and State was continually engendering the sort of abuse which seems inevitably to result from too close a mix of the religious and the secular. In 1949 came the barefaced *coup* by members of the Knights of Columbanus which brought the avowedly non-denominational Meath Hospital under Catholic control, whereupon senior Protestant doctors suddenly found their services dispensed with – a move so shameless that it mobilised cross-Party political support for the hospital and caused Archbishop McQuaid, with his abhorrence of publicity, to quell the Knights responsible in no uncertain manner.[10] The Order also distanced itself from the members involved and denied that the *coup* had been officially approved – though its credibility in such matters is regrettably low.

In 1950 Noel Browne's unprecedented act of whistleblowing during the Mother and Child débâcle revealed the naked facts of power politics in Ireland. In the same year, on a dark day for the Irish conscience, came the Supreme Court decision in the Tilson case, in which the Irish Supreme Court for the first time gave legal backing to the Catholic *Ne Temere* decree, the rule (applying only to Britain and Ireland) by which the non-Catholic spouse in a mixed-faith marriage must guarantee a Catholic upbringing for any resulting children. The following year's campaign against Hubert Butler during the so-called 'Papal Nuncio affair' (in which much was made of the fact that Butler was a non-Catholic) demonstrated yet again that not only could the slightest public demurral with the orthodox Catholic worldview be dangerous in Ireland but that the individual could expect no assistance from the State against any resulting assault. This was again demonstrated, in an even more spectacular fashion, in 1956, when the assault involved was of a far more physical and nakedly sectarian character.

This occasion was the notorious Clonlara case – the incident in which two Jehovah's witnesses made the signal error of preaching their gospel in public in the eponymous village in Co. Clare. The Hierarchy had viewed the growth of the Jehovah's Witness movement in Ireland with alarm since the movement's first public meeting in Dún Laoghaire in 1950 and in 1955 Supreme Knight and Censorship Board member Christopher J. O'Reilly had called on the Order to 'combat' them.[11] It is doubtful, however, that O'Reilly had in mind the kind of combat that took place in Clonlara, where the (pacifist) Witnesses were waylaid and roughed up by a group that included (and some said was led by) the local parish priest. The Witnesses' proselytising literature, including their Bibles, was publicly burned. As with the Meath Hospital takeover, this was going too far even by Irish standards and the assailants duly appeared in court in July.

It was the court case, even more than the assault itself, which aroused controversy. The sitting was attended by the Bishop of Killaloe, Dr Rogers, in whose diocese Clonlara lay.[12] The defence freely admitted both the assault and the burnings, but the presiding District Justice dismissed the charges and put the assailants on probation. The two Jehovah's Witnesses, however, were not so fortunate: they were found guilty of blasphemy and bound to the peace on bonds of £200 each.

Dr. Rogers's interest in the case did, as might be expected, arise from concern for the victims; the odd aspect, to modern eyes, is his view of who exactly the victims *were*. The bishop's views on this issue, unknown to the public at the time, were made clear in a letter he wrote to the then Taoiseach, John A. Costello. In his letter, Dr Rogers berated the leader of the Irish Government because that Government had dared to drag one of his priests into court 'for upholding and defending the fundamental truths of our treasured Catholic Faith ... Are we to have legal protection in future against such vile and pernicious attacks on our faith ... your Attorney General prosecutes one of my priests for doing what I and all good Catholics here, regard as his bounden duty and right. The matter cannot rest.'[13]

For Costello, it was a highly embarrassing situation. Thanks to the intercession of Archbishop McQuaid, however, the Clonlara matter did 'rest'. But Costello's embarrassment is highly revealing. Only half a decade before, he had not hesitated to knife Noel Browne after the Hierarchy's intercession and few seriously doubted that this decision had directly contributed to the fall of Costello's Government shortly afterwards. In matters which he did not think lay in the Hierarchy's proper sphere, however, Costello's reaction to a bishop's diktat could be quite different and common assault was (obviously) one such area. The public face of Catholicism in Ireland might still be monolithic, but in private the Hierarchy was perfectly well aware that much of this was due to fear; in the privacy of the polling booth, as Costello knew to his cost, personal conscience played a much greater role. It was an awareness shared by a growing number of Irish politicians in the 1950s, though few showed any great eagerness to act on the knowledge.

Costello found himself back in office at the time of the Clonlara case after the previous Fianna Fáil government had tried to aid the economy with a suicidal budget introduced by Seán MacEntee in 1952. MacEntee had described the country's financial condition as 'difficult, almost to the point of desperation'[14] and a few months later announced unexpected rises in income tax as well as the prices of bread, tea, petrol, drink, milk, sugar and butter – in other words almost every staple item of spending for the average Irish household. Much to his own surprise, Costello had found himself Taoiseach again shortly afterwards. And it was during the period of this second Inter-Party Government, in the same year as the Clonlara incident, that pressure from the Association of Civil Liberties set in train the bizarre series of events which, though hidden from the public, would explode on Oscar Traynor's desk a year later.

24. Incautiously Rampant

Because of his actions during the furore over the Mother and Child Scheme – and of his own later defence of these actions – the popular image of John A. Costello is that of an appeaser of Church demands. In fact, though he was a genuine Catholic who believed that his clergy knew best in spiritual matters, Costello was not always such a pushover. He had clear ideas about where the spiritual authority of the clergy ended and if he did not always behave accordingly it was for entirely political reasons. His relationship with John Charles McQuaid was, to judge from their letters in the McQuaid papers, cordial and at times even warm. But there are certainly recorded instances where Costello, for one reason or another, withstood demands from McQuaid – the fact that the Yugoslav soccer match went ahead at all was one of them – and others where his actions (at least on the surface) went very much against the Archbishop's clear desires.

One incident of each type occurred in 1956. The smaller but better-known of these measures – and one which so infuriated McQuaid that Costello did try unsuccessfully to undo it – was the appointment of the writer Seán Ó Faoláin as Director of the Arts Council in December.[1] Costello offered the position to Ó Faoláin in the presence of the highly respected Thomas Bodkin, director of the National Library.[2] What possessed Costello to make the appointment in the first place has always been a puzzle: not only was Ó Faoláin a banned writer, but his questioning, continental brand of Catholicism was utter anathema to the Hierarchy and had led to his being branded by the Catholic Right as anticlerical.

217

Furthermore his position on the Committee of the Civil Liberty Association was regarded as final proof of his infamy.[3]

Like some other awkward State moves of the time, it is difficult to be sure that the appointment was anything more than an attempt to throw some sop to liberal and especially foreign opinion. As Ireland in its desperation began to turn outward to the world, it became more important to demonstrate – especially to America, where he was held in extremely high regard – that there was some place in the Establishment's scheme of things even for trouble-makers like Ó Faoláin.

Archbishop McQuaid was incensed at the very idea of Ó Faoláin in the Arts Council job and in an unusual move he pleaded with Costello to renege on the offer. Costello, to be fair, tried to obey: he offered the post instead to Bodkin who, horrified by the attempt to do Ó Faoláin out of a position he'd already accepted, immediately refused – he had, he reminded the Taoiseach, been present when the offer to Ó Faoláin was actually made. During a meeting with Costello and Bodkin, McQuaid himself spent over an hour trying to persuade Bodkin to accept and begged him – as his Archbishop – to 'prevent that man from being appointed'.[4] Bodkin refused. Helpless in the face of Bodkin's honour, Costello found himself stuck with his troublesome appointee and wrote apologetically to McQuaid to admit as much. McQuaid, coldly, responded that 'I can only hope that the nominee will not let you down.'[5] The incident – and especially the behaviour of McQuaid and Costello – makes all the more surprising the behaviour of both men during a far more momentous (but clearly extremely secret) set of events which had begun earlier in the year. This was nothing less than the instigation of a secret State plot against what was, by now, tantamount to an unacknowledged Catholic franchise: the Irish Censorship Board.

It was a widely reported address by the Censorship Board's Chairman, Fr Joseph Deery, which can really be said to have set in motion the sequence of events that would end the Knights' hegemony on the Board. The address, delivered at the end of February 1956 to the Dublin Institute of Catholic Sociology (yet another brainchild of that inveterate organiser, Dr McQuaid) was seen by critics of the censorship system as all but laying bare the Board's sectarian agenda. 'One page in a book', Deery told his audience, 'could be more dangerous than fifty in another if it took the form of an attack on the Catholic faith.'[6] Yet another great round of letters in the *Irish Times* resulted – many of them, as fear then dictated, signed pseudonymously. Lord Kilbracken, in a letter published in March, referred to the Board as 'that foetus of totalitarianism',[7] while on March 7th 'Cara na Leabhar' (a Catholic) provided an answer to 'Dear Brutus', who'd written earlier wondering why opponents of the censorship hadn't reacted more forcefully to Deery's speech. 'Cara na Leabhar' suggested that '[t]hey must be too flabbergasted by the reverend gentleman's truly amazing performance, by his contempt for the rights of Protestants and non-Catholics and for the intelligence of Catholics.'[8]

The beginning of April that year saw the mysterious and celebrated *Observer* incident, when the Easter Sunday issue of that newspaper was (depending on who was telling the story) either impounded or not impounded by the Irish Customs, but was in any case left sitting at the airport by the distributor. This weird event has remained a puzzle ever since. A bewildering number of versions of what happened exist, although the most accurate seems to have been that later given by Seán Ó Faoláin: that a mere rumour of the issue's being banned had frightened the distributor away from even collecting it – what Ó Faoláin would characterise (in his list of seven distinct Irish censorships) as 'censorship by fear'. The full story may be found in some letters from the Censorship Board to the Justice Department, copies of which are in the McQuaid papers (though no copies were found in the State's own archives). These make it clear that Ó Faoláin was correct but also reveal that the rumour was deliberately instigated by Brian MacMahon, Secretary of the Censorship Board. They also suggest that MacMahon was acting on behalf of the Board and was employing a new tactic ('preventitive medicine' MacMahon called it)[9] in a manner completely outside the Board's legal remit.

The letters are from MacMahon himself and are responses to telephone enquiries from Thomas Coyne, the Secretary of the Department of Justice, who was clearly investigating the incident. In the first of them MacMahon describes how at the end of March he had, because of a series on family planning then running in the *Observer*, contacted various distributors and 'informed' them that the paper 'seemed' to be 'heading for trouble.' He was acting, according to himself, in accordance with a decision taken by the Board – a decision it had no right whatsoever to make. MacMahon's attempt at intimidation succeeded. When the distributor, a Mr Kirwan, telephoned to report that he had not taken delivery of the *Observer*, MacMahon disclaimed all interest and responsibility.[10]

MacMahon's response to Coyne's enquiry was delivered in a letter at once disingenuous and smug. It did not satisfy Coyne, who rang demanding further details. Obviously MacMahon was deliberately attempting to frighten the distributors into refusing delivery of the newspaper, a common tactic of the Knights in their own campaigns against 'evil' literature. This, however, was different: this was a Government body.

The *Observer* incident caused great anger in liberal circles and a suspiciously well-informed editorial in the *Irish Times* on April 4th placed responsibility for it squarely on the Board. The Board's reaction to the editorial was to plan to sue for libel and Father Deery – who as a priest could not take part in such an action without his superiors' permission – asked McQuaid to allow him to join his fellow Board members in suing.[11] On April 7th Deery himself called on McQuaid and told his side of the story. Deery did not believe that the *Irish Times* would have been so 'incautiously rampant' if it had not had 'support' in the Department of

Justice. Deery had actually visited the Department, where he felt that Coyne had tried to stop him from seeing the then Minister, Everett. When he eventually gained admittance, Everett had immediately (and sensibly enough, one would have thought) blamed the Board for the controversy. McQuaid (who recorded details of Deery's call in his spidery handwriting) took this to mean that '[e]vidently the Minister had been brainwashed.'[12] Throughout the entire incident it is evident that Coyne's attitude to the Board was already, in April 1956, one of deep suspicion.

It may well be that the *Observer* incident sealed the fate of the Knights' control of the Censorship Board. So long as they kept quiet about their control of the Board, it must be doubted that the State would have been overly concerned about it; but this was going too far. In late April the Civil Liberty Association held a public meeting in the Mansion House that would go down as another milestone in the Irish civil liberties struggle. It was a classic occasion, with many Knights of Columbanus attending incognito in their role as espionage agents and members of Maria Duce busy in the street outside distributing leaflets denouncing the Association as a Communist front. It was during this meeting that Ó Faoláin, the Association's chairman, defined his seven censorships of Ireland and remarked that 'Censorship [was] an obstacle race which books have to go through before they reach you. They might be considered as horses and better put before the N.S.P.C.A. than the Censorship Board.'[13]

The Mansion House meeting was naturally of concern to Archbishop McQuaid, whose papers contain (along with two bulky typescript copies of the meeting's proceedings) the intelligence reports of two Knights detailed to watch it. They are not particularly pleasant documents and reek with contempt for most of the speakers at the meeting, which one describes as a 'picked meeting of all the liberal and Protestant elements'.[14]

One of the purposes of the meeting was to find new signatories for a petition the Civil Liberty Association had been organising since March. This called for a Government investigation into the activities of the Censorship Board. As would later be the case with the Pike fighting fund, the organisers felt obliged to assure prospective signatories that their names would remain confidential.[15] Minister for Finance Gerry Sweetman forwarded an advance copy of the petition (and covering letter) to Costello in April, several weeks before the Mansion House meeting.[16] The petition, short and to the point, read:

> In signing this petition, I do so exclusively for the purpose of encouraging a review of the work performed by the Censorship of Publications Board. I consider that the number of works having general literary merit that are banned is so great as to demand investigation. I am in favour of censorship being applied to pornography, but question the widespread banning of books of literary merit found acceptable in other democratic countries where the Christian Faith is practised.
>
> I, therefore, respectfully request the Taoiseach to initiate an investigation into the record and working of the Censorship, with a view to reconciling the protection of morals with the reading habits and interests of the educated public in Irish society.[17]

The petition itself, with a list of 850 signatories, was sent to Costello in early July, with a warning that the list of names was confidential. An accompanying letter from Edgar M. Deale, Secretary of the Association, also informed the Taoiseach that the Association's Legal Committee had 'drawn up a report containing suggestions for improvements in the working of the Act', which it would forward to him when he'd had 'an opportunity of considering this letter and its enclosures'.[18] The letter was acknowledged on the 10th and on the same day its contents and enclosures were copied to the Department of Justice. It was here that the Civil Liberty Association's suggestions would begin to bear very unlikely fruit and the first steps would be taken in a process whose result would be catastrophe for the secret controllers of the Censorship Board. Like seemingly everything else connected with the Board at the time, this process would involve dealings whose murkiness is only partly explained by the gaps in the available documentation. Much of the missing information can be reconstructed from references in the McQuaid archives; but some of the most intriguing – and insoluble – puzzles involve the behaviour of the Archbishop himself. And on the state of the Archbishop of Dublin's knowledge of – and perhaps even passive involvement in – what was about to happen, the McQuaid papers are as silent as any other source.

25. The Villain of the Piece

Thomas J. Coyne, Secretary of the Department of Justice, is one of the most fascinating figures involved in the events described in this book and much of that fascination derives from the still-enigmatic nature of his role in them. The seven-point memo in the released *Rose Tattoo* file, though unsigned, comes more and more to reek of his work as one comes to know him better from papers which are definitely his; since it is the document which seems to have sparked off the whole State assault on the Pike, this ascription – if correct – would seem to make him at least the proximate author of the Pike's misfortunes. To the Catholic Right, meanwhile, because of his role in the events now being re-lated, Coyne would become a sort of bogeyman, the grey emi-nence behind their rout from the Censorship Board. In their view his malign influence over successive Ministers – particularly Oscar Traynor – would pervert the workings of the Department of Jus-tice with the deliberate intent of advancing the aims of a pro-foundly dangerous, radical and ungodly organisation, namely the Irish Civil Liberty Association.[1]

Absolutely nothing in Coyne's known activities would support the Right's later view of him as a dangerous liberal. Certainly his activities as Government Censor during the Emergency[2] had infu-riated such people as Bertie Smyllie, editor of the *Irish Times*, who resented Coyne's abrasive authoritarian attitude almost as much as his censorship decisions.[3] Smyllie had great personal admiration for Coyne, to whom he attributed 'one of the shrewdest and sub-tlest brains in this beloved country of ours',[4] but the war of wits between Smyllie and the wartime censorship became legend. Among many other things, Coyne became unpopular with liberals for his role in the suppression of Lennox Robinson's play *Roly Poly* at the Gate in 1940 – the only example of straightforward theatre censorship by an Irish government until the backdoor attempt to end the run of *The Rose Tattoo* and, interestingly, an action also officially ascribed to 'moral grounds' – a transparent nonsense which Smyllie in the *Irish Times* described as 'baloney'.[5]

In reality Coyne's actions during the 'Emergency' were no more sinister than a man taking the responsibilities of his important job seriously.[6] Paternalistic he most certainly was, authoritarian he certainly could be; but everything known about Coyne then and later suggests that he was, above all, as conscientious as he was efficient – and the part he played in two Governments' actions against the Knightly control of the Censorship Board suggests that he was very efficient indeed. No wartime censor was going to be popular and Coyne was just as heavy-handed in his treatment of the Right – particularly the anti-Semitic, fascist-leaning Catholic Right which clustered around the doctrines of Father Denis Fahey, later founder of Maria Duce.[7]

As has been noted, Coyne's name is largely absent from the papers in the *Rose Tattoo* file. By contrast, he is all over the assault on Knightly control of the Censorship Board. But the documents that reveal most about Thomas Coyne's attitude to censorship do not come from Government archives at all, but from those of Archbishop John Charles McQuaid. They date from 1960 and consist of a remarkable personal exchange of letters between Coyne and McQuaid. Various people connected with the Censorship Board row had been making negative comments on Coyne to McQuaid for years, but in March of that year Brian MacMahon, long-serving Secretary of the Board, had written a long, malicious letter to McQuaid in which, in terms little short of libellous, he had laid out the Right's full paranoid vision of Coyne as puppet master pulling Oscar Traynor's strings and still taking steps to further curb the Censorship Board's effectiveness.[8] On foot of this letter and possibly in an attempt to form his own definitive opinion of Coyne – with whom he had had some official dealings already – McQuaid initiated a correspondence with him at the Department of Justice. In the course of this Coyne, in three thoughtful letters whose language turned gradually from the official to the personal, laid out his thoughts on censorship – 'a subject to which I have given a great deal of thought'.[9]

It is obvious from the contents of the letters – and was obvious even to McQuaid – that Coyne had indeed done exactly that. The voice which emerges from Coyne's letters is an all too rare one in the Irish Catholicism of the time – that of a sane, thinking, educated layman, convinced that some form of official censorship is necessary but also dangerous: that it is literally a necessary evil. He is convinced too that in the last analysis primary responsibility for the control of what people read must rest with the individuals concerned, guided by their spiritual leaders and, in the case of the young, their parents. It is precisely the rarity of such a voice in an era where almost every major utterance by a public figure was marked by one form or another of casuistry, zealotry, crawthumping, humbug or even all four, which makes it both startling and – when it emerges in other, more official documents – recognisable.

In many ways the Coyne of the McQuaid correspondence, as a thinking lay Catholic[10] with an obviously active personal conscience, is ironically much closer to Seán Ó Faoláin's notions of Catholicism than to the unthinking doctrinaire excess which the Irish Hierarchy then preferred.[11] That Coyne was no rabid liberal was blindingly obvious even to McQuaid: some of Coyne's views would have had Irish liberals foaming at the mouth, just as his imagined libertarian excesses were already having the same effect on many on the Right. In the McQuaid letters Coyne makes no attempt to disguise his contempt for such extremists – the 'person or persons behind the so called League of Decency', for instance, he frankly calls 'obviously unbalanced'.[12] He has concluded that if censorship is necessary (and he believes, with regret and misgiving, that in some form it is) then it can only be successful if it is respected and that it will, in turn, only be respected if it is coherent, balanced and sane – all things which the Irish censorship, particularly as it was being carried out by the Censorship Board in the mid 1950s, self-evidently was not.

The first of Coyne's letters was written from the Department of Justice, the later, more personal ones from his home in Herbert Park. After the final letter he received a rare handwritten reply from the Archbishop – in itself a mark of some respect. McQuaid, who had already decided that Coyne was 'clearly on the side of the Angels',[13] now showed what were, by his own standards, indications of something almost like warmth: 'I agree with all that you have written', he wrote, 'and you have written well.'[14] Such a direct statement of approval from McQuaid to one outside his circle – or even within it – is very rarely found in the available papers and it seems certain that he genuinely respected Coyne's thinking, however much he may have disagreed with much of it. He is not, he assures Coyne, among his detractors: 'I am conscious of your work and I am grateful for what you have achieved.'[15]

Exactly what it was that Coyne had achieved, however, and how detailed McQuaid's knowledge of it was, is still not entirely clear. The Right's portrayal of Coyne as a sort of Svengali of anti-censorship is obviously a gross exaggeration; but this most certainly does not mean that its view of his actual activities was entirely untrue. The Catholic Right of the time habitually demonised anyone who crossed them in any way at all; but again and again, in studying the relevant documents, one is struck in this case by the accuracy of their basic information, much of which can only have come from sources within the Department of Justice itself. In casting Coyne as the mastermind of the plot against them, however, what the Right would omit from their vision was Coyne's own lack of hubris. It is clear that Coyne regarded himself as a public servant; if he acted against them, it was not off his own bat.

Up to a point Coyne's part in what was about to happen is quite clear. The major cause for the fog which then descends is the same cause that hampers research in these stories again and again – the papers in the archives suddenly stop at a most suggestive point. Thereafter we have only a record of the actual events and those events diverge from the direction in which Government intentions (as outlined in the available documents) were clearly going. There was a clearly enunciated official course of government inaction towards the Censorship Board on the official front. But there was also a less clear, though equally definite, course of what seems to have been unofficial government *action* with regard to the Board. And Thomas J. Coyne was up to his eyes in the development of both.

James Everett, the actual Minister for Justice in the second Inter-Party Government, was (theoretically at least) in charge of censorship matters, but in spite of later myth among the Knights of Columbanus there is no evidence of his having played any part at all in what now happened. For it was not to Everett that Costello turned for advice in the matter of the Civil Liberty Association's submissions: it was to Coyne. As we have seen, there are indications[16] that Coyne's suspicions of the Board dated back to at least early 1956, so it may be that Costello was already aware of Coyne's interest in the subject. At any rate on July 9th 1956 Costello, in a departure from normal protocol, arranged personally with Coyne by telephone to forward the Civil Liberty Association's material to the Department of Justice for Coyne's consideration. This was done on the following day. A handwritten note added to the accompanying memo notes the writer's understanding that Coyne would 'like to speak to the Taoiseach or to forward written observations, when he has examined this matter'. [17]

A month later, when the Civil Liberty Association submitted its Legal Committee's list of suggestions for amendments to the censorship legislation, this was similarly passed on. Coyne did not respond to the documents until September 3rd. Though the six page response is couched in conventional officialese ('I am directed by the Minister for Justice to reply as follows ...', etc.) there is no doubt that it is Coyne's own work. The document, at first sight a straightforward dismissal of the Civil Liberty Association's calls for reform, is in fact something far more interesting: it is the genesis of all that would follow.

The report begins by declaring that the Minister for Justice is 'satisfied that there is no foundation for the suggestion that the Board has acted otherwise than in accordance with the law'.[18] Therefore, it says, there is no need for an investigation of the Board such as the Association's petition has called for. As with the reasons which would later be advanced for acting against the Pike, however, the reasons given for inaction in this case are entirely political: the Minister 'could not decently lend himself to such an investigation in the absence of any evidence to warrant it', the members of the Board ('and probably the public as well') would resent it and the Minister – having recently re-appointed the Board-members to their positions – would be 'stultifying himself' by investigating them. Or, to put it another way, the Minister did not want to risk alienating the Board members (and possibly the voters) in a way that might be politically embarrassing to himself, when he did not believe he would be able to prove the Board's members had been maladministering the Act.

That there had in fact been some such maladministration, however, is – in clear contrast to the opening denial – then more or less admitted. 'Whether the Board has been too strict in the exercise of its functions', the report continues, 'is another matter' and in this matter 'it does appear to the Minister, not merely from the high proportion of cases in which the decisions of the Board have been reversed[19] but from what he has heard from persons whose opinions he respects, *that censorship may be being applied unreasonably and in excess to works of literary and artistic merit.*'[20]

However carefully phrased, this is the first known concession by an Irish State representative – and, nominally at least, by the

Minister actually responsible for the Censorship Board – that there is genuine substance in the claims of the Board's critics. This admission would not, of course, be conveyed to the Civil Liberty Association – at least not officially.

What comes next marks nothing less than the beginning of the end for the organised domination of the censorship process by the Catholic Right. Coyne begins by making some statistical remarks on the success rate of appeals (which he puts at 80 per cent) and contrasts it with appeals in civil court proceedings (50 per cent).[21] He contrasts too the 'more exactly regulated' dispensation of justice possible in courts with a censorship system where 'Legislature has left it to a jury of five ordinary citizens to determine the matter in question by common sense and in accordance with their individual judgements' – hardly an accurate description of the current board, who were by no means 'ordinary citizens' and whose 'individual judgements' were frankly guided by the pronouncements of the Archbishop of Dublin.

It is then that Coyne makes the crucial suggestion: '[T]he existence of two vacancies on the Board now offers the possibility of providing against excessive tendencies by the appointment of two broad-minded persons to fill the vacancies.' Why? Because 'no prohibition order can be lawfully made if it is opposed by two members of the Board. In the Minister's view this should be done.' This is clear enough. But in the light of the actual situation and what was to happen, it is tempting to read some significance into the further statement that the Minister 'would like to discuss the matter of personnel with the Taoiseach before making any particular appointments'. One reading of this – and it hardly seems extreme – is that the Minister (or his Departmental Secretary) wants to talk about something that he doesn't wish to put in writing. Certainly there are definite indications elsewhere that there was, in this matter, a parallel (and unrecorded) decision process going on outside the official record.

Whether such a discussion between Everett and Costello ever

took place, or even whether further written communications ensued, cannot be known: at this point the records effectively cease. There are only two further items from the period in the relevant file and in the light of later developments both are tantalisingly eloquent. One is a clipping from the *Irish Times* of November 7th 1956 which, under the heading 'Minority view needed on Censorship Board', reads:

> In a lecture to the Criterion Club in Dublin, Mr Christopher Gore-Grimes, a council member of the Irish Association of Civil Liberties, said that he was hopeful that when the two new appointments were made to the Censorship of Publications Board at least one of them would be a member of the minority religion.
>
> Mr Gore-Grimes said that in recent years there had been a break in the praiseworthy traditions of appointment to the board, which for the past 10 years had been an entirely Roman Catholic board, with a parish priest as its chairman.[22]

The final relevant document in the file is a draft letter to the Civil Liberty Association's Secretary, Edgar M. Deale. The draft was drawn up as early as September 9th, less than a week after Coyne's report. It simply states that the Taoiseach, following consultation with the Minster for Justice, 'is satisfied that there is no foundation' for the Association's claims and 'therefore no case for the suggested investigation'. The rest of the letter dismisses, in no great detail but in the nicest possible way, the Association's proposed amendments to the legislation.

The most interesting thing about this letter is that it was never sent. An appended handwritten note, signed with initials which cannot be deciphered, is dated November 13th. 'File returned to me about 10 days ago,' the note says. 'I have today ascertained from the Taoiseach that he desires that further consideration of the question of sending a reply to the Association should be deferred indefinitely unless we hear again from them on the matter.'[23]

There is no indication that the Government did so hear, nor of why the process, hitherto progressing slowly but regularly, should have simply fizzled out. The potential – noted in Coyne's report – of embarrassment to the Government was an obvious reason for disinterest in taking a legislative route towards reforming the Board. Then again, if the presence of three senior Knights on the Board was known, it can only have seemed that there was a direct, if hidden, McQuaid connection and that would be a can of worms far too potentially explosive to open. In either event the lack of Government interest is, in political terms, perfectly understandable. But the willingness of the Civil Liberty Association to let the matter drop, when they had staged a dedicated campaign on it for most of the year, is inexplicable. Men such as Ó Faoláin and Gore-Grimes were virtually tireless campaigners against the excesses of both Church and State and for months they had devoted a great deal of their energy to the campaign to reform the Censorship Board: they were highly unlikely to just forget about the issue. Yet this is, from all appearances, exactly what they did. There is, of course, one good reason why they might do exactly that and that would be if – precisely as the Right would later claim – they received some satisfaction. And this – although Government papers are silent on the subject – is apparently what happened.

It would appear that the second Inter-Party Government tried to pull a political stroke against the Censorship Board, or rather against the Knights' control of it. It remains unclear as to the extent to which the Civil Liberty Association was involved or even knew about the exercise. Indications are, however, that they knew a great deal more about it than they ever admitted.

In the course of his vituperative 1960 letter to McQuaid, Brian MacMahon, the secretary of the Censorship Board, would recount an event which supposedly happened at around this time, when Christo Gore-Grimes 'in an unusually expansive moment' told MacMahon of a meeting between Coyne and a deputation from the Civil Liberty Association. At this supposed meeting, Coyne had reportedly told the deputation that there was no prospect of having the Dáil change the censorship laws and the 'only hope' lay in getting control of the Board by having two 'suitable' members appointed to it. Through what MacMahon terms an unfortunate mistake by Father (by 1960 Monsignor) Deery, Coyne was – by an extremely odd coincidence – presented with exactly the chance for which he was waiting.[24]

There is no indication of when Christo Gore-Grimes (who must, indeed, have been in a *very* expansive mood) made the mistake of disclosing this information to MacMahon. Certainly there is no record of a meeting such as he described in the available Government files. But neither is there any real reason to doubt that the meeting did take place – Gore-Grimes had no reason to lie and MacMahon was hardly likely to invent stories when writing to McQuaid. The point about 'suitable' members is also precisely the one made by Coyne in his report to Costello. What it *sounds* like is that Coyne met the deputation to explain to them the political impossibility of an official move against the Board and to sell them on his own preferred solution to the problem.

As to *when* such a meeting with the Civil Liberty Association might have occurred, this can only be inferred. If the deputation was concerned with censorship then it seems logical to presume that it met Coyne sometime in late summer or autumn 1956, when the Association was campaigning heavily for censorship reform. But a letter written to McQuaid as early as February 1956 by Fr Deery, Chairman of the Censorship Board, had already mentioned rumours of a meeting between Gore-Grimes and someone at the Justice Department: 'he is said to have interviewed the Minister (or Secretary)'.[25] The same letter speaks of Coyne in no flattering terms and creates the definite impression that he is already, in February – i.e. even before his interest in the *Observer* incident – taking what Deery regards as an unhealthy interest in the Board. This is the only such implication that has been found and since it is sometimes difficult to penetrate the deliberately obscure, conspiratorially euphemistic language employed by many of

McQuaid's correspondents, it only serves to tantalise. At one point Deery even seems to suggest that Coyne has been responsible for some of the letters attacking the Board which had then been appearing in the *Irish Times* (often, tellingly, anonymously) though it is impossible to be certain that this is what he actually means. It may be that Coyne was suspected of leaking to the *Times* the true facts about the *Observer* incident, which the paper then used in the eerily well-informed editorial for which the Board members had contemplated suing. It may even be that he had indeed done precisely that – it is simply impossible, in this Cold War world, to say. MacMahon's letter does, however, indicate that Coyne was already (for whatever reason) a suspect figure in the eyes of the Right, some seven months before he wrote the report suggesting the means by which they would ultimately be dispossessed. What it cannot do is indicate how justified the Right's suspicions were.

There is also the odd matter of the unsent dismissal of the Association's claims, drafted a matter of days after Coyne's report was delivered. Costello first delayed in sending the letter and then, in mid-November, said it should never be sent unless the Association made further representations. Why the initial delay? More importantly, why the later indefinite postponement? One logical hypothesis is that somewhere between early September and mid-November 1956 some private arrangement had been made, perhaps at a meeting with an Association deputation, which Costello thought would satisfy the Association's demands. This may, of course, be nonsense. It is a fact, however, that the Association never did make further overtures and that shortly afterwards it began to declare itself happy with the Censorship Board and indeed would, by the end of 1957, have been transformed into the Board's staunch defender. What is also fact is that in December 1956, in a shock move, Costello would offer O'Faoláin, the civil libertarian, the Arts Council job, an offer which (however Costello later tried to retract it) might be seen as a token of some kind of *rapprochement* between the State and the Civil Liberty Association.

What brought about the transformation in the Association's attitude to the Censorship Board? That at least is no mystery: on December 5th 1956, just three weeks after Costello deferred indefinitely the sending of the negative response to the Association's requests, two new members – Andrew F. Comyn and Robert Figgis – were appointed to the Censorship Board. Precisely in line with the hope expressed by Christo Gore-Grimes in the newspaper cutting of November 7th, Figgis was a Protestant; precisely in line with Coyne's suggestion in September, the new members turned out to be 'broad-minded' – so broad-minded, in fact, that from the first they were opposed by the incumbent Board members. This opposition grew until, on the evening of May 8th 1957, it arrived at the first of several explosions, though the matter was successfully kept from the public eye until later in the year. So began the process which would end in a nationwide campaign of vilification of the Censorship Board and the Minister for Justice, directed now not by the literati or civil libertarians but (of all people) by the Catholic Hierarchy and the Knights of Columbanus. Before that the stalemate on the Board would last, growing ever more edgy, through the summer and autumn of 1957, before reaching its second, greater explosion in December. Until then, the public would know absolutely nothing about any of this: instead they would be following, avidly, quite a different censorship matter – the far more titillating matter of *The Rose Tattoo*.

Everything indicates that what happened on the Irish Censorship Board was, in the grand Irish tradition, a stitch-up and one of which Thomas J. Coyne was essentially the architect. It seems extraordinary that a Government would feel compelled to plot secretly against a bloc which was illicitly dominating a State body and indeed – as the *Observer* incident would suggest – so losing restraint that it was beginning to use that body as a mere extension of itself. But there is compelling – though circumstantial – evidence that some such plot existed and given the dysfunctional nature of Irish society at the time the scenario is all too plausible. What is impossible to say is just how far the plot extended and who was aware of it. Although James Everett, the Minister for Justice, was nominally responsible for the Board, he seems to have played no part at all in the plan. By contrast the Taoiseach, John A. Costello, certainly did – in fact he may be said to have partially instigated it or at least allowed Coyne to get on with the job. And there are possibilities, too, that this particular plot may have had a final twist: paradoxically there are elements of the whole story which really only make complete sense if the Government, in acting as it did, felt that it had the implicit approval of Dr McQuaid himself.

26. Deep Waters

On the face of it this last twist seems simply crazy. And yet there are knots in the story which point to other levels behind the documented (and in this case even the undocumented) one. It has been noted that, despite his image in popular mythology, John A. Costello was perfectly capable of standing up to Dr McQuaid in areas he felt were not the Archbishop's legitimate concern. Now it may be that Costello felt censorship to be such an area, but on the other hand he was anything but a stupid man: whatever his own feelings, he could not doubt for an instant that Dr McQuaid and, indeed, the entire Catholic Church – at least as represented by those who mattered in that institution – believed censorship to be very much their business and would fight tooth and nail against anything they saw as Government attempts to emasculate it.

Thus if only for practical political reasons it seems impossible to take seriously the idea that Costello, of all men, would deliberately cross John Charles McQuaid in such a sensitive area. Apart from anything else, he had for the most part quite a cordial relationship with the Archbishop. Resisting McQuaid's interference was one thing; actually moving to weaken censorship was quite another. Yet Costello did personally ask Coyne to look into the Civil Liberty Association's complaints, a move which resulted in the suggestion – later acted on – that 'broad-minded' members should be inserted on to the Board. What is more Oscar Traynor, writing about these appointments to Eamon de Valera in 1957, specifically claims that they 'were really Mr Costello's appointees' and that Costello had 'recommended Mr Everett to appoint them'.[1] In the light of every shred of information available about John A. Costello, the seemingly unavoidable implication is that Costello did not believe that, in acting against the Board, he was acting against the Archbishop *per se*. Given the popular and essentially accurate image that the Knights were McQuaid's men, this raises several intriguing possibilities, the most obvious being that the preponderance of senior Knights on the Board was not known or alternatively that Costello believed that McQuaid would tolerate such interference.

The presence of a Knightly bloc on the Board had never been admitted and the pursuit of a sectarian agenda was always strongly denied; but the presence of individual Knights on the Board, acting in a supposedly private capacity, would have been unexceptionable during this era: Costello must have known that O'Sullivan and O'Flynn at least were senior members of the Order. The Knights are never mentioned by name in the official documents relating to the matter, but this is hardly surprising – the subject was extremely sensitive and you never knew who might be reading. Even Oscar Traynor, writing about the Evil Literature Campaign a year later, only named the Knights as such in writing directly to de Valera himself – in the many less private documents generated during the Campaign, the Order's name is conspicuous by its absence.

But the notion that McQuaid might have had some prior indication that a move against the Board was in the making and that he stood still for it seems downright bizarre. Yet his behaviour at several key points throughout this whole story shows inconsistencies with what might have been expected from someone with his great interest in the censorship field. These anomalies may nowadays seem no more than slip-ups or straws in the wind. Yet in the complex dance of Church–State relations in that era slip-ups, as such, were extremely rare, especially on McQuaid's part. Similarly what seem to be straws in the wind to us now were quite often, in an era of painfully indirect dialogue between the pillars of Irish society, kites flown quite deliberately by one side or the other and were fully regarded as such by both sides. So before continuing our story of the events of 1956–7, we will cast an eye on some of these straws, or flags, or whatever it was that flew in the wind in 1956; because, deep though the plot-making waters already encountered may seem, there appear to be deeper ones still all around them.

The situation which made the assault on the Censorship Board possible may have been taken advantage of by Coyne, but his opportunity arose through what Brian MacMahon, in his 1960 letter to McQuaid, would refer to as Fr Deery's 'unfortunate' mistake. In March 1956, shortly after the existing members of the Board were re-appointed by Everett, Professor O'Sullivan, a member of the Censorship Board since 1949, died. O'Sullivan was clearly not part of the Knightly cabal: Deery, the Board Chairman, writing to McQuaid in February, was not much bothered about him either way: 'Professors Pigott and O'Reilly and Mr O'Flynn are accepting re-nomination. I have asked Justice O'Sullivan to do so and I think that he will. Anyway, *Mr Coyne would hardly let him go*. His presence or absence matters little to the achievement of the Board's purpose.'[2]

Deery's reference to Coyne here would seem to suggest that O'Sullivan was, if anything, seen as Coyne's man – which in turn would suggest that Coyne had already been taking an interest in the Board even before February. The reason why O'Sullivan's presence or absence mattered little was of course that the unified votes of the other four Board members overruled his opinion. A party with an agenda did not to have every member of the Board on their side: to exert complete control they needed exactly four of the five votes, which is what the Knightly bloc had. This is what Deery clearly has in mind when he dismisses the importance of O'Sullivan – which is odd, because within four months Deery would somehow appear to have forgotten the significance of this fact. O'Sullivan's death took place in the middle of the Civil Liberty Association's campaign against the Board. The failure to appoint an immediate replacement was later portrayed as being a result of Everett's dithering in the face of this campaign, but in the light of the evidence now available it is evident that behind the scenes there was far more going on. And it was – bizarrely – Deery himself who provided the opportunity for someone to really put the cat among the pigeons; and there is something that does not sit quite right about the way in which this happened.

With the vacancy caused by O'Sullivan's death still open, Deery was promoted from parish priest of Mount Merrion to Vicar General of the Archdiocese of Dublin. Now Monsignor Deery, he resigned from the Censorship Board in June – only months after his contentious speech to the Institute of Catholic Sociology had given such ammunition to the Board's critics – citing the increased workload of his new position as the reason. On the face of it this is straightforward, but in fact Deery's resignation raises several questions. The position of Vicar General was obviously in the Archbishop's gift, so Deery was in effect promoted by McQuaid. In addition Deery would not conceivably have resigned from the Board without the Archbishop's permission. And it is simply not credible that McQuaid, with his tortuously machiavellian mind, did not realise how vulnerable Deery's resignation left the Knights' control of the Board itself. With the Civil Liberty Association focusing attention once again on censorship and Deery suspicious of Coyne's interest in the Board as far back as February, the last thing on earth the Knights needed was another Board vacancy. There is no evidence that the Archbishop himself ever commented on the matter at that stage, but in the light of his abiding interest in censorship this is in itself peculiar. As so often in both the stories told in this book, in fact, it is precisely the silence which is most deafening.

There is another very striking event in the strange world of Church–State communications in the 1950s which might provide a clue. This is an address given in University College Cork by Dr

Lucey, Bishop of Cork, a man who had worked closely with McQuaid on such sensitive issues as fixing adoption legislation and on the tortuous negotiations surrounding de Valera's Mother and Infant Scheme – a bishop, in other words, whom McQuaid obviously regarded as reliable. Dr Lucey's address concerned censorship and an *Irish Independent* report of it would later be used as back-up in (of all the unlikely places) Oscar Traynor's explanation to the Cabinet of his own actions against the Censorship Board. This explanation, while delivered by Traynor, was again written by Coyne. For reasons which will become obvious, Coyne's familiarity with Dr Lucey's speech is one of the fascinating things about it.

Lucey's address, which nominally concerned freedom of speech, was given to UCC's Thomas Aquinas Circle in March 1956. The address contains sentiments which are so completely at odds with the views invariably expressed by the Catholic Hierarchy and the lay Right in that era that they are, so far as can be discovered, quite unique.[3] In fact it contains views which sound oddly like those Thomas J. Coyne would express four years later in his correspondence with Archbishop McQuaid. More to the point, the address also expresses an idea which Coyne would suggest less than six months later in his report to the second Inter-Party government:

> Most Rev. Dr Lucey said those who disliked the Catholic Church saw … censorship as in the main religious censorship; those who disliked State authoritarianism saw it as, in the main, political censorship; their would-be intellectuals decried it as in the main literary censorship.
>
> 'In point of fact', said His Lordship, 'it is just censorship of the indecent or obscene – that and no more. Yet how few, particularly abroad, realise this. Indeed, how could they when the propaganda against the censorship emanating from the publicists here keeps darkly hinting at the hidden hand of the Church, at censorship by State appointees behind closed doors, at the literary

classics in danger of being banned.'

Since the then-current censorship was – precisely – being conducted behind closed doors by State appointees with hidden Church connections and since numerous literary classics had indeed been banned, this may seem a bit rich. But it is what Dr Lucey went on to say next that is, in the context of the time, the source and the circumstances, downright astonishing:

> It may be that censorship here is too strict. If so, the remedy is to press for mitigation, not for abolition. It may be that there is no hard and fast rule, as between one generation and another, or one country and another, as to what really tends to deprave and corrupt the average person and that too much is left to the discretion of the Board in coming to a decision …
>
> If the objection to the censorship is that the members of the Board are too narrow-minded, the remedy is to have more broad-minded censors, not to have none at all.[4]

Leaving aside a certain paper tiger irrelevance – absolutely no one in Ireland was publicly calling for the abolition of censorship – this is a genuinely remarkable speech. If anything even vaguely like it was made by any other Irish bishop in the 1950s (or by Lucey himself on any other occasion) then it is a well-hidden fact. These are, basically, the sentiments of the Civil Liberty Association, but coming from the mouth of a bishop who enjoyed the confidence of John Charles McQuaid. McQuaid must have been aware of the speech in advance. Indeed, given the mechanics of Church–State communications in 1950s Ireland, many at the time would most certainly have read Lucey's words as a kite-flying exercise by McQuaid himself.

Although it seems impossible that the nobbling of Professor Pigott's Censorship Board was done with the complicity of McQuaid, there remains the undeniable fact that McQuaid's actions both in promoting Deery and in permitting his resignation from the Board were precisely what made the Knights' position on

the Board vulnerable. Lucey's words here in March, directly reflected in Coyne's suggestions to the Government in September,
provide the only indication that the thinking of Church and State
– and even of the Civil Liberty Association – was, in this instance
at least, not so far apart as other evidence (and other speeches)
would suggest.

If there really was McQuaid complicity in the 1956 events on
the Censorship Board, from what unlikely thinking might it have
come? Certainly one can rule out any idea that the Archbishop
had relented in any way on the censorship issue – by the end of
the following year he would have launched the most sustained ever
Catholic attack against 'evil literature' in Ireland. One thing which
will immediately suggest itself to anyone familiar with Dr
McQuaid, whose priorities remained remarkably consistent
throughout his entire career, is that the Board was becoming too
obvious. With many of McQuaid's actions one can trace motiva-
tion back to one simple, overriding thing – the avoidance of damage to the Church's public image or, as it was then known, 'giving
scandal' to the Church. From inaction on child-abusing priests
and on the horrors of the Industrial Schools system – both of
which he seems certainly to have had at least some knowledge[5] –
to his summary termination of the 1950 takeover of the Meath
Hospital by a rogue group of Knights, his crushing of Maria Duce
and his suspicion of the League of Decency, this single thread of
continuity unites many of the Archbishop's most seemingly dispa-
rate actions and greatly contributed even to the liking for secret
intervention which his opponents so came both to fear and to de-
spise.

Equally dear to the Archbishop himself was circumspection.
Dr McQuaid loved to exercise control and even seems to have
taken some small pleasure in the wildly exaggerated notions of
how powerful his personal influence was; but he hated to be *seen*
exercising control or to have the mechanics of his influence exposed – his manner of having the League of Decency checked out

by having a third party get a fourth party to report on its Secretary was a classic McQuaidism. The Knights who had seized control of the Meath Hospital had engaged in an immediate triumphalist reduction of Protestant staff. That case had very quickly become a public scandal, from which (whatever the truth of the matter) McQuaid and the Order itself had distanced themselves in great haste, humiliating the Knights involved. If there now seemed a genuine danger of the Censorship Board being investigated – which was what the Civil Liberty Association was agitating for at the time Lucey spoke – then there was potential for a simply enormous scandal. If the Knightly *coup* on the Board came to light, liberals would depict it as a re-run of the Meath Hospital débâcle, except that this time, with both the Supreme Knight and the Provincial Grand Knight for Leinster involved, it could not be excused as a venture by any rogue group. Nor would the subversion be of any mere private hospital but of an official State body. The scandal would make headlines around the world and no words would begin to describe the fury of the Government. And there was simply no way in which the whole thing would not rebound, in the fullest possible measure, on the Church itself – and, indeed, on the entire censorship system, which would be completely discredited and, very possibly, abolished. Perhaps there is even an echo of such thinking in Lucey's statement that 'the remedy is to have more broad-minded censors, not to have none at all.'

Looked at from this point of view, it is certainly possible to see how McQuaid might be tempted to at least permit the State to reform the Board: any genuine investigation into its workings posed a far greater risk both to the Church's image and to the institution of censorship itself. Nor can there be any real doubt that McQuaid was as capable of hanging the Knights of Columbanus out to dry as he was of doing the same thing to anyone else: his concerns were not of this world and when it came to the image of the Church no transient human attachment would weigh heavily with him. Like Coyne, he did his job; and protecting the Church's image was something he saw as a definite and indeed essential part of that job.

If McQuaid did agree to stand by while the job was done, however, it would explain some of the deepest mysteries involved in the initial Government assault on the Board – not least Costello's willingness to carry it out at all. It would also explain Deery's sudden loss of interest in being Board Chairman, not to mention McQuaid's own curious lack of interest in the stalled Board during the latter half of 1956. Fascinating though these possibilities are, they must, for lack of evidence, remain a matter for speculation. Back in the real world of events, matters on the Censorship Board took what seems – at least in retrospect – their almost inevitable course.

27. Bust-up

It was now June 1956 and *The Respectable Prostitute* was running at the Pike Theatre. Joseph J. Cooney was expressing his outrage to the Archbishop's Secretary, Christopher Mangan, and (on a more practical level) to the Gardaí. On the Censorship Board, following Deery's resignation, the three Knights were the only remaining members. With Deery's departure they found themselves, thanks to Everett's failure to nominate new members, suddenly powerless: the absence of two members meant that the Board had no quorum for meetings and thus, according to the terms of the Act, could make no decisions at all. Summer and autumn passed without new appointments being made, a fact which the quick-witted *Irish Times* pointed out in both July and August.[1] Calls were made for Everett to act. Michael Adams notes that the delay 'was interpreted as a sign that the Minister ... was grateful for the opportunity to put a curb on the censorship and to choose new censors with the greatest care'. Writing without access to the relevant papers, Adams suggests that '[I]t is equally likely that various persons influenced by the unpopularity of the censorship refused his invitation to act on the Board.'[2]

The new appointments to the Board were finally made in December, the same month in which Ó Faoláin's appointment as Arts Council chief so angered and distracted McQuaid. Of the two newcomers, A.F. Comyn was a Catholic solicitor from Co. Cork; R.R. Figgis, a Protestant graduate of Trinity College, is described by Adams as a 'company director and man of wide literary interests'[3] – the latter in itself enough to make him suspect in the eyes of the existing Board members. The welcome the appointments received from Christo Gore-Grimes, who expressed his pleasure in the pages of the *Irish Times*,[4] would certainly have put the Knights on their guard. Neither of the new appointees had previously expressed any known interest in censorship matters; neither, so far as can be ascertained (and in spite of what the Right would later repeatedly insist) seems to have had a direct connection with the Civil Liberty Association. To all appearances Comyn and Figgis were two intelligent, sane, literate men – precisely the sort of 'broad-minded persons' whom Coyne's September report had envisaged.

Whatever the truth of their affiliations, one thing is certain: if Comyn and Figgis genuinely had been part of some backroom conspiracy and had deliberately set out to get up the collective noses of the Old Guard on the Board, they could neither have gone about their task more wholeheartedly nor succeeded in it so completely. From the very first there was severe friction between the new members and the remnants of the old Board. It centred on the issue which, since its inception, had drawn most liberal criticism to the Censorship Board: Comyn and Figgis simply refused to apply the same standards to literary works as were used on self-evidently pornographic material and whenever it came down to a vote on a book they both voted accordingly. While many accusations and counter-accusations would later be made, this was the central issue in the resulting dispute. It was the prime accusation against Comyn and Figgis which Pigott would make later, when the coming battle finally flared into public view – 'The almost inevitable decision', Pigott told the newspapers in a press statement, 'was three for and two against banning, except in the case of purely pornographic books, which were unanimously banned.'[5]

While Comyn's and Figgis's concentration on literary merit was not unprecedented even on the Board itself, the importance they placed on the matter had previously been confined to – at most – one member, whose opinion could have no effect on the unified votes of the remaining members. But because a four-fifths voting majority was needed in order to impose a ban, Comyn and Figgis now effectively held the whip-hand on the Board. Not only that but they fully realised this fact and – however clear their consciences – proceeded to use their power to the full. It hardly needs saying that this incensed the older members and Board meetings became increasingly fraught occasions. The frustration of the old guard turned to open fury after only two months when the interlopers compounded their effrontery by refusing to automatically ban so-called 'omnibus editions' – books containing several discrete, previously published works by one or more authors. If any work included in an omnibus edition had been banned previously then that omnibus edition had, until now, been itself deemed automatically prohibited. Comyn and Figgis refused to implement such automatic bans. Pigott believed they were disobeying the Act in the matter and obtained advice to this effect from the Attorney General. At the March meeting of the Board, Comyn, on being given the Attorney General's opinion, claimed that it did not constitute 'a definite reply' and asked for clarification.[6] When Pigott requested this through the Department of Justice he received a stinging reply from Peter Berry:

> [W]hile the Attorney General has the duty of advising the Several Ministers on matters of law and legal opinion, it is no part of his duty to advise statutory bodies such as the Censorship of Publications Board ... [7]

Terse though Berry's answer was, it did contain a definite opinion that omnibus editions containing previously banned works were *ipso facto*[8] banned. Yet still neither Comyn nor Figgis would accept this state of affairs and it was this issue which triggered the final explosion. At the Board meeting held on the evening of May 8th, the new members refused to authorise the ban on a pair of omnibus editions. Pigott, his patience at an end, promptly adjourned the meeting, intending to get a definitive view on the matter from the Minister for Justice and settle the issue once and for all. But the Government had changed since the appointment of Comyn and Figgis and the Minister for Justice in the new administration was no longer the Knights' old friend Boland, who had in the past been so accommodating. Instead it was Oscar Traynor, a man with whom the Order had had a very different relationship.

The extent of Traynor's actual knowledge of the situation on the Board at this point is not documented, but he had Coyne to tell him all. Through Coyne or otherwise, Traynor was also aware that several of the old Board members were senior Knights of Columbanus. A life-long, unapologetic soccer supporter in an Ireland where this fact in itself would have been enough to kill the political career of anyone with less cast-iron Nationalist credentials, Traynor had been one of the few political figures not to run for cover in the face of the Knights' concerted attack on the October 1955 soccer international between Ireland and Yugoslavia. On the contrary, Traynor had backed the FAI right down the line, visiting the Department of Justice – he was then in Opposition – on its behalf [9] and even throwing in the ball at the game when the President, Seán T. O'Kelly, suddenly remembered a prior engagement.

In the wake of the Yugoslav match Traynor had become something of a hate-figure to the Knights, though Coyne would soon come to occupy that role. For his part, Traynor clearly felt for the Order itself what one is forced to call loathing – which, as it happens, seems to have been quite a traditional Fianna Fáil view. The Order's own official history preserves a tradition that, in preparation for first assuming power in 1932, de Valera had conducted a secret witch-hunt of his Party, offering Knights State appointments and other inducements to get them to resign and (at least in the Knights' version) punishing those who refused. By the 1950s the Knights, thanks to McQuaid's patronage and their general closeness to the clergy but also to the class-bound exclusiveness of their membership rules, were far too powerful to be treated in such a fashion. At least token membership of the organisation was considered a badge of respectability and social standing among men above a certain social class, including some Fianna Fáil members.[10] An open move of any kind against the Order was about as possible as an open move to separate Church and State. But to old-guard Republicans such as Traynor this *arriviste* group, whose prominence depended so much on class bias, secrecy and Church backing, could never be other than distasteful. Their personal attacks on him at the time of the Yugoslav match had clearly rankled and their meddling in what he considered matters of State offended him. All of this would feed into his forthcoming treatment of the Board and of the later Campaign Against Evil Literature and, though a gloss of innocence lies over most of his official accounts of these events, it seems clear from some of the less public papers that he derived a certain personal as well as political pleasure from this opportunity to both defend the rights of the State and, at the same time, hit the Knights of Columbanus in a place where it so very obviously hurt.

Officially Pigott, having made several unsuccessful attempts to secure a meeting with the Minister throughout the rest of May, finally met him in June – although a document found in the McQuaid papers suggests that there may have been an earlier meeting, in mid-May. At their first meeting – whenever it was – Pigott demanded that Traynor dismiss the new Board members. Receiving no satisfaction from the Minister, Pigott instructed Brian MacMahon to call no more Board meetings until he had received an answer from Traynor. Pigott had by now reached the conclusion he would later assert in his press statement – that Comyn and Figgis were actual agents of the Civil Liberty Association. All during the summer he persisted in his refusal to call meetings of the Board. After this impossible situation had continued until the end of August – meaning there had now been three more months during which, once again, the official censorship mecha-nisms of the Republic ceased to operate – Traynor again (on September 5th) met Pigott, who still refused all compromise: the Minister must choose between himself and the new members and must ask one or the other to resign. The Knights regarded the ball as being theirs; if the game wasn't to be played by their rules, then no one was allowed to play at all. Four days after Pigott's second meeting with Traynor, the Minister wrote to the Professor, very regretfully, asking for his resignation:

> I was sorry to find at our interview of September 5th that your mind had not changed and that you were not prepared to convene a meeting of the Censorship of Publications Board while it remained constituted as at present. That being so, I feel that I have no option but to ask for your resignation.
>
> I am taking this step with the greatest reluctance, but I feel that there is no other course open to me to set in motion again the machinery of censorship established by the Censorship of Publications Acts.[11]

Giving in with remarkable ease, Pigott resigned on September 14th. On the same date O'Reilly and O'Flynn resigned in sympathy. By early October Traynor had three new members appointed to the Board, including Emma Bodkin, the first ever female member.

And that was that: or at least that was the public face of the story as it later emerged and as Traynor would portray it even to the Cabinet. But there was another side to the story – the version of events given by the Knights – which put a very different slant on Traynor's dealings with Pigott. It also suggests that the Irish State (as distinct from any particular Government) had very good reasons indeed for keeping the lid on the Censorship Board story and for avoiding at all costs an investigation into the real history of the Board – and that keeping the full facts of the history of Irish censorship out of the public eye would have been worth almost any price.

28. Stand-off

Though the dealings between Pigott and Traynor would be crucial to the whole story of the Censorship Board crisis, they have left no trace at all in the public archives of the State. Such contemporary State documents as are available – and there are a couple, consisting of Censorship Board documents addressed to the Minister – come from the McQuaid papers, where of course they had no proper reason ever to be. There is evidence in the Archbishop's papers to show that the Knights consulted with him at least once during the period and that on that one very important occasion he advised them on tactics. But the surviving documentation at least would suggest that for the most part, while these critical struggles were going on in this field in which he had such an abiding and consuming interest, Dr McQuaid was simply not there.

Broadly speaking there are two versions of Pigott's dealings with Traynor that summer. One version – Traynor's own – is in the brief account given in the report he delivered to the Cabinet at a special meeting more than six months later during the Campaign Against Evil Literature. This account, undoubtedly written by Coyne, is a bland depiction of the Minister – a patient, fair-minded man doing his best to reconcile warring factions on the Censorship Board – being reluctantly driven to action by the obstinacy of a regrettably extremist Board Chairman. The second version, which can be found scattered over a number of documents in the McQuaid papers, paints a picture of a semi-decrepit old politician being manipulated by his Secretary, Thomas Coyne, into reneging on a secret deal honourably entered into with a representative of the Knights.

The two versions cannot be reconciled. Traynor's account is an obvious whitewash, omitting more or less all of the important facts about the real nature of the dispute on the Board. The Knights' account, meanwhile, is tainted by fury and by the incredible rancour expressed towards Coyne, whom they identified as the architect of their downfall on the Board.[1] But from the details of the Traynor/Pigott meetings given in the Knights' accounts it is at least possible to construct a third version of the story, one far more in keeping with Traynor's profession and with his known attitude towards the Old Guard on the Censorship Board. In this version an experienced and cunning politician, dealing with an extremely delicate matter, plays an intelligent but politically naïve Professor, patiently feeding him the rope with which to hang both himself and his companions and then – when everything is ready – persuading the lot of them to step happily off the end of the gallows under the fond illusion that the ropes are made of rubber and the whole performance simply a charade which will allow the Minister to grant them their hearts' desire.

The Knights themselves believed Traynor had been acting all along in good faith and had only been deterred from carrying out his end of the bargain at the last moment by the dastardly Coyne. But nothing in the later State documentation suggests that Traynor ever had the slightest intention of making any fresh deals with the Knights – or of honouring old ones. And even the Knights' own accounts of what was said make it plain that what Pigott *thought* he heard Traynor promise was not, in fact, what the Minister actually *said* at all. The Knights were sure of the justice of their own position and seem to have regarded the Censorship Board as their actual property; politically, however, they displayed a *naïveté* that seems astonishing in men whose own documents reveal them to have been extraordinarily dedicated schemers.

What the Knights simply did not grasp but is clear from the Justice Department's behaviour was that by now they themselves were seen as the problem. However convoluted the previous Gov-

ernment's actions had been, they had represented a genuine attempt to make the Censorship Board at least slightly reasonable.
The Knights had resolutely stonewalled that attempt. Given this it
is difficult to avoid the conclusion that Traynor at an early stage
decided to end the Knightly presence on the Board completely. It
seems even possible that, right from the start, he (or quite possibly
Coyne) planned exactly how to do it and that the shenanigans of
that summer simply represent the working out of this plan. How
it was done and exactly why politicians of both Fianna Fáil and
Fine Gael felt obliged to treat the sulking Knights with such extreme care, is revealed by the Knights' own papers.

Officially Pigott tried and failed to secure a meeting with Oscar
Traynor in May and only succeeded in meeting him on June 15th.
A letter written by Brian MacMahon on Pigott's instructions,
however, and referring to a meeting of 'the 15th ult.' is dated '4
Meitheamh' (i.e. June 4th). This may or may not be a typing error
although after one has spent much time immersed in the documents of the Catholic Right of the 1950s, news that there had
been a secret meeting in May would not really come as a surprise.
At their first meeting – whenever it was – neither man got any
good out of the other. It was in the wake of this meeting that
Pigott instructed the Board Secretary, MacMahon, not to call any
further meetings of the Board. If Traynor and Pigott's June interview did take place (as later stated by both) and if it was their second interview, then it was almost a re-run of the first. The date of
the first meeting is of less importance, in the context of the Censorship Board story at least, than what transpired at it: on this subject Oscar Traynor at least is of no help. Fortunately the Board
members, although nominally serving the State, were in reality
serving a far higher power; thanks to this we have, from the
McQuaid papers, a very good account of what Traynor and Pigott
discussed. And what they discussed, according to these accounts,
would go a long way towards explaining exactly both why the Irish
State felt obliged to treat the Knights on the Board with such sen-

sitivity and why getting rid of them was at the same time so important.

The actual purpose of the letter Pigott had McMahon write to Traynor – apart from pressing him for a decision – was 'to refresh the Minister's memory on the points discussed' at the first meeting. To this end, McMahon attached a copy of a draft document 'prepared earlier [by Pigott, O'Flynn and O'Reilly] as a basis for his discussion with the Minister'.[2] In other words, the attachment may be taken as fairly representing what the Professor, on behalf of himself and his colleagues, said to Traynor at their first meeting. If it did no more than this, the document would be valuable; but in fact it does a great deal more. In its introductory remarks, intended to remind the Minister of a history its authors obviously expect him to know very well, the document raises the Censorship Board crisis to a whole new level of importance: in effect it does nothing less than call into question the fundamentals of democracy as it supposedly operated in the Irish State for much of its history.

Though this document was among the last we found in our search through the McQuaid papers, and though its contents were the most explosive thing we'd found in the course of our research, its actual existence was in part already known to us, from an intriguing reference in Adams's *Censorship: The Irish Experience*. In writing his book, Adams was given access to Professor Pigott's private papers. Among these was a copy of Pigott's 1957 press release, from which Adams was allowed to quote freely. There was another document, however, with which Adams was not allowed such freedom. This contained what Adams described as some 'incomplete typewritten notes'[3] addressed to Traynor which, Adams surmises, were intended for Pigott's use in his first meeting with the Minister. While Adams was allowed to describe this document and even to quote some selected extracts, he notes that he was expressly forbidden to use all of its contents.

Adams's description of this mystery document precisely

matches the set of notes found in the McQuaid papers, as do the brief quotes he was allowed to put in his book. They are undoubtedly two copies of the same thing. And the slightest glance through the full document's contents explains why Adams was not permitted to quote from it freely: the real surprise is that he was allowed to see it at all. The greater part of the document merely recaps the Knights' version of the events of recent months, including their 'evidence' for believing Comyn and Figgis to be agents of the Civil Liberty Association which, along with 'some disgruntled authors and others of the "arty-crafty" circles' had been maintaining a 'campaign of vilification' against the Board. These charges, however, would be repeated elsewhere, including in Pigott's own later press statement. Nonetheless, the document contains two real revelations. The first relates to what exactly it was that the Knights wanted from Traynor. This, it turns out, was not simply the removal of Comyn and Figgis: what they wanted the Minister to do was to remove altogether the anomaly whereby two members voting together could effectively prevent a book from being banned. The Knights wanted the Censorship laws adjusted yet again since their last rewriting of them had not turned out as planned. Even this, however, comes as no real surprise. It is the second revelation made in these notes that is the really important one and it concerns not the future but the past.

It is mentioned quite casually, in the document's opening paragraph, in a recapitulation of censorship history which the authors thoughtfully provide as a reminder to the Minister – a Minister who (to quote Pigott's condescending sentiments as transmitted in McMahon's covering letter) 'only recently assumed control of a Department of which he has had little previous experience'.[4] It should be stressed that there is no suggestion that anything they are saying will be news to the Minister – they are simply refreshing his mind as to the realities of the censorship situation. The paragraph is well worth quoting in its entirety:

Section 6 (6) of the Censorship of Publications Act, 1929 (substantially repeated in Sec. 11 (c) of the 1946 Act) which empowers any two members of the Board, working in unison, to impose their will on the entire Board was considered by the first two Chairmen of the Board to be contrary not only to democratic usage but to the will and intention of the vast majority of the Irish people. On different occasions they discussed the matter with at least two Ministers for Justice when the question of various amendments to the Act were mooted and were always assured that the matter was immaterial as care would be taken to ensure that at no time would there be two people representing the anti-censorship interests on the Board at the same time. This arrangement was maintained for 26 years and has now been broken.[5]

What this actually says – although so casually that one had to read it several times to take in its full significance – is that since 1929 the Irish State had supported a tacit, extra-legal deal with the censorship lobby, which essentially consisted of the Order of the Knights of Columbanus and its clerical allies and masters, guaranteeing that lobby control of the censorship mechanisms of the Irish State. What makes this truly outrageous is that the Order was precisely the kind of special-interest group which had been specifically excluded from participation in the censorship process by a democratic vote in the Dáil – a vote taken after a clause allowing the participation of such groups in the censorship process mysteriously appeared in the wording of the proposed legislation. In fact, since the involvement of the Order in the original push for legislation was known or suspected by many at the time, the exclusion of special-interest groups by the lawmakers may very well have specifically referred to the Knights. What is being said here, in either case, is that since 1929 the Irish State had kept a secret pact the nature of which was not simply questionable but which flew in the face of the clearly demonstrated wishes of its own supposed lawmakers. According to this, the entire Irish political Establishment – no matter who was in power – had basically spent 30 years colluding in an arrangement which rendered its own laws farcical. The post-war Knightly coup is revealed as not a *coup* at all but, following the departure of the last token Protestant from the Board, the completion of a project that had been under way for decades – the copper-fastening not merely of covert control but more or less of State-permitted *ownership* of State censorship by the Catholic Church. This was infinitely worse than the likes of Ó Faoláin and the Civil Liberty Association had ever imagined.

As must be said of so many matters in this book, the dearth of available documents makes it impossible to be definitive about Government thinking at that stage; but it is not difficult to understand, in the light of this claim, exactly why any Irish Government would feel the need to treat a dispute about censorship with the Knights very, very carefully. If the revelation of the Knight's domination of the Board would have been enough to cause a major scandal, it is actually difficult to think of an appropriate term for the effect that *this* news might have had if it became public. Quite apart from the fulminations of liberals or the attentions of the wider world, there would be political implications involved. These were pretty hysterical times, in a country in dire straits. The Government, in the face of what contemporary observers deemed an extremely serious IRA threat to a punch-drunk State already tottering on the brink of ruin, was precisely poised to introduce a series of draconian legal measures, including internment without trial. No notionally democratic State could credibly act in such a manner unless it could portray itself as the final upholder of the Law: that was the bottom line. It is part of the very essence of such actions to insist on the fundamentally criminal nature of the opposition and to contrast it with the State as the very embodiment of Law – exactly as the British had done to many of the men now in Government, including Traynor himself, during the war of independence. If it became public knowledge that the Irish State had been conniving for decades in the flouting of its own laws, what credibility would its campaign against the law-breakers in the IRA have?

Any overt attempt to forcibly remove the Knights from the Board would meet with a predictably ferocious response. On the evidence of the McQuaid papers, the orchestrated public campaign and the secret fix were the two main weapons in the Order's armoury. What Pigott wanted from Traynor was what Magennis before him had sought from Boland – the secret fix. If the attempt to secure it failed, it was reasonably predictable that the Order would ensure that (in however convoluted a form) the row entered the public arena. Whatever Dr McQuaid's opinion may have been on the necessity of reining in the Knights' excessive – and thus scrutiny-attracting – zeal on the Board, he could hardly be expected to approve of their complete removal from it. It would in any case have been politically impossible for him to stand completely aloof while such important allies fought alone in a field with which he was so closely associated. Thus any row might be expected to draw in Dr McQuaid and with him the whole Catholic Hierarchy. It would be a Church–State clash of enormous proportions – the very sort of fight whose mere possibility had always unnerved previous Governments. And in any such conflict, there would be a danger of the Knights repeating in public the 'facts' they had laid before the Minister in private.

But *are* they facts? Is the document's claim plausible or even credible? With the best will in the world, it must be said that it is both. The 1920s were years when the fledgling State, struggling to recover from the Civil War and desperate for stability and respectability, was most open to influence from Catholicism – a fact which there is every indication that the Catholic Hierarchy, to name but one, used quite ruthlessly. Some modern historians have even posited the existence of a basic, deeply secret *rapprochement* between the Irish rebels and the Church actually predating independence, but certainly the twenties were a decade when the new, insecure, *petit bourgeois* (and of course Catholic) regime which wound up inheriting the fruits of Ireland's revolution enacted a whole series of laws favouring the majority religion – indeed, the original moves to introduce a censorship had been viewed with deep suspicion by some (including W.B. Yeats) as a backdoor attempt to introduce precisely one more sectarian Catholic measure. The existence of such a deal would be entirely consistent with the state of Ireland in 1929; the idea that this particular arrangement existed fits perfectly with the actual history of the censorship and with the persistent complaints of its critics. It would also fully explain the difficulties foreseen by the previous Government in doing anything *official* about the Board situation: Costello and Coyne – two of the most powerful men in Ireland – had taken it for granted that even an official *investigation* of the Censorship Board situation was too politically dangerous and had been reduced to cloak and dagger plotting in order to effect change on the Board. The Order's prestige and connections might well have ensured that this was the case anyway, but it seems that the true danger lay not in what the Knights might *do* in response to a threat but – because of what they knew – in what they might *say*.

Even to refer to what is being said as a 'claim' is incorrect: it is a quite casual statement of fact, a reminder of something the writers assume that the Minister will know perfectly well, which occurs in the preamble to the document's real purpose – 'proving' the perfidy of Comyn and Figgis. But the acid test, surely, is Traynor's reaction after he was presented with the document. Whatever the Knights themselves may have thought, it is clear that at some senior level in Government a decision had been made that the Old Guard on the Board must be winkled out of it completely. Their own written claim that the State had been party for decades to an illicit pact would, if untrue, have been a perfect means of discrediting them: the claim, after all, was either true or a complete fantasy – there seems little room for anything else in between. Although Pigott did not realise it, handing this document to Traynor was – if the story of the secret pact was untrue – the equivalent of handing him a loaded gun: all Traynor had to do to make the Knights look completely crazy was to publicise their own words.

Traynor, however, did nothing of the sort. Instead he spent the summer treating the situation on the Board with great care, as though handling something very delicate and very dangerous. From the evidence supplied in the accounts of the Knights themselves, however – evidence whose significance they do not appear to have realised – it seems obvious that Traynor was working towards a very specific end: not simply the removal of the Knights from the Board, but their removal in a manner which would neutralise their ability to do damage. It was an extremely delicate matter, which Traynor (no doubt advised by the able Coyne) handled with truly admirable skill. For however politically naïve the Knights may have been, still it took a silver tongue indeed to dislodge them from a position they considered theirs by right and to remove them from the Board in the one manner that left them quite powerless to resist: namely, with their own connivance.

29. Mr Traynor and Professor Pigott

At their first meeting, whether in May or June, Traynor responded to Pigott's demand that the new members be removed by pointing out the limitations of his own power in the matter. The Minster could appoint people to the Board; but he did not have the power to ask for resignations unless the relevant member or members 'were absent from a number of meetings without a valid excuse, or proved unsatisfactory'.[1] Pigott claimed that the two new members were indeed unsatisfactory, since they 'were making the literary, scientific or artistic merit of a book the final consideration'. But as Traynor pointed out, Comyn and Figgis had declared themselves perfectly willing to attend meetings and otherwise carry out their Board duties: those were the only criteria he could act on.

That is the story as it emerged in public, but we know from the Knights themselves that they in fact wanted far more from Traynor than simply the removal of Comyn and Figgis: they wanted nothing less than the ending of the 'undemocratic' anomaly whereby two united votes could prevent a book from being banned. This would have required fresh legislation and no Justice Minister, given the difficulty which had attended the framing of censorship legislation in the past, would be in a hurry to go down that particular road. What *Traynor* wanted was what every Justice Minister for almost 30 years had probably wanted: he wanted the whole subject of censorship removed from the political arena. And as long as the Knights were involved in the Board, it seemed, this was not going to happen.

Over the summer, while the Minister was engaged elsewhere –

most publicly with his Department's pursuit of the Pike Theatre, most importantly with putting in place measures to destroy the IRA – the Knights fumed and Pigott still refused to call meetings. By doing so, however, the Professor was putting himself – technically at least – on increasingly vulnerable ground. By refusing to call meetings, he himself was irrefutably obstructing the workings of the Act; and by the end of August he had also, for a reason whose legitimacy the Minister seemed disinclined to accept, not only missed but actually prevented several meetings from taking place – which were exactly the criteria on which Traynor *could* act against a Board member.

This fact does not seem to have been entirely lost on Pigott. In early September, with internment for the IRA in place and the *Rose Tattoo* case awaiting its High Court hearing, the Minister found time for a second (or third) interview with the Professor. The meeting was scheduled for September 5th and on September 3rd Pigott called on Dr McQuaid to discuss matters. Whether there were other such visits that summer is unknown, but we know about this one because McQuaid himself preserved a record of it, in the margin of his copy of McMahon's June letter to Traynor. The purpose of the visit was to discuss the situation on the Board (which had, McQuaid records, 'become impossible') and to plan a strategy for Pigott's meeting with the Minister. The Professor seems to have expected Traynor to ask for his resignation: at least the eventuality was discussed. Dr McQuaid's notes, though terse, are clear on his own reaction to the prospect: 'I warned Chairman not to resign, but if needs be, to allow himself to be removed with his two colleagues.'[2]

Pigott next asked the Archbishop to approach the former Taoiseach, John A. Costello, 'who appointed Comyn' and 'ask him to have Comyn resign'.[3] McQuaid (possibly recalling the failure of his own attempts the year before to have Costello keep Seán Ó Faoláin from the Arts Council job) said he 'feared Mr C. would not wish to have such a proposal put to him'. McQuaid's behaviour here and later might be cited as proof that he cannot have known anything about the original plot to dilute the Knights' influence on the Board; in fact it proves nothing of the kind. Though he would fight so long as there was a chance of victory, the Archbishop was far more of a realist than many of his fellow bishops and certainly more so than many of the lay zealots of the period: as the incident with Ó Faoláin had shown, he might not always show good grace when bowing to the inevitable, but he was quicker than many in his camp to recognise it and move on to the next battle.

A dilution of Knightly control of the Censorship Board was one thing; it would be enormously regrettable, but infinitely preferable to a major scandal that reflected badly on the Church. The complete removal of the Knights' influence, however, would be a matter of much graver concern to the Archbishop. The Knights were not only his eyes and ears but they were not infrequently his strong (if clandestine) right arm: their removal from the Censorship Board would be an appalling blow in an area very important to him. And yet his refusal of Pigott's request is striking. The Archbishop was surely correct in presuming that Costello would not welcome a request to intervene; but given the questions surrounding Costello's and perhaps even McQuaid's own part in the original move against the Knights it is tantalising to wonder at McQuaid's actual reasons for thinking that 'Mr C.' would dislike any request to butt in. More revealingly, McQuaid was evidently regarding Traynor's summoning of Pigott as part of a pre-existing Government strategy: he was thinking beyond the immediate situation to one where the public presentation of the facts might become a factor. In that event, the Knights' claims on the moral high ground would be greatly weakened if they simply resigned now. If they forced Traynor to remove them against their will, however, that fact could be turned to their advantage in future propaganda, where they could be portrayed as martyrs. The exchange suggests that McQuaid at least was thinking in terms of a

Government stroke and also of a resulting public campaign.

The second meeting between Traynor and Pigott duly took place on September 5th and again has left no contemporary record in the State archives; fortunately the later accounts of the Knights themselves remedy the deficit. For the most part, as Pigott himself later said, the two men 'travelled over the same ground'.[4] It was obvious by now that there was no hope at all of any compromise and Traynor, with every show of reluctance, eventually said that he would be forced to ask Pigott to resign. It was open to Pigott to refuse and thus to blow the whole issue – which had thus far, thanks at least partly to the huge publicity generated by the *Rose Tattoo* case, remained out of the public eye – wide open. It was precisely the point on which McQuaid had warned Pigott two days before; but Traynor, having regretfully flourished his Ministerial stick, now held out a far more appetising carrot:

> I had already suggested to [the Minister] that, since he could not ask a member to resign, he should dissolve the Board and appoint a new Board. He now asked me what would be the attitude of Professor O'Reilly and Mr O'Flynn in the event of my resignation. I told him that I did not know, but it was possible that they would resign in protest against my forced resignation. 'In that event' said the Minister, 'I would have sufficient justification for dissolving the Board.'[5]

This was the crucial point: it is clear from the Knights' later accounts that Pigott *interpreted* these words as an offer – a way out of the current impasse that would let him restore the Knights to their 'rightful' position on the Board. Comyn and Figgis showed no intention of resigning; but if the three Knights themselves left then Traynor – who had already made a point of telling Pigott the limitations of his own powers in the matter – would find himself with a Board that had fallen apart. He would then be free to appoint a completely new Board – without the troublesome blow-ins and (one must suppose) without the galling veto. But it should be noted that, even in Pigott's own version, Traynor did not commit himself to dissolving and reconstituting the Board if the three Knights resigned: he simply said that he *would have justification* for doing so. There is (as the good Professor would soon discover) a world of difference between the two. Professor Pigott would soon learn the famous problem with verbal agreements: they're not worth the paper they're written on.

Four days after this meeting, Pigott received Traynor's official request for his resignation. A week later – a week for which we have no record at all of the actions or thinking of *anyone* involved in this story – Pigott resigned. The other two Knights, as he had foreseen, resigned – supposedly in protest – within 24 hours. One presumes that they then waited for Traynor to carry out his end of the secret 'deal'. If so, they waited in vain: far from dissolving the truncated Board, Traynor immediately moved to replace the departed Knights and by early October had three superlatively respectable and quite unimpeachable new members on the Censorship Board – as well as Comyn and Figgis.

Whether Traynor really hoodwinked the Professor is, finally, impossible to say; but the circumstantial evidence seems convincing. And, given the reliance that the documents show him to have placed on Coyne during his Ministry and Coyne's tactical ability, it is difficult not to see his hand in the affair. The Knights certainly believed that Traynor had given them a nod and a wink and continued to believe that (at least during the actual meeting) he had done so in good faith. Dermot J. O'Flynn, in a set of notes on the crisis sent to Dr McQuaid in April 1958, seems to imply that even the resignations of O'Reilly and himself had been not so much foreseen as almost pre-arranged: he reports that Traynor '[g]ave [Pigott] to understand that if Messrs O'Reilly and O'Flynn resigned in sympathy – it would give him an opportunity to dissolve the entire Board and set up a new group of 5 – "without prejudice!". Messrs O'Reilly and O'Flynn resigned to give the Minister a free hand.' In O'Flynn's preferred version of what followed, Traynor had subsequently been 'dissuaded' (evidently by Coyne) from reconstituting the Board as he had promised.[6]

This view shows a touching faith in Traynor but is not terribly persuasive. The obvious care with which the new Board candidates were chosen and the speed with which Traynor had them in place (barely three weeks after the Knights' resignations) speak of careful preparation. Nor can there really be any doubt that it would have given Traynor a certain personal satisfaction to put one over on the Knights, while it would equally have satisfied Thomas J. Coyne, that enemy of zealotry (who would, moreover, within six months be writing gleefully to Traynor of leaving the new Board's critics – essentially the Knights themselves – 'lepping mad').[7]

Quite apart from the sinful pleasure its architects might take in codding God's agents, such a stroke would have an eminently practical, entirely political result: it would remove all of the Knights from the Board without a potentially highly dangerous public row, such as they would almost certainly have caused had Traynor attempted to remove them in any other way. Even if such a row erupted now, it would be possible to depict the Knights as having essentially abandoned their duty in a fit of pique because they couldn't get their way – precisely as Traynor/Coyne would later portray them to the Cabinet.[8] Anything they chose to claim could be dismissed as the product of sour grapes. By tricking them into removing themselves, Traynor would effectively leave the three without a leg to stand on in any later public row – precisely as McQuaid had clearly both foreseen and explicitly warned them against.

The new Board was by no means composed of flaming liberals, but on the other hand it was no longer covertly monopolised by a group with a shared secret agenda. It would – in the long run – encounter nothing like the controversy caused by its predecessor. Yet in the short term it would encounter a great deal of controversy indeed, although of a very different kind. When Michael Adams writes of this Board that 'if lack of controversy implies public confidence and support, this Board was … more successful than any previous Board had been' then he is surely – even in terms of what was known in 1968 – being disingenuous. The events of 1957 would indeed meet with a reaction and a very large and hysterical one at that. It would not, however, come from the liberals and it would not address the actual area of dispute. Only Professor Pigott himself would try to air at least some of the real issues involved; and his bitter voice would be lost in the clamour of the much bigger campaign that would begin at the end of the year and which has gone down in history as one of the last great Catholic campaigns of the era – the 1958 Campaign Against Evil Literature.

30. Protest and Protect

Wherever one turns in examining the social mechanics of that time and place, one finds strangeness piled upon strangeness and secrecy piled upon secrecy. This is not simply a case of 'different times, different people': much of the strangeness seemed every bit as peculiar to its contemporaries as it does to us. But very often the oddity was only superficial and came from the fact that what the public saw was merely the tip of an iceberg, the brief, unavoidable emergence into the light of some underground struggle, or fix, or negotiation among the powerful. For all their apparent strangeness, these dealings were ultimately almost invariably about cold-bloodedly practical matters of power. A fuller picture of some of these affairs may be found in Government archives; an even fuller picture may be found in the McQuaid papers. Again and again, particularly while reading material gleaned from the latter, I found myself thinking of the words a friend had said to me at an early stage in the research, when I'd been trying to explain our growing sense that the *Rose Tattoo* case hadn't been about theatre at all but about something else. 'In Ireland back then', he said, '*everything* was about something else.'

'Everything was about something else': the phrase might serve as an epitaph for the era, were not that particular aspect of its legacy still showing such signs of life in some areas at least of modern public life. But both the phrase and its context are highly relevant here because, so far as the general public was aware in 1957, very little that you have read in the previous 100 pages or so had ever happened at all.[1] There had indeed been an enormous furore over

Irish censorship that summer, but it had not been about print censorship – it had, of course, been about theatre censorship, namely about an 'indecent' play running in the Pike Theatre. Not a word of the potential crisis on the Censorship Board had leaked out and if anything the usual sources of censorship agitation had been almost preternaturally quiet.[2] But this had been the case for quite some time – since the Spring of 1956 even the usually predictable stream of Church and Church-related calls for *more* censorship had dried up. As Traynor's *Memorandum for the Government* would happily point out some months later (after that silence had been broken in the most astonishing way) the only major exception to this had been Bishop Lucey's unprecedentedly warm welcome for the idea of actually *relaxing* censorship.

Thus the general public could be forgiven for being amazed when, very early in December 1957, an enormous and very obviously pre-arranged public campaign against 'evil' literature erupted (there is no other word for it) throughout the entire country. To the average person, the campaign must have seemed to come out of the blue. Its central plank was the contention that Ireland was awash with pornography and that this situation was a recent development resulting from failure by the Censorship Board. It hardly needs saying that it was actually about something else entirely.

The many hysterical and farcical elements of the Campaign Against Evil Literature are the ones generally stressed in the few and invariably brief accounts of it given in general histories today; but its significance for anyone who has studied the material from which the previous part of this book was drawn is simply enormous. The Campaign Against Evil Literature was the first occasion on which an Irish Government felt confident enough to face up to a full-frontal, nationwide public campaign by the Catholic Church and its lay allies, using all of the mechanisms of propaganda, political trickery and back-door influence built up over 30 years of dedicated work. That sheer size of the campaign is evident even from the papers preserved in the National Archives; that it was a co-ordinated effort to bully the State, seen as such in the Department of Justice and treated as an inherently political battle, is demonstrated time and again in the same place. It is clear that the Department was the main engine of State defiance and fought the battle with the deftness and skill one had by now come to expect from the combination of Coyne and Traynor. Both seem quite clearly to have viewed the matter as being about one fundamental question: who was to run Ireland, the Church or the State? Though Coyne and Traynor were very different men in many ways, their instinctive answer to this question was identical: Ireland would be run by those democratically elected to run it.

In some ways the Catholic propaganda machine had developed a great deal from the sort of thing that had fuelled the passing of the original censorship legislation in 1929. A far greater number of organised bodies took part, for one thing – if only for the simple reason that John Charles McQuaid in particular had, in the interim, busied himself founding Catholic organisations through his clerical network and through the Knights of Columbanus. Though many of these organisations were primarily founded to prevent Catholics having to mix socially with Protestants (a practice Dr McQuaid regarded as dangerous) they also gave the Archbishop the same advantage that they gave the lay religious groups – that of having at his disposal groups which could act in his interests but for whose actions he could deny responsibility.

The basic mechanism of such a campaign was to create, via a great deal of frenzy and froth, the impression of a huge surge of popular concern about the relevant issue and indeed to whip up such concern through sermons, meetings and publications (whether printed especially for the purpose or planted in existing magazines and newspapers). Trusted lay spokesmen would make speeches and call meetings, the teeming hordes of sodalities and Catholic Associations and guilds and leagues and organisations and so forth would pass resolutions, as would the various rural or provincial committees-for-whatever chaired (almost invariably) by the local parish priest and with local Knights as highly placed members. Organisations whose interest in pornography was minimal suddenly found their committee meetings dominated by the subject and parliamentary questions were planted in the Dáil.

The ultimate intended audience was the politicians – mainly those in power, but also those in opposition for whom such a controversy represented a chance to pillory the Government. The authorities themselves would be inundated with 'spontaneous' communications from the public in support of whatever the Hierarchy wished to support or condemning whatever the Hierarchy wished to condemn. Clergy of all ranks would give sermons, lectures and addresses on the relevant issue, rousing support in a society where people had been encouraged for 30 years to see their clergy rather than their political leaders as the arbiters of right and wrong and where the average person, having received an education in a system dominated by the Church, still left school at 12 years of age.

It was, in many ways, campaigning by numbers; but by 1958 the State knew the numbers very well. By then the notion that such a campaign was spontaneous was patently ludicrous to all but the most self-deceiving observer. The clear purpose was to underline to those in power the electoral clout of the Church. But in 1957–8, while the power of the Church was still certainly enormous, its actual political ability to destroy a Government had never been tested and, to many, was in some doubt. The one Irish Government whose fall from power had involved its relationship with the Church had been Costello's first coalition; and in that case it hadn't been defiance of the Hierarchy's will, but a perceived over-eagerness to placate the bishops, which was seen as having disgusted many voters. The most recent comparable Church campaign, too – the more localised frenzy against the Yugoslav football match – had been anything but an unqualified success. Its excesses had worried many thinking Catholics and the match had not only gone ahead in spite of it but had given over 20,000 people a chance to display their embarrassing disaffection with the Archbishop of Dublin by attending the game. Still a Church-inspired campaign, with its suggestions of Government moral laxity and its capacity to ignite the passions of the latently crazy – not to mention the endless opportunity it offered to any half-awake parliamentary Opposition – was not something to be risked lightly; the Evil Literature campaign would make the attack on the Yugoslav match look like a bun-fight.

If the undoing of Knightly control of the Censorship Board is surrounded by ambiguity or simply absent from the State archives, then the records of the Evil Literature campaign are far more complete. Whether or not this is because the papers serve mainly to discredit the campaign is impossible to say, but certainly they do tend to serve that purpose. The papers show Traynor, deftly advised by Coyne, rebutting the complaints against himself and the new Censorship Board at every turn. Not only that, but Traynor had to steel de Valera himself when the Taoiseach seemed to be wavering under the Campaign's first blast. What the documents also comprehensively do is bury any lingering notions that the Department of Justice under Traynor was frightened by the Hierarchy, at least when it was not politically opportune to be so – such a rationale for its activity in the *Rose Tattoo* case (by now more than half a year old) is shown up as nonsensical. Open contempt in the documents is reserved for examples of lay Catholic zealotry, but the attitude shown towards the Hierarchy itself is reminiscent of nothing so much as the sort of mixed feelings normally reserved for a mad old maiden aunt given to throwing tantrums, but who must still be occasionally humoured because she might otherwise burn down the house.

Coyne, writing in Traynor's name two months later, would describe this first period of the Campaign and relate it directly to events on the Censorship Board:

> Subsequent to the re-constitution of the [Censorship] Board ...

there was an interval of some two months when little or nothing was heard of the changes in the personnel of the Board or the question of censorship generally, but on the 4th of December it was reported in the Press that, speaking at a Conference in Dublin, the Archbishop [of Dublin] had referred to 'the unquestionable evidence proving that very many foul books have been made available for open sale in the city of Dublin' and that the Conference had passed a resolution on the subject. This was followed next day by a report in the Press of a lengthy statement by Professor Pigott giving his version of the circumstances in which he had resigned from the Censorship Board ... No sooner had the Archbishop and Professor Pigott spoken than there was a spate of publicity about the supposed shortcomings of the censorship and rhetorical references to the 'tide of filth' that was said to be 'inundating' the country.[3]

'Spate' doesn't quite cover the actuality: 'tidal wave' might better describe it. If the 'flood of evil literature' was largely fictitious, the flood of complaints, calls for action and planted newspaper stories was certainly not. As soon as McQuaid's call for action hit the newspapers, in fact, the hounds of reaction were out of the traps with their tongues hanging out. The *Irish Independent* on December 7th carried a report of the protest letters sent to Traynor by the Catholic Youth Council of the Catholic Social Service Conference. 'We protest strongly', wrote Mr G. McGurk (who signed the protest on behalf of the Council's GAA football leagues) 'against the dangerous immoral literature at present being allowed into our country.' The necessity for Christian censorship was borne out strongly, he said, 'by the recent unfortunate breaking down of barriers which had let through a flood foreign to our national and religious ideals'. A Mr D. O'Donohoe, who had signed on behalf of the Council's soccer leagues, demanded that the Minister take 'immediate and effective action with all the powers available to you to give protection to our youth from the flood of filthy foreign literature pouring into our city. It is our duty to protest. It is your duty to protect.'

Professor Pigott's press statement of December 5th, which received wide coverage, gave a highly partial account of events on the Board earlier that year and contained the central assertion that Comyn and Figgis were agents of the Civil Liberty Association. Like all other individual accounts of what had happened on the Board, Pigott's mixes fact with useful silences, skating around the Board situation prior to 1956. But Pigott and his supporters were not to have the field entirely to themselves. Seán Ó Faoláin, in his capacity as President of the Civil Liberty Association, was first to respond to Pigott. The same issue of the *Irish Independent* that reported the Catholic Youth Council's call also carried Ó Faoláin's response to the Professor's statement.[4] Like Pigott, Ó Faoláin ignored some parts of the story, but for the most part he stuck with indisputable facts. He also made an assertion that, though much more politely phrased, would feature prominently in Traynor and Coyne's account of events on the Board: 'The fact seems to be, on the Professor's own showing, that he resigned in a huff because he failed to bully the Minister for Justice into allowing him to interpret the Act in his own way.'[5]

Many of the protests from 'Catholic organisations of every sort and description' that would feature in Traynor's February report are preserved in the archives. The developing trend of these is more revealing than any of the individual examples. At first the protests are general: the Chaplain of St Joseph's Catholic Boys' Brigade, for instance, wrote to the Taoiseach on December 20th, forwarding a motion passed by the Brigade Council on the 15th, protesting 'most emphatically against the flood of evil literature to be had so easily by boys and girls in city shops and at street corners', and demanding 'effective action'.[6] This is typical of the first stage in the campaign. By late January, the Holy Family Branch of the Catholic Young Men's Society had a much more specific agenda, building on the earlier calls: having passed the by-now standard resolution calling for immediate action 'to stem the unprecedented flood of filthy written matter', the Holy Family

Branch explained to the Minister exactly how this might be achieved:

> That immediate proposals for legislation be drafted for the recasting of our completely inadequate Censorship of Publications Act, under which new legislation a permanent full time Censorship Department will be set up, which will be directed by a Board fully representative of the community where majority decisions will operate.
>
> FURTHER RESOLVED:
>
> That we are of confirmed opinion that a Censorship Board, where a minority can exercise the power of veto, is farcical in the extreme, is a negation of democracy and flouts the spirit of the Constitution, the Preamble of which invokes the name of God.
>
> We therefore call upon the Taoiseach and all Public Representatives to see that, pending the introduction of proposals for legislation, Emergency Powers are taken to deal summarily with the importers and vendors of the filth.[7]

This extraordinary call was anything but unique. In fact the schedule of the carefully orchestrated campaign is reasonably transparent. First the nation would be portrayed as knee-deep in filth, with a weakened Censorship Board unable to cope; then a serious assault on the Board itself – as currently constituted – would begin in earnest. The Government would again be softened up with a storm of protest made in general terms and then the campaign's specific aims would gradually be introduced. Following this the Hierarchy itself would move in directly – as it duly did, only four days after the C.Y.M.S. resolution was passed, with a list of its own considered recommendations on how to remedy the evil literature 'crisis'.

Government concern about a backlash naturally pre-dated the Hierarchy's eventual move. There can be no doubt that antennae had been up from the time the new Government first learned that there was trouble on the Board. But the blizzard of propaganda and protest did clog up the machinery at the Department of Justice. The Department's resentment, frustration and scorn at the 'flood of protests' which reached it would be evident in the consciously bathetic catalogue included in Traynor's *Memorandum for the Government*:

> First of all there were protests from Catholic organisations of every sort and description such as the C.Y.M.S., the Catholic Boys' Brigade, Secondary Schools' Past Pupils Unions, various Football Clubs and Associations affiliated to the Catholic Social Service Conference and even from an odd Conference of the Society of St. Vincent de Paul and from the Legion of Mary in Wicklow. A number of these were date-lined the 4th December, 1957,[8] and were in common form ... A protest from the Belvedere Newsboys Club ... expressed concern at 'the present apparent inactivity of the Censorship Board' and voiced the opinion that 'the Board as recently constituted was not properly fulfilling its function.' On the 7th December, there appeared in the Press a letter from the Parish Priest of Ballyfermot on much the same lines ... in which there was a reference to 'the sham of the present system in which two members can out-vote three' and there was a postscript to the effect that the statement ... would be read at Masses in Ballyfermot on the following day ... Finally, to round off the story, various local bodies[9] have joined in the chorus with cries of outraged morality.[10]

It went on and on throughout December and January. Provincial papers featured articles on the mortal danger being presented on every street corner to the youth of small Irish towns; Urban Council meetings neglected their normal business to debate the flood of pornography flooding into the country. Many of the written protests were directed to the Taoiseach's office and at first de Valera was obviously rattled. He raised the matter at a Cabinet meeting on December 31st and 'tentatively' asked whether

(1) a public statement should be issued on the matter and

(2) the Garda Síochána should be instructed to visit places in

which such literature is being sold or offered for sale and, where appropriate, to prosecute the offenders.[11]

Dev was cagey though: he 'did not press for a decision on either of these suggestions' and was afterwards told by Traynor that using the police was impracticable. Traynor reminded the Taoiseach, almost tartly, that there were perfectly adequate channels in place through which members of the public could complain about any material they found dubious.[12] He made the same point when responding to a resolution from the County Dublin Libraries Committee: the Gardaí, he said, were always willing to prosecute, but 'little or no evidence had come from the general public, from whom there had been few specific complaints.'[13] This stress on the fact that the censorship machinery was now at all times fully operational (for the first time in some 18 months), but was receiving few actual complaints, was to be a feature of Traynor's own counter-offensive.

The letter from the Standing Committee of the Hierarchy – the point towards which the entire agitation had been leading – was sent January 30th and resulted (at least theoretically) from the Committee's deliberations at a meeting held on January 14th. This meeting had considered the 'great increase of evil publications' available in Ireland (as evidenced by the propaganda campaign which its own allies had begun) and had (like the Holy Family Branch of the C.Y.M.S.) reached certain conclusions (oddly enough, in fact, the very same ones). The letter, which was signed on behalf of the Committee by its Secretaries, the Bishops of Raphoe and Achonry, conveyed these conclusions to de Valera.

The Standing Committee had thought long and hard about the parts played by the police and the Censorship Board in the censorship process. The 'existing regulations', the Committee deemed, provided the police with 'ample powers to deal with the importation and sale of the commercialised crime and sex fiction'. But these were only effective '[i]f ... applied with vigour', which their lordships obviously felt was not being done: they 'earnestly request[ed] that the necessary steps be taken to ensure this vigorous application'.

It was the status of the Censorship Board, however, for which the bishops – unsurprisingly, perhaps – reserved their true ire. They expressed understanding of the unfortunate Government's position:

> [T]he bishops recognise that your Government has inherited a difficult situation. This situation has arisen because this Board has been submitted to procedures and regulations which are not applied to other Government Boards.
>
> To none of these Boards are people appointed who are openly and avowedly determined to obstruct and frustrate the attainment of the public aim for which the Boards were founded. The Government does not, for instance, appoint to the Turf or Electricity Boards persons who seek to limit, restrict and confine the operations of these Boards ... Secondly, in none of these Boards is a minority of members given a right of veto over the decisions of the majority ... Thirdly, in none of these Boards is there an Appeal Board to review its decisions.

Their Lordships, while holding that the current Board was failing in its duty, naturally did not blame the Board members themselves, but felt that

> it is quite unrealistic to expect a Board of five voluntary and parttime members to cope with the vastly increased number of books which require to be submitted to the Board ... If, as [we] assume, the Government is in earnest in desiring that the object of the Censorship Board be attained ... the Bishops beg to submit that certain slight administrative changes would notably conduce to that end – firstly, that membership of the Board be substantially increased to, at the least, the number of 20; secondly, that each book be submitted to a group of three members and the decision be by a majority in each case; thirdly, that no members of the Board have the right of veto and that revision of the decision of the Board be reserved to the Appeal Board.[14]

Leaving aside the notion that a fourfold increase in the size of the Board could be called a 'slight administrative change', the letter is a remarkable document. Basically it is a call to completely redraw the rules of the game, made by the side which had essentially drawn up those rules themselves, because they turn out to have drafted them less cleverly than they thought: the other team has (as the bishops see it) had the temerity to actually score. Taken with the calls for Emergency police powers and the existing use of Customs officials to pursue suspect material, it is a perfectly serious call for the introduction of a censorship regime the likes of which had never been seen outside a totalitarian regime. What world opinion would have made of such a daft exercise in the late 1950s, quite apart from the reaction of groups such as the Civil Liberty Association in Ireland itself – not to mention the difficulty the Government might expect in getting such patently insane legislation through the Oireachtas – almost defies imagining.

On the day after the Standing Committee's letter was sent to de Valera the newspapers carried a statement issued by the Committee, clearly meant to turn the heat still higher. While it nowhere mentioned the Censorship Board, the statement seems designed to give the Bishops' imprimatur to the impression that Ireland was in imminent danger of drowning in what to them passed for hardcore pornography.

> There have been widespread complaints confirmed by the strongest evidence that our country is being flooded with enormous quantities of books and magazines which are detrimental to public and private morality. These publications describe in a vivid, suggestive manner and often with illustrations, crimes of violence and unchastity ...
>
> Every right-minded person must regard with great concern the rising tide of juvenile delinquency and the decline of moral standards which are sure signs of decadence ... Our Catholic people need no reminder that one of their most important obligations is the defence of Catholic morality especially in that sacred

sphere where the health and vigour of the race, the purity of domestic life and the sanctity of marriage are involved ... We remind all parents that they have a strict duty to preserve their children by due warning and discipline from the dangers of these evil books and magazines. Parents would regard with horror any contact of their children with physical filth or physical poison; moral filth and moral poison are greater evils.[15]

The view of Irish parents on the matter is not recorded nor was it ever sought; but in a land where depopulation through celibacy and emigration seemed a very realistic prospect, one can only imagine that Irish parents had greater fears for their children's future than tides of filthy literature which seem to have been invisible to all eyes except those of clerics, whether ordained or lay.

On receipt of the letter from the Standing Committee, de Valera phoned Traynor. Details of the conversation were not kept, but its contents are clear from the follow-up letter Traynor wrote to his leader on February 4th. In this letter, relieved of the need to express himself in careful officialese, Traynor gave the position as he actually saw it, as well as offering a few trenchant suggestions (in at least some of which one must yet again suspect the hand of Coyne) on how the aged Taoiseach might once more do what Dev at his best excelled at: gut those opposing him. By now Traynor had been on the receiving end of the campaign for two full months and he was plainly annoyed:

Dear Chief,

Further to the conversation I had with you yesterday ... concerning the representations you have received ... I want you to know that any increase [in the amount of 'indecent' books available] ... took place ... during the period when the Board was not active for want of a quorum as well as during the period when the dissensions between the members were very live and active and when only three meetings took place ...

[F]rom the moment when I was forced to call for the resignation of ... Professor Pigott, because he had brought the work of the Board to a standstill by a refusal to convene any meetings, I have been flooded with protests as part of a campaign that had undoubtedly been worked up amongst Catholic organisations such as confraternities and sodalities and even in such unlikely places as the Conference of St Vincent de Paul and sodalities connected with football clubs and athletic associations …

This campaign was started off by a public statement by the Archbishop of Dublin … and it was spearheaded by the Knights of Columbanus, an organisation in which the two other members of the Board who resigned with Professor Pigott are prominent and of which he himself is almost certainly a member.[16] And I am sure that the campaign would never have been started at all but for the fact that His Grace was not consulted by the former Taoiseach or by me about recent appointments to the Board …

Be that as it may the present campaign will do some damage to the Government and the Party if it is not handled with courage … [Y]ou ought to make an effort to spike the guns of this type of opposition and to rally the responsible members of the various parties in the Dáil to the support of the institutions of the State … Fortunately [the Hierarchy] have provided you with an excellent opportunity … by the references … to the Censorship Board in the fourth and fifth paragraphs of the Bishops' letter … which are tantamount to an attack on the persons appointed by my predecessor who were really Mr Costello's nominees. What I suggest is that you should ask Mr Costello to come and see you … and ask him if you can count on his support against this line of attack …

[T]here is no truth in the suggestion that the two persons concerned viz. Messrs. Comyn and Figgis, are 'openly and avowedly' opposed to censorship … and … the former Taoiseach was at pains to satisfy himself on that score before he recommended Mr Everett to appoint them. I think … you should take the step I suggest. I have already got notice of two Dáil questions on the subject … and I expect that there will be a spate of those … followed by a debate on the adjournment unless it is made known … that what the Hierarchy appear to be aiming at is to discredit the former Government's nominees.[17]

A less official, unsigned and undated document in the same file is even less careful in its speech. After an account of the Board crisis which is nakedly critical of the previous Administration's handling of the affair (and couched in frankly party political terms) it concludes with the lament that the whole thing is '[a]nother Coalition mess left behind for Fianna Fáil to clear up!'[18]

Traynor was right to suspect that he might be bothered with Opposition questions, but even he can hardly have suspected how devious his opponents really were: according to letters in the McQuaid archives from Dermot J. O'Flynn, one of departed Knights, the Order was not simply prompting Dáil questions but was in some cases – at least in the case of Knight-TD Joseph Blowick – actually framing them.[19] The O'Flynn letters give a fascinating insight into the detail in which the whole 'evil literature' campaign was planned and the sheer amount of industry involved – securing Dublin Corporation resolutions (using other organisations as fronts),[20] initiating censorship correspondence with de Valera himself in an apparent attempt to secure evidence of the Government's moral turpitude,[21] targeting importers and distributors (of material which was not in fact legally outlawed),[22] planting newspaper stories[23] etc., etc., etc. The letters also indicate just how well-placed some of the Knights' informants were: O'Flynn could report to McQuaid on many sensitive Censorship Board and Justice Departmental matters, including the text of Traynor's *Memorandum for the Government* and secret measures taken by Coyne to further weaken (or streamline, depending on one's point of view) the censorship process and clear the backlog left by the 18 months of virtual Board inactivity.[24] It is a tribute to the Knights' energy that, while all this was going on, they still had enough energy to begin a campaign against the 1958 Theatre Festival[25] and keep a vigilant eye on the activities of the Jehovah's Witnesses.[26]

31. Defenders of the State

Many of the documents bearing Traynor's name in the archives are obviously in large part the work of Thomas Coyne. We have some of Coyne's notes and explanations to the Minister and also the distinctly Coyne-like sentiments that repeatedly appear in the finished documents. Dermot J. O'Flynn, who had access to inside knowledge, claimed to McQuaid that Coyne prepared the entire *Memorandum for the Government* delivered by Traynor in February 1958 and there seems little or no reason to doubt this.[1] It is also more than possible that Coyne was behind some of the counter-measures taken during the Campaign Against Evil Literature. It seems reasonable to identify such involvement from Traynor's suggestion that de Valera should enlist Costello in the fight. A subsequent memo by de Valera's private secretary notes that de Valera did precisely this, meeting Costello privately in the Taoiseach's office on February 10th. No record was kept of the conversation, but 'Mr Costello had expressed confidence in the [Censorship] Board as now constituted.'[2] Given the cloudy but central part Costello had played in the whole sequence of events this is hardly surprising and while Dáil pressure on Traynor did not stop still it noticeably eased.

In early February 1958 Coyne wrote a memo to provide Traynor with material for use in responding to a Dáil question from Fintan Coogan, TD. Coogan meant to ask the Minister to 'state what steps he had taken to prevent the sale or circulation of undesirable books'.[3] Coyne's advisory document is a model of efficiency that begins with a machine-like exercise in number-

284

crunching, demonstrating the plain silliness of claims about Board inactivity; then it shifts to almost philosophical ground and immediately we hear the clear voice of Coyne as it would sound more than two years later in the McQuaid correspondence, voicing very similar sentiments:

> To prohibit a book without just cause is an infringement of a fundamental human right of freedom of expression as well as the property-rights of authors and publishers ... it is not possible to go into detail on the problems involved: problems which have exercised some of the best minds in the civilised world and which arise ... whether the standards adopted are extremely liberal or extremely narrow. There are only two classes of persons for whom no problem exists: one is the class who say there should be no State interference of any kind, the other is the class who hold that authors should not be allowed to publish anything which might possibly cause offence to anybody who might possibly read it, no matter how young or how innocent of life. For the vast majority of persons who do not subscribe to either of these views, the problems are real and will not be solved by pretending they do not exist. Nor will they be solved by an approach which seems to deny all individual responsibility and, in particular, the responsibility of parents and guardians to supervise the reading matter of their children.[4]

Sensible though much of this would have seemed to most people even at the time, it is manifestly clear from their own words that such sentiments would have been dangerously radical in the eyes of the zealots of the old Board and it is in this light that their depiction of Coyne as a wild liberal should be viewed. From these musings Coyne, in his notes to Traynor, moves to summary which dismisses as 'facile' the Right's argument that the Censorship Board is undemocratic because two members can prevent a ban ('if it is [undemocratic], trial by Jury must also be "undemocratic" as one in twelve can prevent a verdict of guilty'). Coyne finally suggests that the Minister include in his Dáil reply to Coogan a tribute to the members of the new Board ('The Members are working extremely hard and richly deserve a tribute to their public-spirited decision to carry on their task in the face of unwarranted criticism'). In Coyne's covering note, addressed personally to Traynor, we see a wily and intensely *political* Coyne, who suggests that the Minister use the information he is providing sparingly, so as to 'hold [his] fire' for the reply to the Hierarchy's letter (then recently arrived). Coyne's suggested wording for the Minister's answer to Coogan included the required tribute to the Board, whose members were 'now working together in complete harmony'. The covering letter concludes by crowing that '[t]he reference to the harmonious working of the Board will make its opponents lepping mad!'[5] As it no doubt would have, except that they were clearly 'lepping mad' already.

Throughout February Coyne worked on two linked projects: a response to the Hierarchy's letter and the *Memorandum for the Government* which Traynor might deliver to the Cabinet, explaining the situation and justifying this response. De Valera had asked Traynor for these on January 31st, as soon as the Hierarchy's letter arrived.[6] By the time the *Memorandum* was delivered to the Cabinet, on February 25th, it was a massive 25-page paper. It was not a particularly liberal document nor (in that it conveniently omitted many pertinent details from the history of situation) could it even be called a particularly honest one, but, as one might expect from Coyne's work, it is shrewd and efficient. On February 20th Traynor officially requested to have the matter placed on the agenda for the forthcoming Cabinet meeting on February 25th, certifying that the matter was urgent and further certifying that the time required to carefully consider it had prevented 'the usual period of notice being given'.[7] The *Memorandum* was circulated to the Cabinet in advance of the meeting, at which it was duly discussed. There is no available record of the discussions.

The main body of the *Memorandum* begins by setting out the background to the situation as the Department chose to report it.

Only many pages later would it clearly say that in 1956 'the Government of the day was satisfied that the time had come to replace some of the existing personnel of the Board by more broadminded people with a view to preventing the wholesale banning of serious works of literature and the resignation of Monsignor Deery and the late Justice O'Sullivan' gave them the opportunity.

It recounts now how there had been a six-month delay in filling the vacant posts on the Censorship Board, how there had then been friction between the new members and the old, how Pigott had refused to call meetings after May 1957 and how – as a 'result' of this – he had been called on to resign in September, the other two 'old' members resigning with him. In the course of this simple account a good deal of subtle misreporting and character assassination are carried out. Pigott is above all depicted as a man who refused to comply with the legislation ('apparently resenting the requirements of the law'). The friction on the Board is treated as resulting from a straightforward struggle between broadmindedness and conservatism.[8] Pigott's insistence that resignations be called for is referred to as an 'ultimatum', while the account of the resignations of Pigott, O'Flynn and O'Reilly give the impression that these were a form of dereliction of duty carried out in a fit of pique.

The new Board, naturally, is praised to the skies. The newest members – Judge Conroy, Mr O'Reilly and Miss Bodkin – 'were selected for their evident culture, good sense and respect for morality'. More to the point, 'Miss Bodkin is a member of a family … which included two Carmelite nuns and a Jesuit priest. She herself … is a most active member of the Legion of Mary,' while F. T. O'Reilly 'is a 1916 man' and 'an exemplary Catholic and well known to be such'. Of the new Chairman, Judge Conroy, meanwhile, 'nothing requires to be said'.[9]

Turning to the Evil Literature campaign itself the document tells how in December 1956, after a quiet couple of months during which the new Board got down to work, the Archbishop of

Dublin made a public reference to the number of 'foul books' on sale and identifies this speech as 'the signal for numerous protests from various Catholic organisations, apparently acting in concert'. Thereafter the *Memorandum* proceeds to utterly demolish the campaign's pretence to being in any way, shape or fashion a spontaneous expression of anything at all. The document is perfectly clear about two fundamental things: that the campaign was co-ordinated and that the 'flood' about which it complained did not exist. Those who maintained that it did are represented quite frankly (though the word itself is never *quite* used) as liars: of the many planted newspaper articles, for instance, the *Memorandum* says that:

> certain sections of the Press featured articles about the prevalence of immoral literature about which it was alleged little or nothing was being done and *to lend these articles verisimilitude,*[10] some of the writers affirmed that they had on their desks, as they were writing, specimens of publications that were 'foul beyond description' which could be freely obtained in city bookshops. But the writers concerned did not bring these books, *if they were not a figment of the imagination,*[11] to the notice of the police or lay an information against the supplier as they could have done.

On the orchestrated nature of the campaign, the *Memorandum* is unequivocal:

> That this is an organised campaign admits of little doubt. The timing of the campaign, the way it has been worked up, the concerted action of the participants and the stereotyped nature of the protests strongly suggest that the attack on the Censorship Board and the sudden concern with the problem of obscene publications were a direct consequence of the action of the Minister for Justice in calling for Professor Pigott's resignation. That this was a case of cause and effect is made all the plainer by the fact that throughout the period of nearly 11 months, when the Censorship Board was not in a position to function at all, there was not a word from the Archbishop of Dublin, or from the Hierarchy, to suggest that the

censorship of Publications Acts were in need of amendment or that there had been any change in circumstance in relation to the number of obscene publications in circulation.

Here the one exception to this silence – Dr Lucey's bizarre call for more broad-minded members on the Board – is po-facedly pointed out.[12] Then the *Memorandum*, though having found much of the scaremongering to be obvious twaddle, nonetheless sets out (in a professed spirit of fairness) to examine the claims about greatly increased levels of 'evil' publications. Unlike the campaigners, it seeks to establish a rational basis for such an examination and settles on two things that its author feels will act as indicators: 'an evident deterioration in public morality' (such as 'one would expect any such increase to be reflected in or accompanied by') and 'an increase in numbers of complaints from members of the public'. On both counts it finds nothing unusual. On the first:

> [t]here has been a progressive decrease in the number of illegitimate births and there has been has been no increase in sexual offences during the last few years. Statistics of sexual offences by juveniles are not compiled but the Chief Probation Officer, who is in a position to know, has expressed the opinion that such offences, which are always rare, are no more frequent now than they used to be.

The use of public complaints to the Censorship Board as a yardstick – a particularly rich joke given the Campaign's frequent suggestions that the normal complaint mechanisms be ignored – yielded similar negative results. There had been 17 complaints from the public in the years 1956 and 1957,[13] nine of them in connection with books (of which five had turned out to be already banned). Since the Archbishop's speech there had been eleven complaints 'some of which have already been fully examined and found to be unsustainable: the others are being examined'. A special investigation made (at the Department's request) by a Garda

Inspector had found that it was simply untrue that 'obscene publications were prominently on display in bookshops' – having said which and possibly for fear of giving hostages to fortune (or the Hierarchy), the Memorandum hurries to stress that 'a policeman is not qualified to act as a censor of literature and cannot be expected to rummage the bookshelves and thumb his way through pages and pages of possibly questionable publications.' (It is impossible to resist the urge to point out here that for the previous eight months or so the State – and indeed this very Department – had, in open court, been insisting that policemen were perfectly qualified to act as censors of literature if the literary work in question was a play by Tennessee Williams called *The Rose Tattoo.)*

There follow several paragraphs delineating precisely the powers of the police and Revenue Commissioners in the matter of obscene material, aimed at demonstrating that the Bishops, in writing of the 'ample powers' of the police in the matter, are talking through their mitres – the police simply do not have the powers to search bookshops at will, as the bishops seem to feel they do. Nor are the courts reliable instruments in the matter: any trial resulting from a seizure of obscene material will technically be for obscene libel, an indictable misdemeanour which must be tried by jury. In this regard the memo suggests that 'in most countries juries are slow to convict' – a rather astonishing statement coming from the Department then pushing for precisely such a trial for Alan Simpson.

Having by now demonstrated pretty comprehensively that a) the Minister had been justified in asking Pigott to resign; b) there was no genuine increase at all in 'indecent' literature; c) the current campaign was orchestrated, Catholic and fraudulent and d) the Hierarchy's call for police action was based on ignorance of the law, the *Memorandum* turns to a more general consideration of the whole question of censorship. It is here that we hear again clearly the voice of Coyne, as his different personae – the philosopher, the stickler for detail and the political stroke-puller – combine to frame a draft reply to the Hierarchy's demands.

32. The Response to the Standing Committee

As regards the actual reply to the Hierarchy's letter, the *Memorandum* suggests this must depend on the Government's conclusions; the Department's own view is summed up perfectly well in its suggested draft in the appendices. While couched in the most respectful terms, this is a point-by-point rebuttal of the Hierarchy's letter – the Government will of course 'continue to see to it' that police powers are used to suppress the traffic in 'evil publications' (from which scourge the Government thinks Ireland is 'freer than any other country in the world'). But the draft reply embodies the *Memorandum*'s contention that their Lordships seem to have an exaggerated notion of the actual extent of these powers. In reality police powers are fairly restricted and 'these restrictions ... are not accidental but represent the deliberate policy of the law in a difficult matter that requires sensitive handling.' As regards the claims about Comyn and Figgis, the Government 'have no evidence that any person has ever been appointed a member of the Board who is "openly and avowedly determined"' to obstruct the Board's aims. The Bishops' analogy between the Censorship Board and other State bodies is termed a false one and 'the right of an adult person to choose his own reading is such a fundamental freedom that there should be no interference with that right by those who have been entrusted with ... censoring publications unless they are substantially agreed that the common good requires it.'

One may suspect that Coyne – if this is indeed his work, as it seems certain it is – derived a certain amount of malicious satisfaction from composing the draft response. The points that the Bishops had raised are treated with absolute seriousness, in the certainty that what their Lordships had publicly written was not at all what their Lordships had privately meant. The hysterical campaign leading up to their letter is praised as a help to censorship rather than damned as an attempt to subvert it. The knife is twisted in the wound of the Right's injured dignity by a reminder that such difficulties as the new Board is having (and it is admitted that these exist) are due mainly to the backlog caused by its recent inactivity. The draft twists the knife in the Hierarchy itself by pointing out that the Standing Committee's recent public statement 'will no doubt have a significant effect' – 'one substantial importer of paperbacked novels', it is pointed out, 'has already given up this business altogether.' Catholic organisations are now far better informed about the correct procedures for complaining about 'evil' books – knowledge which, to judge by their recent complaints, they had certainly not had before. 'For all these reasons', the draft cheerfully concludes, 'the Government think that … the pressure on the Board will soon ease and that the situation will be restored to normal before long.'

Absolutely none of this was what the Irish Hierarchy wanted to hear, nor was it in fact what they *did* hear – at least not in so many words. Although the draft response was the ultimate basis for de Valera's actual reply to the Standing Committee's letter,[1] Dev's version was infinitely more diplomatically phrased and omitted most of the draft's comments on censorship and pastoral responsibility (which would certainly have incensed the recipients). The final response laid out existing Garda powers and praised the existing Censorship Board (a dangerous enough ploy), which 'has, I am informed, been working harmoniously and well'. The Pigott-enhanced backlog became 'the arrears that resulted from the difficulties concerning [the Board's] membership and functioning'. The draft's rebuttal of claims about Comyn's and Figgis's intentions became 'to the best of my belief, each member of the Board desires to perform his duties ... in a conscientious manner and is endeavouring to do so.' The false analogy between the Censorship Board and other State bodies was ever-so-tactfully adverted to 'Their Lordships will appreciate ... that the functions [of the other Boards] ...are fundamentally different'. The *Memorandum*'s dismissal of their Lordships' suggestions for a greatly enlarged and more complex Censorship Board was softened and the emphasis completely shifted: such arrangements might result in adverse publicity for the censorship process itself – the enlarged and infinitely complicated Board suggested by the Bishops would find it 'very difficult to maintain uniform standards of judgement and ... in consequence of this, there might be a serious growth in adverse criticism of the censorship arrangements'.

On the whole the actual reply, as preserved in the archives of both Church and State, is a classic example of the patented de Valera approach to communication. A comparison of Coyne's draft with the letter actually sent reveals that while most of the draft's points do get mentioned in the eventual letter, it is often in such a transformed manner that they are almost unrecognisable. The actual reply is above all a masterpiece of understatement,[2] to the extent that, to the uninitiated, it would require not so much clarification as outright translation. In this instance, of course, all involved were anything but uninitiated: they were up to their elbows in the intrigue which had led directly to this point. And no matter how politely and diplomatically phrased, however carefully all direct mention of these intrigues was avoided, de Valera's response unequivocally refused the Hierarchy's just-as-carefully phrased demands.

This is perhaps the most significant point about the entire Censorship Board controversy: not only was it the first occasion on which an Irish Government explicitly rejected a demand from the assembled Hierarchy of the Irish Catholic Church, on an issue to which the Hierarchy attached great importance and considered to lie within its sphere, but it was the first occasion on which an Irish Government actually felt in a position to do so. Previous Governments had railed privately at Church interference and had – as de Valera himself had done with his Mother and Infant Scheme only a few years before – haggled over detail before effectively conceding to the Hierarchy's demands. But none, so far as can be traced, had actually faced up to the combined might of their Lordships and simply said 'No'. That the Government could do so now was simply a matter of circumstances, many of which were created by the Hierarchy's (and particularly McQuaid's) own fear of candour. Nonetheless the opportunity was taken and the line crossed.

There is no particular date on which the great Evil Literature campaign may properly be said to have ended. The main hullabaloo died down gradually in mid-1958, though clerical calls for action continued with growing hollowness right into next decade. The Knights of Columbanus were still busily collecting 'evidence' of the tide of filth swamping Ireland all through 1959, even though the Government had decisively dismissed the whole notion as a chimera. The supposed misdeeds of Coyne, meanwhile, were still being reported to the Archbishop in 1960 by various figures involved with the issue – notably O'Flynn, by now Supreme Knight of his Order.

If the 'end' of the Evil Literature campaign is impossible to pinpoint, there is no such difficulty in identifying the point after which it became an essentially hollow undertaking: early March 1958, when the Hierarchy received de Valera's letter repudiating their call for action. The full import of the message may have taken a while to digest, but digested it was: so far as can be ascertained, the Hierarchy subsequently dropped all their official approaches to the State. Certainly they stopped feeding the fires they had lit under the Evil Literature campaign. De Valera's reply to their letter, for all its ameliorating vagueness, had been a clear shot across their bows. The only option remaining open to the Hierarchy was a direct appeal to the people over the heads of Government. That was a truly nuclear option and a road that nobody at all wanted to go down. Apart from anything else, it is evident both from their behaviour and from many of their private comments that their Lordships' faith in their own power over their flock was less complete than many of their public statements would suggest. Nobody at all would benefit from the full Censorship Board story coming out. The confident Government dismissal of their calls had indicated to the Hierarchy that they were, politically speaking, in a hole. With a degree of common sense unusual for any Irish institution, and certainly far greater than their allies in the Knights had recently shown, their Lordships promptly stopped digging, at least on any kind of high-profile official level. True to form, the Knights of Columbanus themselves had played no high-profile part in the Campaign, at least under their own name. There had been no appeal to the sanctity of any past secret deals. With the Board now Knight-free and the only written record of the deal being a mention made in a document written by one of their own, it would have been all too easy for the State to make them look mendacious or insane: What secret? What deal?

Given the decided preference of all involved for secrecy and the incomplete state of the documentation, there is no way of knowing much about further informal or confidential contacts between Church and State, except to say that – unless all concerned suddenly underwent a positively miraculous reform of their habitual behaviour – these certainly took place. There is even an almost accidental record of what was very likely one of the most important of these contacts: sometime before May 20th 1958, Thomas J. Coyne paid a long visit to John Charles McQuaid in the Archbishop's Drumcondra headquarters. There is no record of what was discussed at this meeting – indeed, there is no official State record, at least in the archives, of its ever taking place. The meeting's existence is known only from references in letters in the McQuaid papers.[3] Whether it was part of some confidential wrangling process is unknowable, but it certainly concerned censorship and it is very difficult to see it as anything other than some kind of peace conference. All we know for sure of the event is that McQuaid presented Coyne with three books as samples of the debauched reading available on the streets of Dublin and that after the meeting Coyne wrote a letter (largely uninformative from our point of view) to the Archbishop.[4]

As late as December 1959 McQuaid himself was writing menacingly about the 'present' censorship Board to Fr Roland Burke-Savage, SJ: 'I wish you to know that the matter causes me the acutest anxiety … If I make up my mind that it is my duty as a Bishop to take action, I will take every means open to me as a Bishop to remedy the evil.'[5] But the ominous-sounding words concealed a fact which by that stage must have been perfectly clear to the Archbishop: that the means now open to him were, at least in this potentially dangerous case, strictly limited. More to the point, they had already quite comprehensively failed. And while nothing in Coyne's writings for an instant suggests that he was the wild libertarian portrayed by the Right, there is no doubt that he was largely responsible for that failure.

Given this, the story of the McQuaid–Coyne relationship had a surprising coda in the form of the 1960 correspondence between the two men, in the course of which the Archbishop would seem to try – quite possibly for the first time – to really understand the other's point of view and would indeed end by praising much of what Coyne wrote. What developments (if any) might have come from this will never be known: within the year Coyne's beloved wife died and he himself was diagnosed with a serious illness. The last letter in the correspondence in the McQuaid papers is a sad note written by Coyne in December 1960, in response to a lost communication from McQuaid. Someone had told the Archbishop of Coyne's distress and McQuaid – whose quiet, private kindnesses, it must always be remembered, were legion – had written to him. Coyne's response was a brief, touching note from a broken man:

> I was never more conscious of the need for God's blessing ... I
> have no longer the support of my dear dead wife to sustain me. I
> never thought to survive her and my hope and prayer is that I
> may not have to do so for very long ... I am not yet incapacitated
> but go out very little – just for a couple of hours when the
> weather is not too severe so that I may not have to take to my bed
> any sooner or for any longer than needs be.

In some fashion McQuaid had suggested the possibility that he
might personally visit Coyne – an honour rarely extended even to
senior Government Ministers, who normally waited on the
Archbishop in his offices. Of this suggestion Coyne says 'I neither
expect nor deserve such an honour but if there was any question of
your Grace's doing so perhaps you would ask one of your secretaries to let me know before hand so that I could be sure to be here.'[6]
It is not known whether the visit ever took place. The incident
seems as convenient a point as any at which to mark the end of
this account of a certain kind of Catholic approach to censorship
and of the remarkable and now half-forgotten civil servant who,
more than any other single individual, was responsible for ending
its covert monopolisation of the censorship machinery of the
State. Thomas J. Coyne, former censor of Ireland during World
War II, expertly, humbly (and terribly efficiently) sowed the seeds
which make it possible, almost half a century later, for you to read
books like this one.

The Knights of Columbanus continued to report to the
Archbishop on their efforts to combat filth – they spent much of
October 1960, for instance, campaigning against the staging of
Brendan Behan's *The Hostage*. But it was a far cry from the recent
attempts to pressurise an entire Government and it was more than
a merely tactical change. For all the bitterness of later campaigns
on other issues, there would never again be anything quite like the
Campaign Against Evil Literature. Just as the State would not in-

volve itself in direct theatre censorship after its fingers had been charred in the *Rose Tattoo* case, so the Hierarchy would fight shy of so wholeheartedly committing itself to involvement in such a wide-scale public censorship campaign in the years ahead. The rebuff from Government had been too complete: a repeat, apart from anything else, would be too humiliating. De Valera's response to the Hierarchy's demands, however mistily phrased, marked a sea change in relationships between the two great pillars of Irish society. It had been, in its way, a tacit acknowledgement by the State that Irish society itself had changed and it marked the Hierarchy's cards as effectively as District Justice O'Flynn's scathing summing up in the *Rose Tattoo* case a few months later would mark the State's. The lessons were not lost on either recipient. From now on they would go about things a bit differently.

PART FOUR

1957 REVISITED

'Turning backwards is how the way moves'
Lao Tzu

33. Ar Ais Arís

There are many peculiar stories in the history of mid-twentieth-century Ireland, buried in unmarked graves in dusty archives, occasionally with the archival equivalent of stakes through their hearts. As time passes, and more facts are revealed, one of these stories occasionally bobs to the surface, to the wonderment of all. Were we really like that? Is that really how things were?

To some of its readers this book may seem to contain two such stories, connected only by the coincidence that central events of both took place at the same time. It will be obvious that this is not what the present writer believes. The second of these stories did not 'bob to the surface' – it (or something very like it) was deliberately sought out and it was sought out because the facts of the State's initial action against the Pike seemed to make sense only if the theatre had become inadvertently involved in some pre-existing row of sufficient size, and with players of sufficient importance, to make the State feel that such unheard of action was necessary.

Nor was the existence of this theoretical row 'revealed' by the papers eventually released on the *Rose Tattoo* case; it was, rather, inferred from the contents of those papers and – more importantly – from lacunae and inconsistencies in the story that they seemed to tell. Though we could dimly see an outline of this phantom story and even hazard a guess as to the location of its unmarked grave, still our initial search for its burial place was undertaken, as much as anything else, to ascertain whether what both the history books and the archives seemed to tell us – that it did not exist –

301

was correct. Mainly we wanted to discount the possibility of its relevance so that we could look for more promising areas of research.

In fact it is the present writer's belief that the well-buried story behind the battle for the Irish Censorship Board is the single most important element in the answer to the most fundamental riddle of the *Rose Tattoo* affair: why the Irish Government felt obliged to take any action at all against the Pike, as distinct from any other theatre running any number of far more controversial, far less celebrated, far more complained-of shows. For, until the State's own assault on the theatre became public knowledge, there simply *was* no controversy about *The Rose Tattoo*; in terms of the supposed law of the land, there *were* no known complaints about it.[1] Indeed one of the bitterest ironies of the matter is that, had Joseph J. Cooney not become disenchanted with the normal complaints procedure – had he trotted along to a Garda station, as he'd done the year before in the case of *The Respectable Prostitute*, and registered a complaint about *The Rose Tattoo* – then all the available evidence suggests that he would have been fobbed off and told that the play had been vetted and that, yes indeed, it was terrible, *terrible*, but … what could the police do? And anyway (he would have been told, as he and others had been told before) it was too late now, the show was over. And there would never have been any such thing as the *Rose Tattoo* case.

One of the few things about the roots of the case that is unequivocally stated in the released State papers is that action was deemed necessary precisely so as to *forestall* not a complaint *per se* but a *demand*: 'a demand – possibly a demand made in public – from any one or more of several sources, including the Archbishop, for action'.[2] We have seen that Dr McQuaid, in spite of what Seán Brady had told Traynor on May 9th, privately denied responsibility for the move against the Pike and seems to have learned of the facts behind the matter (even possibly, given his seeming blind-spot to theatre, of the very existence of the play) only after Alan Simpson's arrest. We have noted the Archbishop's general reluctance to make specific public demands of the sort the Department of Justice feared – a reluctance so extreme that even later, during the Campaign Against Evil Literature, not just his own initial address but the greater part of the entire campaign would concentrate (to its own detriment) on generalities, side-issues and demonstrable fantasies, thus avoiding the real causes of dispute. Nor had Seán Brady, TD – in his witting or unwitting transmission to the Justice Department of information about *The Rose Tattoo* that seems to have been simply untrue – made any mention at all of a threat by McQuaid to issue a public statement. This whole chimera, at least on the evidence we have, came from the imaginations of men in the Justice Department who were, as we have also seen, anything but religious zealots on one hand or, on the others, nervous nellies given to twitching fearfully at the mere invocation of the Archbishop's name – they were perfectly level-headed men, quite capable of resisting even highly organised, nationwide attempts by the Irish Catholic Church to pressurise them into taking actions that they did not want to take. Except in this one single instance, when a mere unsubstantiated rumour of Dr McQuaid's interest would appear of the face of it at least to have sent them into a tizzy.

Why?

The known history of May 1957 offered no explanation that was even vaguely credible; but when our second story was un-earthed, brushed down and put on the table beside the now-public record, we found ourselves looking at an answer that was not only credible but – at least in terms of the players involved, the known relationships between them, the subsequent events and indeed the whole story of 1950s Ireland – entirely logical. The Department of Justice had feared intervention by John Charles McQuaid, we concluded, because at that precise time – the third week of May 1957 – the Department lived in anticipation of an enormous fight. It anticipated a fight with the Knights of Columbanus, and very possibly Dr McQuaid, over control of the Irish Censorship Board. And, precisely because it *did* know its opponents well, the Department expected – as it couldn't afford *not* to expect – that the fight would be both indirect and dirty.

One of the basic moves the Department might have expected from its opponents was an attempt to undermine the Department's own credibility in the field of the dispute by indicating that the Department – with its 'inexperienced' Minister, Oscar Traynor – was not (to use terminology common at the time) 'sound' on the whole censorship 'question'. And, in turn, one of the most effective ways for Dr McQuaid and the Knights to do this would be for them to shoot first – to find a censorship issue on which the Archbishop could attack the Department or at least hold out the threat of such attack. The actual text of any 'demand for action' on *The Rose Tattoo* would be irrelevant – indeed, The *Rose Tattoo* itself would be irrelevant, except in so far as it provided an excuse for the attack. What would matter – what would be meant to matter – was the subtext of the Archbishop's statement which would be: 'Here is a Justice Department, and a Government, that encourages and even subsidises filthy plays in the theatres of Dublin: how can anything it says about censorship be taken seriously?'

There were two ways open to the Department to prevent such a call being made. One was to give Dr McQuaid what it might expect him to want – a restoration of Knightly power on the Censorship Board. The other was to neutralise the danger at source, by moving quickly to quash the play that would provide McQuaid with the excuse to speak out. We have seen the later actions of the Minister towards the Knights; it seems clear that, even if these had not been decided on by late May, the Department was at least minded to keep its options open and not to yield immediately. So the Department chose the latter course and thus set in motion what would go down in history as the *Rose Tattoo* case. This, in a nutshell, is our answer to what we have identified as one of the most fundamental questions: why the Department of Justice took any action against the Pike at all.

This would make both technical and political sense, for Church–State relations in the era were entirely a matter of politics and both sides behaved accordingly. But would any Irish Government, however cynical, put innocent people through all that Simpson and Swift endured on such grounds? Would it legally persecute them – or *need* to persecute them – for over a year, and destroy their theatre, just for the sake of neutralising a perceived threat from an opponent in a political fight in which the Pike was completely uninvolved?

We shall leave the theoretical answer to that question to the taste of the individual reader. As it happens, it need not concern us here: for our answer to the second basic question about the case – why State action took the form it did – is quite a different matter. It is perfectly clear from the seven-point memo that the Department of Justice never expected any of these things to happen and equally clear from the actual events of the *Rose Tattoo* case that the Department was as surprised as anyone else by the way the affair developed. Though it has always been taken for granted that there was at least some element of conspiracy behind the events of the *Rose Tattoo* case it is obvious, even from the material now available, that the public events of the whole case were, at least in part, the result of a monumental cock-up.

When Carolyn Swift and I set out to research the roots of the *Rose Tattoo* case, we had not sat and talked about what exactly it was that we were looking for. Later we realised that, in looking for *an* explanation – for a single fact or wellspring that would explain the many oddities of even the public facts of the case – we were being as simplistic as the media had been in its easy acceptance of the suggestion that Dr McQuaid was *the* cause of the case. Everyone likes an easy answer, and – where an injustice has been done – everybody likes to find *a* villain. The State's *Rose Tattoo* file was released shortly after the appearance of John Cooney's monumental biography of Dr McQuaid, with its exhaustive depiction of the Archbishop's views, acts and methods, so deeply at odds with our own supposed pieties. After years of semi-neglect, Dr McQuaid had returned to the spotlight and in the period of the State Papers' release it had become well-nigh fashionable to ascribe to his influence all the teeming ills of Irish society during his long reign as Archbishop. Here, seemingly, was a villain one could hiss: and he was duly hissed, by all and sundry.

Real life, of course, isn't like that; certainly the agonisingly complex, tortuously indirect real life of the competing Establishments of Ireland in the 1950s wasn't like that. If looking for a single person responsible for the case had been naïve, then looking for a single explanation for all of the various anomalies that emerged over its long life would also be a mistake. If the State's case against Alan Simpson seems a shambles, this is quite simply because it *was* a shambles, an *ad hoc* response thrown together by a State which found itself in an situation it had never expected to arise and for which, as a result, it was completely unprepared.

The best way to explain what we think happened in that summer of 1957 is to retrace the path of this part of the *Rose Tattoo* story with (as it were) some of the holes filled in. As told in the first part of this book, the story was given from what might be called the *outside*: from the point of view of the Pike Theatre and the public record. The absence of the State's own point of view was regrettable but inevitable given its conscientious refusal ever to say anything about the case. For all the publicity they received at the time of their emergence, the released State papers in themselves do little or nothing to alter that situation: if anything the selective nature of the release means that the overall effect of the State file as it stands is actively misleading.[3] Looked at in the light of the disinterred Censorship Board story, however, the events of that summer seem quite different; looked on in that light, they even begin to make a twisted kind of sense.

In the course of its long, almost surreal existence, the *Rose Tat-*

too court case came to take on something like a life of its own, and to touch on matters – such as a defendant's right to have access to information on his case – which are not central to this book. Apart from anything else, a detailed study of the entire, year-long trek through the courts would demand a book several times the size of this volume. So we will concentrate here on the two truly essential elements of the story: the decision to make a move against the Pike and the reason that this move ended up taking the form that it did – on how, in short, Alan Simpson came to find himself, on the morning of May 24th 1957, the first and so far last Irish theatre owner and director to be standing in the dock of an Irish court facing indecency charges. These, finally, are the elements that combine to form the real 'riddle' of the *Rose Tattoo* case. In the last analysis, what follows can claim to be no more than a theory. Due to the paucity of papers, our interpretation of events must remain just that – an interpretation. In terms of hard evidence, it cannot claim to be more than a plausible scenario – though this in itself marks a very distinct advance, since plausibility is something that has been singularly lacking from all accounts of the *Rose Tattoo* case for almost fifty years.

No doubt some of this scenario remains, for want of fuller information, only partially accurate. A few elements may be downright wrong. Some questions must remain open and these are noted in the relevant places. This imprecision is beyond our control: the absence of meaningful information on what the State really thought it was doing makes it ultimately impossible to say whether what follows is *the* truth about what it *was* doing. More than two years of research and reflection, however, have convinced both the present writer and Carolyn Swift that it is at the very least far closer to the truth than either the self-evident nonsense produced by the Chief State Solicitor's Office in court in 1957–8 or the extremely partial version of events suggested by the file released to public scrutiny in January 2000. If what follows must remain speculation, still it is very highly informed speculation, taking into account the established behaviour patterns of all concerned and based on substantially more information than was available to anyone who has previously written on the case – including the present writer, when he first wrote part one of this book.

34. May 1957: Take Two

The Fianna Fáil Government that returned to power in March 1957 did not need a censorship crisis: any incoming Irish Government at the time would have had more than enough on its plate with a foundering economy, a flood of emigration and what seemed like a major upsurge of armed political violence on its single (and very politically sensitive) land border. A censorship crisis in the making, however, was exactly what the new government inherited from its predecessor. The anonymous, unaddressed and undated summary of the situation, written in early 1958 and found with Oscar Traynor's 'Dear Chief' letter in the National Archives[1] lays the blame for the situation fairly and squarely on the previous administration: '[i]t was apparent ... that when filling the vacancies [on the Censorship Board] the Coalition Government were aware of the likelihood of divergence of opinion on censorship as between the old and the new members and hadn't made the slightest attempt to find out if [they] would cooperate in working the Act.'[2]

Quite what Oscar Traynor himself knew about the Censorship Board situation before it really went critical, or when he learned it, is impossible to say. But it would have been remiss of Coyne not to brief the incoming Minister on the situation, which had always been an almost guaranteed source of some kind of trouble; and from what is known of Coyne he seems the last man to be remiss in his duties. Compared to the fight against the IRA, Traynor can hardly have deemed the Censorship Board situation a priority – so long as it stayed quiet. Still, Departmental antennae will have been

309

up and ears open for any whisper of trouble from the Knights or
the Church. Already by March the disagreement on the issue of
omnibus volumes had caused Pigott to contact the Department in
search of a ruling from the Attorney General, so the Department
will have been quite well aware of the growing friction on the
Board.

Early on May 9th 1957 Seán Brady, TD for Dún Laoghaire-
Rathdown and a trusted Party loyalist, came to see the Minister
with news of a terrible thing. An 'unquestionably indecent' play
was to be produced in Dublin the week after by the Pike Theatre.
According to Brady, the play's production had already been 'prohibited in several American cities and … in France',[3] and
Archbishop McQuaid had not only 'called for the script' but was
aware of Brady's visit to the Department.[4] Four decades later, a
certain amount of condescension towards Brady was apparent in
some of the media coverage that followed the release of the *Rose
Tattoo* file and there was some amusement evident at the picture
of a TD running to the Minister with tales of indecency. But Seán
Brady had no history of zealotry in the censorship area and it is
quite unclear from the papers what exactly he placed greater emphasis on – the play's 'indecency' or McQuaid's supposed interest
in it. It may well be our modern interpretation of events that is at
fault and that the point of Brady's visit was not to complain of the
play, but to warn the Minister of McQuaid's seeming interest.
There is at this stage no way of knowing one way or the other; but
given that a row with the Archbishop would be unwelcome at any
time, the latter would be a perfectly reasonable thing for Brady to
do.

Be that as it may, in that era of cryptically indirect communication between Church and State the 'fact' that McQuaid knew of
Brady's visit can only have seemed particularly significant – perhaps the most significant thing about Brady's 'news'. Complaints
about 'immoral' plays were perhaps new to Traynor, who may
have expected that the Justice Ministry involved other things; but

they were anything but unknown to the career civil servants in his Department for whom such complaints were pretty much routine. That this particular 'complaint' – if Brady's news can be called that – came from a ranking Party member would have guaranteed it a hearing, nothing more. What would make the Department take the issue seriously at the best of times was the involvement of McQuaid – and not simply his involvement, but the fact that he seemingly wanted them to know that (in effect) he had his eye on them. The fact that McQuaid had never before shown such interest in theatre, and the unusual manner of the apparent approach, will have flagged the matter as significant and – even if only as a matter of routine procedure – an attempt will have been made to figure out what exactly it was that Dr McQuaid actually *wanted*.

Given the situation on the Censorship Board at this time, it is simply not possible to believe that it did not *at the very least* cross Departmental minds that Brady's visit was somehow connected with the Board situation. Dr McQuaid's own interest in censorship was as well known to the Department as to everyone else; if he had ever, in any form, agreed even tacitly to allow a dilution of the Knightly monopoly, it was obvious by now that the experiment had not worked. There is no reason to suppose that anyone in the Department as yet knew of the acrimonious break-up of the previous evening's Board meeting, but any suggestion that McQuaid was taking a particular interest in a matter of censorship – *any* matter of censorship – can only have rung Departmental alarm bells.[5] If the link with the Board situation *was* made at this point, what will have seemed at least very possible – *in the context of these men's experience* – is that the Archbishop's supposed expression of interest was an instance of a classic tactic of the Catholic Hierarchy to which they were also well used – the lateral approach to the real issue of concern.

If this did strike the men at Justice, then it will have seemed not simply a normal but also a logical ploy for McQuaid to use: we are not talking religion here, but politics. It would be potentially dangerous for the Archbishop and his allies to take the Minister directly to task over the Censorship Board – there were questions they themselves would not want raised on the subject. An indecent *play*, however, was something that might have been tailor-made for use in applying pressure to the Minister at this time: a safe opportunity to imply – even in public – that the Department was unreliable on the whole censorship issue.

To younger readers this may all seem quite insane and in some senses of course it is; but the civil servant who did not subject 'news' such as Brady's to such an examination would have been considered to be falling down on the job. Nothing in Brady's story, at this early stage, suggested that this was the opening salvo in an actual attack. Instead it would seem like a preliminary jockeying for position on the potential battleground, lest combat become necessary. It was, however, indisputably a threat: a reminder of where the moral high ground lay and an announcement that the Archbishop was both ready and willing to launch a first strike should it become necessary. The ball was in, the news said, and the game was on; what the Department needed to know, before it started playing, was the state of the pitch.

Regardless of what Brady's news portended, the *exact* needs of the Department at this point were three in number: firstly it needed to know precisely what action against the Pike might be open to it, in case *some* overt action should turn out to be needed in a hurry; secondly, as an insurance measure, it needed to instigate some kind of activity on the matter immediately – to demonstrate afterwards, if need be, that the authorities had been on the ball and had responded quickly to McQuaid's concerns. With these measures safely in place it would then, thirdly and most importantly, need to figure out – if it did not already know – what exactly McQuaid really wanted, so as to gauge the seriousness (or otherwise) of the threat represented by *The Rose Tattoo*. What we actually see in the released May 9th documents – the communications between Berry and the Attorney General's office – is, at least in part, the first two of these things being done and being done with an ostentatious display of promptness. The real measure of the Department's normal reaction to complaints about plays is the glaringly obvious fact that it had absolutely no idea what – if any – measures were available to it for use against a theatre. The supposed McQuaid approach had completely blindsided it – which, if anything, can only have made it appear more authentic, since this was the sort of thing the Hierarchy specialised in. [6]

An attempt was made within the Department itself on May 9th to find a mechanism that could be used to stop performances of *The Rose Tattoo* at short notice if this proved necessary. A couple of possible excuses were found but no one was sure how effective they would be; so Peter Berry wrote to the Attorney General's Office, sounding out the viability of both methods. The first option – which seemed the most reliable – was to close the theatre itself because it was operating without a licence; a second possibility (mentioned briefly and almost as an afterthought in the final paragraph of Berry's two-page letter) was a prosecution for indecency.

The reply from the Attorney General's office suggested that neither was actually ideal for the intended purpose. To close the Pike because of its lack of a licence was perfectly possible but politically thorny since every other theatre club in Dublin was in precisely the same position. The second option, however, looked slightly more promising and there was even a more-or-less relevant law on the books that could be interpreted as covering the case.

With this sorted, a decision was made that police should be set to watch the Pike production after it opened. Seán Brady was informed of this decision and later that same day he in turn conveyed it to his own original informants, Cooney and O'Farrell.[7] It may well be that, since they appeared to have the ear of the Archbishop, or even to be acting on his behalf, this news was meant ultimately for Dr McQuaid. The exact nature of the orders given to the police observers remains as secret now as it was in

Dublin District Court 45 years ago. In a way, however, the nature of the orders is irrelevant – the mere act of sending observers to the Pike was quite meaningless in itself and neither more nor less than the response Joseph J. Cooney – a member of the lowly League of Decency – had received to his complaint about *The Respectable Prostitute*. It was a way of being seen to do something about a complaint: whether or not it was more than this in the present case (at least at the time it was first done) must at least be open to question.

From the point of view of documentary evidence, silence now descends on Government thinking, a silence not broken until the writing of the seven-point memo almost two weeks later. But we do know two very important things that happened during the silent period. The first, though we cannot date the event, is that the Department learned the situation on the Censorship Board had gone critical, with the May 8th Board meeting breaking up acrimoniously and Pigott demanding an interview with the Minister. It must be presumed that Coyne at least had been keeping an eye on the situation he had done so much to engineer, so news of the row cannot have come as a complete surprise; but still the possibility that the can of worms would spill out into public view can only have been very unwelcome. And – whether or not our own reading of the situation is precisely correct – it cannot but have put Dr McQuaid's sudden apparent interest in theatrical censorship into an entirely different light. The fact that his 'approach' to the Department followed immediately in the wake of the Board Row, taken with everything else, can only have made it seem like a distinct possibility that it was a direct consequence of the row. That would make Brady's visit seem like a shot across the Department's bows and would make his 'news' appear very much like an immediate threat.

Given the deafening silence elsewhere, it is very tempting to take the date typed on Brian MacMahon's 'June' letter at face value and suppose that a secret meeting between Traynor and Professor Pigott did take place on May 15th. But though this would usefully add another exact date to a sequence of events otherwise lacking many, all other sources agree that the first meeting between the Chairman and the Minister took place in June and it seems likely that MacMahon, writing at the beginning of July, simply wrote down the name of the previous month without thinking. In any case there was no need for a face-to-face meeting: we know that, after the break-up of the May 8th meeting, Pigott spent the rest of the month attempting to see Traynor. His suspicions about Comyn and Figgis will (unless Coyne was sleeping on the job) have already been known at the Department.[8] What will also have been clear to the Department, even before any meeting took place, was what is obvious from the accounts of the Knights themselves: their utter unwillingness to give an inch on the whole Censorship Board issue.

In itself the Pike Theatre was, like *The Rose Tattoo* itself, unimportant from the Department's point of view. What the Department needed to know was what part, if any, McQuaid intended to play in the dispute over the Censorship Board. What they could not do – since the situation did not officially exist – was simply ask him; so they were forced to decide the matter themselves. The supposed McQuaid interest in the Pike was highly suspicious. If it *were* connected to the Board dispute, it meant that Dr McQuaid was positioning himself for a possible public fight – he was very possibly preparing, via a statement condemning the Department's inaction on an indecent play, to give the moral high ground to his allies.

The usual Irish State reaction in such a situation, historically speaking, would have been to shilly-shally, put a brave face on things and then essentially cave in. On this occasion, however, the previously normal thing did not happen. The practical arguments against leaving the Knights with complete control of the Board remained the same as they had been in 1956: they'd had their chance and they'd been unable to restrain their appetite for excess.

If they refused under any circumstances to share control of the Board, or to mitigate their ultra-conservative (and, much worse from a State point of view, patently *obvious*) policies, then they must go. Getting rid of them without a public row, though, would be a delicate process and it would take time. In these circumstances, the prospect of having Dr McQuaid sniffing around any censorship issue at all would be doubly worrying. The prospect that he might be about to wade into the dispute on the Knights' side would seem calamitous.

The second thing that happened in this silent period – and the thing that turned *The Rose Tattoo* into an issue demanding an urgent decision – is mentioned in the seven-point memo itself: on May 20th, ads appeared in the newspapers announcing that, due to popular demand, the play would transfer to the Gate Theatre for a further week's run at the end of the Theatre Festival. The question of whether or not McQuaid's 'interest' in the Pike was a political ploy now became a vital one. The transfer would ruin any Departmental alibi to the effect that the play had reached the end of its run before action could be taken against it. Dr McQuaid might have been dissatisfied with such an outcome, but there would have been nothing he could practically say against it: a paper trail existed to demonstrate the Department's immediate response to the matter on May 9th. A transfer to the Gate, though, was quite a different matter: that the play had been permitted not only to continue its run but to move to a major city-centre theatre, in spite of Dr. McQuaid's 'message' to the Department, would look like open defiance – or could be so construed, if the Archbishop wished to construe it in this way. And if his 'approach' had indeed been part of a bigger plan related to the Censorship Board, then that is exactly how he would wish to construe it. Suddenly the Pike Theatre was no longer a side issue: it was a problem that needed action *now*. But what action?

The contents of the seven-point memo have been quoted at length in these pages, many chapters ago now; but it seems suitable at this point to repeat the relevant section, which reads quite differently in the light of what we now know to have been going on:

> 4. It now appears from advertisements in the Press that the play is being transferred from the Pike Theatre to the Gate Theatre at the end of this week, where, in the ordinary course it would be shown to a much wider audience than the 70 odd persons who can be accommodated nightly in the Pike. This makes the question of the continuance of the play much more important.
>
> 6. … if there is any delay in taking action you may be faced with a demand – possibly a demand made in public – from any one or more of several sources, including the Archbishop, for action and … you would then be put in the position of having either to take no action – though the play is believed to be indecent – or to give the impression to the public that you acted only at the dictation of the Archbishop or of somebody else.[9]

The Minister, in other words, would be in what we would now call a no-win position. If it is simply impossible to believe that Knightly domination of the Censorship Board came about by some bizarre series of coincidences, or that the Board's eccentric behaviour during the period of their complete hegemony was somehow unrelated to their dominance, then it does not seem one whit more likely that what began to happen now to the Pike was unrelated to the broader censorship situation. And this, rather than *The Rose Tattoo* itself, is what the seven-point memo is actually 'about'. While the memo is without doubt the one central, vitally important document in the released file on the Pike case, it is also something else: it is a plan outlining how the Minister can neutralise a major weapon in his opponents' arsenal and, at the same time, completely turn the tables on his opponents. For by closing the play, by hook or by crook, Traynor will not only forestall the expected criticism but will actually appear *strong* on censorship. The question of how the whole thing will affect the Pike is never even considered; like the Knights themselves, the Department is working for a Greater Good. Unfortunately, the Pike Theatre is standing in the way.

35. Action

What is the really striking thing about the seven-point memo but also the aspect of it that is all too easy to overlook, is that it nowhere envisages the arrest of Alan Simpson, still less his prosecution. The memo concludes that the run of *The Rose Tattoo* must be stopped and that this will arouse some comment. But there is no suggestion that Simpson be arrested or that the old law found to 'justify' stopping the play should actually be used. It is proposed that a uniformed police inspector should have a quiet word with the management of the Pike and – basically – put them in an impossible position: they are to be told that, if the play is not either taken off or 'expurgated', they will be prosecuted. As Cathal O'Flynn would point out over a year later, this was an unreal choice: with no indication of what was being objected to, the only option really being presented was to stop the play. The message was clear – or at least it *should* have been clear. The question of what will happen if the Pike refuses to comply is never raised: the memo simply takes it for granted that the visit from the police will do the trick and that the Pike will stop performance of *The Rose Tattoo*.

The seven-point memo was written on May 20th or 21st – after the announcement of the Gate transfer and before Ward's visit to the Pike. The method chosen for use against the Pike was uncannily similar to the method Thomas Coyne,[1] as wartime censor, had used against the Gate to close Lennox Robinson's *Roly Poly*. During the Emergency, however, Coyne had had draconian wartime powers at his disposal with which to threaten the Gate; in

319

1957, following the Attorney General's advice, the Department was reduced to using the ancient law against indecency. This, however, was at most a minor matter: almost any old law would do, since there was no expectation that anything beyond a threat would be necessary.

On May 21st the Deputy Garda Commissioner, Garrett Brennan, received (still-unavailable) instructions from the Department of Justice,[2] and that evening a uniformed Inspector Ward went to the Pike and did precisely as the memo recommended. It was at that point that the reactions of Simpson and Swift – which the Department of Justice had equally failed to take into consideration – came into play and the quick fix concocted by the Department came unstuck. Because Simpson and Swift did not move in the same world as those at the Department, they failed to understand the message they were being given. They were used to living in a world where the fact that they had done nothing wrong actually counted for something. So they thought the Inspector's presence had to be a mistake, of the kind that reasonable people could sort out, and, having an audience waiting inside, they refused to do as they were told. This simple act, which neither Swift nor Simpson considered particularly defiant, can only have confounded the entire Department of Justice. The police visit had been treated as an important but still relatively minor matter: the State would tell the Pike to stop the play and the Pike would stop the play, end of story: there *was* no plan B.

It is evident that there was an unusual degree of official activity following Ward's failure to stop the play quietly. Ward himself wrote his report on the visit next day and Garret Brennan immediately sent it, along with other documents in the case, to the Chief State Solicitor's office.[3] This high-level attention right from the start of the matter is of course in itself an indication of how sensitive it was felt to be. May 22nd and 23rd were the days Alan Simpson spent frantically trying to contact everyone he could think of who might help rectify what he and Swift still thought of as the police 'mistake', but there can be little doubt that there was a certain amount of panic at the Department too: the nobodies at the Pike had actually done the unthinkable and defied the law – what to do now?

It was on the morning of the 22nd that Florrie O'Riordan dug into the matter and – 'much shaken' – reported back that 'Dev himself wants action taken against you'.[4] If the involvement of high officials is an indication that the matter was being taken seriously, then the involvement of de Valera would indicate that its real significance was not legal, but political. The decision itself, however, is unsurprising: an overt move against the Pike had been made, however quietly and had failed. If this became public, then the action designed to display the Department's censorship credentials would backfire badly. So really there was no option but to persevere: the Department was caught in a trap of its own making.

A decision was clearly being taken on May 22nd–23rd; but again it was not necessarily a decision to prosecute Alan Simpson. Because an appearance in court followed Simpson's arrest, it has always been assumed – even by Swift and Simpson – that these were part of a single sequence of actions (as, indeed, they are legally supposed to be). But there is more than one valid interpretation of exactly what Alan Simpson's arrest was meant to achieve. From the State's point of view there was much more to be said *against* an attempt at prosecution than in favour of one: prosecution would effectively guarantee the maximum publicity for the whole affair. Even worse, the government's case would stand a good chance of failing if it even got as far as a trial: the state's received wisdom, as later stated in Traynor's *Memorandum for the Government*, was that an obscenity trial was very difficult to win.[5] And in the unpredictable forum of the courtroom there was every chance that the questionable roots of the Government's own interest in *The Rose Tattoo* might emerge, which would defeat the point of the whole exercise.

The visit from Inspector Ward, though dressed up in the language and uniform of legality, had basically been an exercise in para-legal intimidation, an attempt to use the law as a form of blackmail – in the same way that the police visit to Lord Longford, also suggested in the seven-point memo, was designed to use a different law to the same end. The attempt on the Pike failed because – almost comically – neither Simpson nor Swift had ever experienced this kind of intimidation and so did not recognise Ward's visit for what it was. Simpson had been told – after a fashion – to close the play; he had refused. From the State point of view the situation could not be left like that. But Ward's visit had been an attempt to put the frighteners on the Pike, not a valid attempt to enforce the law. As such, the next logical step wasn't an attempt at prosecution – the logical next step was to increase the degree of intimidation. And the more one considers Alan Simpson's arrest, the more this seems to have been its intended effect and the more likely it seems that, far from being a precursor to an intended court case, the arrest was in fact an attempt to avoid one.

To understand the sense of this we need to look not at what happened but at what was *supposed* to happen – because once again the Department simply failed to take into account the kind of people they were dealing with. The very public nature of Simpson's arrest was the Pike's doing, not the State's. Left to themselves, the police clearly intended to waylay Simpson as he went to the theatre on the evening of the 23rd and arrest him quietly. Once in the back seat of one of the unmarked police cars, Simpson would have been whisked away to the Bridewell and the first Swift would have known about the arrest would have been when she heard it through Con Lehane, the only person Simpson would be allowed to contact under the terms of the extraordinary warrant deliberately used. From Swift's point of view, Simpson would effectively have disappeared.

In the event Simpson's entrance through a back garden took the detectives completely by surprise and they actually had to be told that he had arrived at the theatre – news that cannot have pleased them at all. When they did finally approach the Pike the police did so cautiously, first sending two scouts who were astonished to find a reception committee of reporters and cameramen. When their attempts to lure Simpson to the privacy of the end of the lane failed, there followed a long wait as the detectives debated what to do – or, as seems much more probable, sent for instructions. The presence of the newsmen meant that the police couldn't just withdraw – the matter was going to go public now whether the Department liked it or not. To have visited the Pike twice and been repulsed each time was simply unthinkable. So the arrest had to go ahead. But even when the police cars finally came into Herbert Lane the detectives' first thoughts were to get Simpson into the privacy of the box-office – a privacy they were so determined to have that they dragged him there when he refused and almost broke Aidan Maguire's wrist when he tried to stop them closing the door.

The heavy-handed manner of Simpson's arrest and detention was always an aspect of the case that seemed particularly inexplicable. Even by the robust standards of the time, it seemed very much a case of using a sledgehammer to crack a nut. No plausible explanation – beyond mere bullying – has ever been advanced for the police behaviour. To the modern eye, however, certain things about it seem relatively obvious. For one thing it is safe to assume that the police were following orders, and that these orders (to judge by the facts of the 21st) came directly from the Department of Justice and were almost certainly specific. Precisely what the orders were does not, in the last analysis, matter: what matters is the effect that their being carried out was intended to have.

The manner of Simpson's arrest – the intended manner, before the Pike's theatrics spoiled it – makes no sense as part of a legal process. It makes perfect sense, however, as a continuation and intensification of the policy of intimidation. From Simpson's point of view, he would be surprised on his way to the Pike, bundled into a big black car, driven away and held virtually incommunicado in a prison cell. What all these circumstances suggest is that Simpson's arrest, which would form such a dramatic element in the mythology of the *Rose Tattoo* case, was intended as a straightforward application of one of the oldest para-legal tricks available to police forces anywhere: having failed to bully Simpson into stopping *The Rose Tattoo* by just ordering him to do so, it looks very much as though the State now decided to soften him up with a night in the cells.

Although its elements vary over time and place, the classic version of the night in the cells is extremely simple. The subject is usually someone who has declined to give required information or carry out a desired course of action. He or she is detained, threatened,[6] then left incommunicado in unpleasant solitude to ponder the possible consequences of their failure to co-operate. In the morning, when the subject's morale is at its lowest, he or she is again offered the opportunity to play ball, promised release if they do and threatened with truly dire consequences if they still refuse. There is nothing mysterious about the technique itself: it is one of the oldest tricks in the book and while it is of course unofficial it remains in common use in most countries because it is, from the authorities' point of view, so often incredibly successful.

If Alan Simpson's experience in the Bridewell wasn't a deliberate use of the tactic then it had, in almost every detail, an astonishing accidental resemblance to it. In a dark cell, cut off from communication with all but his lawyer, Simpson spent the hours of darkness considering his position. He had time to think of many an appalling vista before day broke and by his own account of that night he thought of every single wretched one of them. When morning came he'd had no sleep and his morale was at its lowest ebb. It was just then that Con Lehane was sent in, with the State's extraordinary offer to drop the whole thing if Simpson immediately stopped production of *The Rose Tattoo*. This was the requisite carrot and it was backed up by a big, ugly stick: if Simpson refused, the State would not only press charges but would also oppose bail, leaving him – though proven guilty of nothing – in jail for anything up to six weeks.

Simpson now had a very clear choice, the first plain, unequivocal choice with which the State, finally dropping its obscurity, had actually presented him. The choice was at least admirably simple: he could stop *The Rose Tattoo* dead in its tracks, or risk ruining his entire life. It was an offer the State can hardly have expected him to refuse; but, amazingly, he *did* refuse, thereby wrong-footing the Justice Department yet again.

It was at that precise moment – and at no point before – that a court appearance, if not a *Rose Tattoo* 'case', became inevitable. Simpson's very success in securing publicity for his arrest had removed the State's room for manoeuvre and compromise. The original move against the Pike had been felt necessary because the move to the Gate, by promising yet more publicity for *The Rose Tattoo*, seemed to make a McQuaid attack more likely: but the stage-managed arrest had given the play more publicity than a whole year at the Gate would have done. If the State withdrew now, having come so far, the move against the Pike would – quite farcically – have resulted in the very thing it had been designed to prevent. Furthermore, the Department of Justice's credibility on the matter of censorship would, of course, have been destroyed.

So the initial hearing proceeded. But even then the State offer – by now perhaps best thought of as a plea – was repeated one final time in open court. When Simpson again rejected it, the prosecution, as threatened, did oppose bail. And in the prosecution's bluster and animus on that first court appearance – patently obvious from the court reports even four and a half decades later – it is very hard not to see an element of genuine anger at the frustration of the latest game plan … plus an attempt to disguise the fact that the prosecution didn't have a leg to stand on – and knew it.

District Justice Rochford, who heard the case on that first day, foiled the prosecution's resistance to bail by finding a colleague willing to hear the case immediately. Whether Rochford made such an unusual effort because he did not like the State's behaviour is impossible to say; but such few indications as there are seem to suggest that he, like O'Flynn after him, did not like the smell of the case at all. Certainly Rochford's promptness in finding a judge is itself possibly the best indication of this, since he must have had a shrewd idea of the effect it would have. His action threw the prosecution into disarray – they clearly had no idea of how to react to this development, which deprived them of their most potent immediate threat.

For all that the arrest had been treated as a matter of major importance, the State had made no preparations whatsoever for an actual court appearance – surely the final proof that they hadn't expected one. Having been forced to rely on little more than a repeated claim of Simpson's guilt throughout this first day in court, the prosecution was now reduced to offering lame excuses for its inability to proceed with the case proper – the book of evidence wasn't ready, counsel said, and the witnesses were scattered. In reality, of course, the State *had* no evidence beyond the reports of its own policemen; even six weeks later when the case returned to court, the supposed evidence (following various attempts to find more) never amounted to anything beyond the unsupported claims of these same witnesses – all of them the very type of person whom Traynor and Coyne's *Memorandum for the Government* would within a matter of months be describing as unqualified to act as censors.

After that first day, all attempts at doing any kind of even tacit deal with Simpson were pointless. The cat now was out of the bag and the State found itself committed to a legal process that it can never really have hoped to win. The carrot disappeared from its bag of tricks, though the threat of the stick remained. Some of the authorities' subsequent actions really only make sense as part of a pattern of continued intimidation and a public demonstration of the Department of Justice's deep commitment to decency. The heavy police presence at the Pike on the remaining nights of the play's run are very much part of this pattern – in spite of the individually delivered (but very carefully phrased) police threats to all involved with the production it is simply not possible to believe that there was ever a serious intention of arresting anyone there. The ridiculous presence of Southern detectives in the audience for the play's Belfast visit is also inexplicable in any other terms.

Even Ó Caoimh's threat to initiate a prosecution of Simpson no matter what happened in the District Court, while it seems to have contained an element of plain nastiness, must finally be seen as another part of the intimidation process, though Simpson and Swift – as they had to – took it very seriously indeed.[7] If there was ever any real question of Ó Caoimh's initiating a prosecution, it is inconceivable that he would have been allowed to proceed after O'Flynn's comprehensive rubbishing not just of the prosecution case but of even the charges. The prosecution in any subsequent trial would be forced to rely on the same 'evidence' O'Flynn had dismissed and the whole public airing of the matter would have prolonged the State's exposure to the thing power in Ireland has, until recently, always feared far more than any legal battle – ridicule.

36. Last Thoughts on Licensed Premises

While we have said that we will not pursue the actual court case in detail beyond the question of how it ever happened – of how Simpson came to be in court in the first place – some general comment on later events does seem necessary. Because although the State's behaviour suggests that it did not wish the matter to ever get as far as the courtroom, there was no sign of the prosecution's holding back once the battle was joined. And while some of the prosecution's seeming zeal can be put down to State annoyance at what must have seemed like Simpson's impudence, there is a factor beyond this that the present writer at least finds far more disturbing.

The released file gives no indication one way or another as to what the Government's actual game plan in the court case was; but there can be no denying that, in the light of our new knowledge about the Censorship Board battle, the very public nature of the *Rose Tattoo* case was – however coincidentally – in some ways extremely *handy* for the Department of Justice. In fact if one accepts even in part our scenario of events so far, then it becomes difficult not to think of the continued attempt to prosecute Alan Simpson as, in a very special sense, a show trial – a process which the State knew it was unlikely to win, but one whose real purpose was never to send Alan Simpson to trial but to demonstrate, in the most public fashion possible, the Department of Justice's deep commitment to protecting the Irish nation from 'indecency'. Profoundly and unpleasantly ironic though the thought may be, the inescapable conclusion would seem to be that the attempt to prosecute Alan Simpson may in the last analysis have been a piece of political theatre.

If, at any time before May 23rd 1957, the Department of Justice's worst-case scenario had come true – if the Knights of Columbanus and/or Archbishop John Charles McQuaid had publicly attacked the Minister for being soft on censorship – then there would have been very little Oscar Traynor could do to defend himself against the charge. Though on occasion the censorship system had been useful to the State, in general it was treated by all Irish Governments as an embarrassment and certainly something with which they did not want to deal – one of the prime *political* reasons for Boland's 'reforms' had been to get the whole subject of censorship out of political life. Hence his instituting of an Appeals Board to take over what had formerly been a Ministerial function. There was also an international aspect to the matter: foreign public opinion had – despite profuse denials – become increasingly important to the State and the repetition of grotesque episodes such as the *Tailor and Ansty* debate in the Senate could only convince the wider world that the Irish Republic was every bit as barking mad as some believed. The plain fact of the matter was that Traynor, like almost every Justice Minister before him, didn't give a tuppenny damn for the Knights' form of censorship, any more than (as both the Hierarchy and the Knights seem to have been basically well aware)[1] did the great mass of the Irish people, who had more important things to worry about. But what might be felt and what might publicly be admitted were, in that Ireland, two radically different things and as such neither Traynor nor his Department would have any credible defence to offer in the face of a Knightly accusation of disinterest.

If the attempt to quash *The Rose Tattoo* had begun as an attempt to buy time, it had soon turned – however inadvertently – into something more. The arrest of Alan Simpson turned the Government, out of the blue and literally overnight, into outright *champions* of censorship. By the end of May, and certainly after the international media coverage the affair received during the court sittings in July, this Government (and in particular this Justice Department) were widely regarded as being downright ferocious censors, who had taken Irish censorship beyond anything previously known. That demonstrably unfanatic civil servants and politicians went out of their way to deliberately acquire the backward image this gave them internationally has always been a source of surprise to many commentators on the case; but the discovery of the buried Censorship Board story puts this behaviour in a completely different context and suggests that the State's posturing did in fact have one immediately beneficial (and entirely political) effect. With the Department of Justice publicly demonstrating to the world in open court its deep concern about Irish morality throughout the summer of 1957, the Knights of Columbanus had simply missed the boat: attempts to portray Traynor as soft on censorship in the wake of the *Rose Tattoo* case would have appeared silly. And the fact that overt attempts to portray him personally as such were surprisingly lacking from the public face of the later Campaign Against Evil Literature would suggest that, by then at least, his opponents had cottoned on to this fact.

The $64,000 question, which remains completely unanswerable, is how great a part – if any – was played in the *Rose Tattoo* case, as it eventually played out in court, by the Justice Department's domestic need for precisely such censorship credibility at this time. It is still hard to read the heavy-handed State actions *after* Simpson's arrest as anything other than further attempts at intimidation; but whether this very public intimidation was itself, at least in part, a self-conscious attempt to demonstrate the Department's deep commitment to rooting out 'indecency' will probably never be known.

The usefulness of the *Rose Tattoo* case, whether fortuitous or otherwise, lasted throughout the summer of 1957. The appeal to the High Court in July usefully kicked the whole matter into the long grass for several months, during which Traynor and his men got on with the far more important business of breaking the IRA border campaign. On the Censorship Board front, Pigott and company. were left to stew in their own juices: with each day that Pigott refused to compromise and with each meeting he refused to call, he very clearly obstructed the operation of the Censorship Board in the most literal way imaginable and put himself ever further in Traynor's power. With each passing month the moral high ground slipped a little further away from the Knightly cabal and it became a little more possible to portray Pigott as being derelict in his duty – a duty which was of course terribly important to that by now well-known pursuer of pornographers, the Minister for Justice.

By the time the High Court took up the State appeal in the *Rose Tattoo* case on October 11th even the Censorship Board matter was, at least for the moment, sewn up in a neat little bundle: Traynor's new appointees had taken their places and the Board had resumed operation. There was at any rate nothing to fear from the High Court sitting, which did not concern the events at the Pike at all, but was about legal technicalities. Simpson and Swift's decision to appeal the High Court ruling was (almost perversely) even more convenient for the State, since it kept the case *sub judice* while the worst of the Campaign Against Evil Literature was raging. The Evil Literature campaign, unable to refer to the real bones of contention, lost its way in technical criticism of the censorship apparatus and demonstrably wild exaggerations of the 'filth' situation. At the end of January the Hierarchy played its cards; in March, his resolve stiffened by Traynor and (presumably) the rest of the Cabinet, de Valera called their bluff. The two matters had, in any case, become quite distinct: the *Rose Tattoo* case had come to revolve around matters far beyond censorship and to focus on things which really did matter to the State – such as its own freedom to treat other people exactly as it had treated Alan Simpson without being subjected to scrutiny.

Once that matter had been decided the *Rose Tattoo* case was of no further possible use to the State. By now, in fact, the case was something of a Banquo's ghost: an unpleasant reminder of past dirty dealings. And when the case returned to Dublin District Court in June 1958 the most noticeable thing about the State's attitude was precisely its lack of interest. The by-now-familiar police evidence was trotted out, the prosecution went through the motions on autopilot and then everyone waited. Cathal O'Flynn's summing up was scathing, but its conclusions cannot have been unexpected, at least by the prosecution. In fact, although this really turns the accepted view of the matter on its head, the worst possible outcome from the Justice Department point of view would have been if Cathal O'Flynn had somehow allowed Alan Simpson to be sent for trial. The long, long silence had turned the case into old news: the newspapers, both at home and abroad, had found a whole string of other topics to cover, even Irish ones – by now the Fethard boycott, the second Theatre Festival row and the Evil Literature campaign itself had all come and gone; and even the IRA was on the run.

A trial for Alan Simpson now would rake over all the old dubious ground yet again and renew interest in the bizarre State conduct which, when all was said and done, was the *Rose Tattoo* affair's most striking feature. The prosecution would be reduced to trotting out the same non-existent evidence, now being dismissed by a District Justice; and this time it would be trotted out in front of a jury. A trial would also return censorship to the front pages at a time when, though the dispossessed Knights were still seething, the State felt no further political need to pose as the champion of decency. In what is perhaps the ultimate perversity of the whole thing, O'Flynn's refusal to send Simpson for trial may well have been almost as big a relief to the Department of Justice as to Simpson and Swift.

After it had ended, the one remaining useful thing that the *Rose Tattoo* case could do for the Irish State was to go away. The State duly forgot about it; everyone else did not. But the State's selective amnesia and the utter lack of any common sense in the events of May 1957 left a vacuum that rumour rushed to fill; over the years the case accrued a seemingly unbreakable shell of myth and half-truths. If the first part of this book even puts a few dents in this shell, it will have achieved something.

Among those who did not forget about the case were, naturally, Simpson and Swift. Unlike the State, they could not simply pretend that the whole thing had never happened. Alan Simpson was vindicated in court, but he would always be regarded as vaguely *suspect* from then out; most of the rest of his professional life would be conducted outside Ireland and after the closure of the Pike he would never again have a theatre of his own. He would die in May 1980, a week before the 23rd anniversary of his 1957 arrest. And though it would continue for a while and even have successful productions, the Pike was effectively dead after the *Rose Tattoo* case It had been bled white by costs that could not be recovered, and profits that would once have gone towards its fund for a new theatre now went towards paying Simpson's legal debts. The theatre's club membership base was literally decimated by the court case and the attendant scandal. Its proud record of venture-some performance had been irreparably crippled by the long need for caution. Its glorious flight was effectively ended and the Pike Theatre Club was dead in the water; it just took it a while to lie down.

This, then, is the narrative of the *Rose Tattoo* case arrived at by myself and Carolyn Swift after two years of study. Whether it is credible is for its readers to decide. The present writer became involved in the project, and persevered with it, in the hope of finding a solution that would finally satisfy Swift herself, who has spent not two but almost 50 years pondering these events. The conclusion to which our research led us cannot have been an easy one for her to accept, since it may seem to detract from the one positive thing she and Simpson derived from the entire experience: the idea that, at whatever personal cost, they had won an important victory against a State attempt to censor yet another area of the arts in Ireland. This feeling was very general: even the Knights of Columbanus believed it.[2] In our scenario, of course, the State never gave a damn about *The Rose Tattoo* as such. In our theory, the importance of the play lay in the imagined relevance it had to an issue of conflict which, however obfuscated by the issue of religion, was, at base, about political power. And in this scenario too, though it flies in the face of all previous readings of the *Rose Tattoo* case, the State – although it had to assume some unfamiliar postures and to endure some embarrassing moments – substantially got everything it wanted from the affair.

But it would be a mistake to think that our theory in any way detracts from the importance of the stand taken by Simpson and Swift in 1957. However obscurely, the State told Alan Simpson and Carolyn Swift to do something; believing they had done no wrong, they refused. It may be that, had they understood exactly what was going on, they would in some way have modified their behaviour – Swift denies this forcefully, but Simpson at least seems later to have felt that, if he had been approached in an even slightly reasonable fashion, some compromise could have been reached. Reason, however, is a variable concept and one with whose use the various powers in 1950s Ireland seem on occasion to have had some little difficulty. The immediate instinct of Church and State alike, when dealing with those they deemed susceptible, was not to reason but to order: compromise – at least when dealing with 'unimportant' people like mere members of the '"arty-crafty" set' – seems to have been as alien to the State as it would appear to have been to the Knights or indeed to their Church.

At any rate Simpson and Swift did take a stand and they did not bend before State action both licit and illicit, before prosecution, intimidation and moral blackmail. Perhaps the most revealing thing about the whole story is that, faced with a principled refusal of unreasonable demands made basically for the State's own convenience, taking these actions would appear to have been the only response the State felt able to make.

Nonetheless this theory does turn the Pike from being the centre of attention to being at best a sideshow in a much bigger power struggle, one that was – as befitted the status of the combatants – conducted well away from public view. It also suggests that, by 1957, Irish society was being run along lines that were not simply complex but were, by any meaningful standards, completely and utterly dysfunctional. This latter suggestion at least seems more amply borne out the more we find out about the period; to the present writer, it is most tellingly symbolised by the fact that, in May 1957, on the basis of documentary evidence, it simply was not possible for the Irish Department of Justice to contact John Charles McQuaid, ask him a straight question and believe his answer. It would be difficult to find a more potent symbol of lack of communication. Yet in terms of what is known about the mutual (and, it must be said, not unmerited) mistrust between Church and State by that time it is no mere symbol and is not even particularly surprising.

If we initially approached the mystery of the *Rose Tattoo* case as a 'whodunit' – if we hoped to find a single villainous individual or institution at whose door responsibility for the event could be laid – then we soon learned the pointlessness of such hopes. In our researches we came across much rank duplicity, flagrant abuse of power, subversion of democratic process, extraordinary callousness and a very great deal of cynicism among the great and good of Irish society, both clerical and lay. But we came across no villains, only humans who, for better or worse, believed themselves to be acting in what they felt to be the best interests of Ireland. Many of their views seem quite bizarre to us now and many of their definitions of what constituted Ireland's best interests seem appallingly self-serving; but perhaps our own views will seem the same to those who come after us and our failure to live up to them as glaring.

The final rights and wrongs of the *Rose Tattoo* case are thankfully not our concern here, nor are its politics. The government which happened to have the Censorship Board crisis land in its lap was a Fianna Fáil one; but the previous administration had clearly decided that action needed to be taken and had in fact initiated the sequence of actions which culminated in the Board crisis of 1957. The architect of the assault on the Knights' monopoly seems quite clearly to have been Coyne, whose continued importance in Departmental planning is manifestly shown in the papers relating to the Government's handling of the Evil Literature campaign; the general absence of his name from the released *Rose Tattoo* file has been noted, but the seven-point memo – the true origin of all that followed for the Pike – seems so very much like his work that, in the absence of any indication to the contrary, it is hard not to believe him its author. Coyne was a career civil servant and a supporter of Fine Gael, so these are certainly not party political matters.

In two years in-depth study of papers generated in the mid-fifties by both Church and State, it has been extremely difficult in the end not to see all the major representatives of one or both – the Ministers, the civil servants, the Knights and even the Archbishop – as being themselves trapped by their places in the deeply strange society which had grown up in Ireland since independence. Like Serafina in *The Rose Tattoo*, the persistence of Church and State alike in attempting to transpose their idealised dreams on to the real world had resulted in a kind of stasis, at once hysterical and lifeless and almost wilfully divorced from the realities of life around them. If the question 'whodunit' is regarded as another way of asking how the *Rose Tattoo* case ever happened, there seems little doubt that the answer is the old chestnut, at once terrifying and clichéd: society done it – or at least that particular society, where so very much of reality was unmentionable, made something like the *Rose Tattoo* case possible. But then it had made far worse things possible, in its time.

Still the effective demotion of the Pike's struggle is the thing Swift finds hardest to accept in what she now regards as the true story of the *Rose Tattoo* affair. That she does accept it and regards our theory as being the only sane explanation so far advanced for what she and Simpson experienced at the time, suggests either that she is a brave person – which hopefully this book at least has shown to be the case – or that she is a deluded old woman, or both. Again, the reader must decide which is the case.

As I write these words, Carolyn Swift is in the middle of a course of radiotherapy treatment for her cancer, which returned in early 2002. The outcome of the treatment is uncertain. She herself has raised the possibility that she may not live to see the publication of this book, which would, in some ways, be the final bitter irony of the whole shabby history of the *Rose Tattoo* case. Because while we believe the theory outlined here to be essentially true, it is obviously not the full truth, which remains unknowable without full documentation. Though even the indisputable facts we unearthed in our search must seem at the very least regrettable, this book was not and is not intended as an indictment. It is, instead, offered in the hope that it will reopen debate on the case – and as part of a plea. That plea is directed towards the Irish State, which holds all the relevant cards. Unless most of the papers in the *Rose Tattoo* file disappeared years ago then the release made in January 2000 was an extremely selective one. The file in the National Archives contains at most a small sample of the documents that the year-long pursuit of Alan Simpson will have produced. More importantly, with the single great exception of the seven-point memo, it contains only scraps relating to the period between May 9th and May 24th 1957 – the period when all of the most fundamental decisions in the case were taken. These are precisely the decisions over which the largest questions remain. Our own theory must perforce rely on those scraps and what can be inferred from them; but if this theory is incorrect in its substance, then Swift still does not know why her and her husband's theatre was ruined.

And though two years of studying State documents have left us with a healthy scepticism about their ability or willingness to tell the plain truth and with a clear awareness of how some of them, even in seeming to tell it, serve only to mislead, still we have also learned that even their simplifications and silences can at least point in truth's direction. The idea of a hidden dispute involving Dr McQuaid still seems thoroughly sound; and if it was not the buried story of the Censorship Board crisis, then we must assume that there is another buried story somewhere, waiting to be discovered. But Carolyn Swift does not feel she has the energy to begin the search all over again; nor, these days, can she be at all sure that she has the time.

Our plea, obviously, would be for a fuller release of the remaining *Rose Tattoo* papers. If our scenario is even partly correct, then the gaff is in any case blown; if it is incorrect, then the remaining documents will discredit it with little difficulty. This is all that Swift herself wishes for: not apologies, restitutions, explanations, honours or anything else – simply an opportunity, if our own explanation of its roots is so wide of the mark, to lay the ghost of the *Rose Tattoo* case once and for all. Looking at the contributions she has made to Irish life for over half a century, the pleasure and knowledge her work has by now brought to several generations of Irish people and her ground-breaking role in so very many cultural areas, it does not seem terribly much for her to ask. Still the plea is made without much hope of its being heeded: if her past experience at State hands is anything to go by then one is forced to suspect that, little though she asks and without malice though she asks it, still it is more than she will receive.

A NOTE ON THE TRIAL OF ALAN SIMPSON

All attempts to write about the *Rose Tattoo* case run up against the problem that the mythology of the case has long been accepted as fact. And one of the main myths about the case is that Alan Simpson – or in some extreme versions the entire cast – was put on trial for staging the play. In the classic, extreme variant of this myth, found in all too many supposedly definitive works, Simpson and/or the cast were put on trial, after complaints from the public, because a condom was produced on the stage of the Pike. Depending on which incorrect version is being used as a source, he or they were found guilty, but won on appeal, or else the case was either withdrawn or simply collapsed. Simple enough though these versions of events are and ubiquitously though some variant of them appears in print, they in fact contain (depending on which mixture is used) a minimum of at least five separate errors. And though Carolyn Swift has tried tirelessly to correct these and other errors for 45 years at the time of writing, they continually reappear.

Swift is by no means merely nit-picking: the truth is quite important, because it emphasises both the dubious nature of the entire process to which Simpson was subjected and the size of the apparent defeat that the State would encounter. Although a complaint from the public about the production was theoretically necessary for the case to take place at all, no evidence was ever offered that any such complaint had been lodged – on the contrary, strenuous efforts were made by the State to prevent all inquiry into the origins of the matter. Furthermore, the State's defeat in the *Rose Tattoo* case would not simply be a matter of Simpson's being found innocent at a trial or winning an appeal or having the case against him in some way collapse through some minor defect. It would, in court at least, be a much more complete rout than that. The Irish State spent a great deal of time and public money in a seeming bid to bring Simpson to trial and in process caused Simpson, Swift and their family a great deal of suffering. But despite passing a great deal of time in various courtrooms, Alan Simpson was never actually put on trial for anything at all. Since this issue is an important one, it bears some explaining, which will be kept as straightforward as possible – though this is not always the easiest thing with legal matters, as many readers will appreciate.

Alan Simpson was the only person ever arrested by the police in connection with the Pike Theatre production of *The Rose Tattoo*. Though Swift, the cast and the Pike's backstage staff would all be individually threatened with arrest, no further legal action was ever taken. As regards the 'trial' error, it is a very easy mistake for a layman to make (a layman, at least, fortunate enough to have had no direct acquaintance with the wrong end of the Irish criminal justice system) but it is equally untrue. The entire *Rose Tattoo* court case, for all its length, was no more than a preliminary hearing of the evidence: a hearing at which the State requested that the accused be *committed* for trial. The difference may take a moment to grasp, but it is extremely important – particularly if you happen to be the person sitting in the dock.

A preliminary hearing takes the form of a statement (by a lawyer for the State) that the accused committed such and such an offence on such and such a date and that the State will produce witnesses who will prove this. The presiding judge (there is as yet no jury) has no power to find the accused person either innocent or guilty: that is not what the judge is there for. What the judge at this stage is sitting in judgement of is not the defendant, but the prosecution: he (or, occasionally nowadays, she) is there to decide whether or not an actual offence in law did take place and whether, if the accused is sent for trial, there is at least a reasonable likelihood that a jury made up of ordinary people will convict him *on the strength of the evidence produced by the State*. The question at issue is whether the prosecution has presented what is known as a *prima facie* case: put at its simplest, a question of whether or not a trial would be both unjust and a waste of time.

Alan Simpson was eventually released *without* trial, not simply because Cathal O'Flynn felt it unlikely that a jury composed of reasonable people would convict him – though O'Flynn did decide that 'no jury weighing the probabilities of this case ... would or ought to convict' – but also on the far more fundamental grounds that that State had failed to show that any offence had ever taken place – 'I am not satisfied that the evidence in this case is sufficient to justify me in committing you for trial. Consequently, I find a *prima facie* case has not been made out.'

This was, of course, a great moral victory for the Pike, but it was also – with a sad irony – its financial undoing. For all its protractedness, Simpson's ordeal had been – in legal terms – no more than a preliminary hearing – the sort of thing District Courts deal with every day. Defendants in preliminary hearings pay their own legal costs. It was simply unheard of for a preliminary hearing to last as long as Simpson's did or for it to wind up going through the entire court system; thus there was no legal mechanism by which Simpson might seek to recover his costs from the State, even though its assault on him had been deemed legally groundless. Interestingly enough, should the same thing happen today, the financial situation of the accused would be identical. Had Simpson's case in fact gone to trial, he would have been able to reclaim costs if found innocent. It is possibly the blackest irony of the whole affair that, precisely because Simpson was morally vindicated in the clearest possible fashion, the State got away scotfree, while the Pike was ruined. In this sense, the question of who actually won the *Rose Tattoo* case must remain at best unanswered.

Notes

1. The Good Daughter
[1] Returning home for the first time after successful cancer treatment, for instance, she'd been mugged on her own doorstep by someone who proceeded to steal her car.

2. Genesis
[1] In his authoritative book *An Age of Innocence: Irish Culture 1930 – 1960*.

[2] Pilkington, *Theatre and State in Twentieth Century Ireland*.

[3] Or to realise how frustrating or occasionally even dangerous a field they could be in which to work.

[4] It should be noted that in many cases this suited the political and social Establishment of the State perfectly well.

[5] Though his papers do show that Dr McQuaid, responding to complaints he received, sometimes had Knights sent to monitor plays which had been brought to his attention and to write reports on them.

[6] Where many of the most ardent Red-hunters were, of course, Catholic Irish-Americans.

[7] Fluency in Irish had, under Blythe, become a condition of employment at the theatre, even for stagehands. Even the headings on Abbey notepaper were in (some said ungrammatical) Irish.

[8] *Irish Times*, 9 November 1947.

[9] Quoted in Fallon, *An Age of Innocence*, p.138.

[10] In whose founding MacLíammóir had, ironically, been instrumental.

[11] The term did not yet exist. Twenty years later the celebrated English drama critic Sir Harold Hobson would tell RTÉ that the Pike was the first fringe theatre he had seen, before the term itself had actually been invented.

[12] Based on Christopher Isherwood's Berlin stories, *I Am a Camera* would of course go on to supply the basis for the musical *Cabaret*. In 1950s Ireland its portrayal of *louche* living in pre-war Berlin – complete with an abortion theme – was considered by many to be degenerate.

3. Progress

[1] *Evening Mail,* August 1953.

[2] It is a telling comment on Irish society of the time that, throughout the various *Follies* shows, some of the other writers who contributed material felt obliged to use pseudonyms.

[3] Swift's memoir of the Pike years, *Stage By Stage* (Poolbeg, 1985), contains a hilarious account of the sardine-can effect of opening-night full house.

[4] Father of the future folk-singer Danny Doyle, who – like other children from Herbert Lane – could frequently be found attending rehearsals. He later described the Pike, in an interview for Aer Lingus magazine, as 'like a rainbow at the end of our lane'.

[5] There would be five series of *Follies* between 1953 and 1958: all but the final one – undertaken in desperation during the Pike's declining days – were enormous hits.

[6] The degree to which Swift revised *The Quare Fellow* is a matter of some dispute, with Swift – who retains enormous affection and sympathy for Behan – denigrating her contribution but several sources, including contemporary accounts and members of Behan's own family, begging to differ. There is no doubt, however, that Behan subsequently broke his financial and contractual obligations to the Pike – he later admitted as much himself.

[7] *Irish Times*, 29 May 1956.

[8] Because of the lack of seats, the Pike lost money every night the play ran and Simpson and Swift felt obliged to forego their own shares of the take. Even so, Behan (who received more money than anyone else involved with the production) got only £25 for the play's four-week run – a deciding factor in his later decision to break his contract with Simpson and Swift and throw in his lot with Joan Littlewood.

4. Omens

[1] Lionel Pilkington's contention that 'the production was intended as provocative' is glaringly incorrect: like most of the small theatres, the Pike regarded the attention of vigilantes as something to be avoided. While some of the little theatres did use provocation in an attempt to attract audiences, the Pike had never – at least to its knowledge at the time – been complained of. And one has only to look at the standards being used by some complainants about plays, and some of the plays complained of, to realise how very little it took to be 'provocative' in the era.

[2] 'Me, I'm no whore!'

[3] *The People*, 29 April 1956.

5. An Inspector Calls

[1] *Evening Press*, 13 May 1957.

[2] Simpson, *Beckett and Behan and a Theatre in Dublin*, p.138.

[3] *Daily Telegraph*, 14 May 1957. Coton noted that the Pike was 'the smallest [theatre] in Dublin and possibly in Europe.

[4] Manchester Guardian, 14 May 1957.

[5] Hobson, interviewed by RTÉ, 1979.

[6] Swift, op. cit., p.247.

[7] Simpson, op. cit., p.139.

[8] Swift, op. cit., p.227.

[9] Simpson, op. cit., p.140.

[10] Swift, op. cit., p.249.

[11] Simpson, op. cit., p.141.

6. A New World

[1] Later Irish Ambassador to Australia, Denmark and Austria.

[2] Swift, op. cit., p.254.

[3] This account is based on Alan Simpson's and there were no witnesses to the meeting. But Simpson later repeated his account both in public and in print, challenging Longford to dispute it; the good Lord never did.

[4] The London *Times*, 25 May 1957.

[5] Anna Manahan, interviewed by Órlaith O'Callaghan, October 1994.

[6] The back wall of the Pike was in effect made up of two large, garage-type doors.

[7] Simpson, op. cit., p.149.

[8] This was hardly surprising: the Attorney General had had to go back 200 years to come up with a charge that appeared in any way relevant.

[9] Simpson, op. cit., p.149.

7. In the Bridewell

[1] Ibid.

[2] Ibid.

[3] Ibid. Simpson's surprise at the fact that a policeman had seen the play would be short-lived: as he would discover, quite a number of policemen had seen it – in the course of their work.

[4] Simpson, op. cit., pp.152-3.

[5] The *Daily Express* later estimated that 'more than 100 actors and actresses packed the public benches' (*Daily Express*, 25 May 1957).

8. In the Dock

[1] *Irish Press*, 25 May 1957.

[2] Simpson, op. cit., p.152.

[3] *Evening Press*, 24 May 1957. The *Press* carried the fullest account of the proceedings in that day's newspapers.

[4] *Evening Press*, 24 May 1957.

[5] *Evening Press*, 24 May 1957.

[6] Swift, op. cit., p.263.

[7] The London *Times*, 25 May 1957.

[8] Both Swift and Kate Binchy distinctly remembered having this impression at the time.

[9] The London *Times*, 25 May 1957.

[10] Almost IR£2000 in 2001 terms.

[11] Séamus Heron was also the grandson of the labour leader James Connolly, executed in 1916.

[12] *Evening Press*, 24 May 1957.

[13] *Evening Herald*, 24 May 1957.

[14] *Evening Standard*, 24 May 1957.

[15] Simpson, op. cit., p.154.

[16] Swift, op. cit., p.264.

[17] Ibid., p.269.

[18] The London *Times*, 25 May 1957. It should be pointed out that it seems highly unlikely that 500 people would physically *fit* into Herbert Lane outside the Pike building.

[19] When Simpson finally returned to Herbert Lane that night he was disturbed to find a group of men in an unlit car parked suspiciously near the Pike. They turned out to be his fellow officers, continuing their vigil.

[20] Anna Manahan, interviewed by Órlaith O'Callaghan, 1995.

9. Tribulations

[1] Swift, op. cit., p.275.

[2] Ibid., p.284.

[3] *Belfast Telegraph*, 18 June 1957.

[4] Simpson, op. cit., p.157.

[5] The Irish Army remained highly supportive of Simpson throughout the *Rose Tattoo* affair.

[6] Swift, op. cit., p.280. Among the named contributors was Lord Longford although, as Swift pointedly remarks, his donation came nowhere near to covering the Pike's outlay on preparations for the cancelled Gate run.

[7] *Irish Times*, 5 July 1957. Author's italics.

[8] *Irish Times*, 5 July 1957. The *Irish Times* provided the most detailed reports of the evidence and all direct quotes are from its pages unless otherwise stated.

[9] In fairness, one lapse of three years between acts did strike Detective Sergeant Martin as worthy of mention.

[10] This last particularly exasperated Kate Binchy, whose lasting irritation was clear more than 40 years later when she pointed out to the present writer that Rosa removes her dress 'because she's going to bloody *bed!*'

[11] 'In those days, when men were expected to shield their womenfolk even from the vocabulary they used every day among their own sex, it seemed wildly funny that he would take his wife to a show he was expecting to be indecent or obscene' (Swift, op. cit., p.290). Speaking on RTÉ radio after the release of the *Rose Tattoo* papers, Mrs Martin would still

insist that the play was filthy. She described her husband as a very 'with-it' man. (*Joe Duffy Show*, RTÉ Radio 1, January 2000)
[12] *Irish Press*, 5 July 1957.

10. Hazy Ideas
[1] The Square Roof is, in the play, a local roadhouse/saloon.
[2] 'When told blackjack was a game of cards, [Martin] appeared so sur-prised we could not help wondering what he had thought it meant' (Swift, op. cit., p.289).
[3] Author's italics.
[4] Carolyn Swift, interviewed by Órlaith O'Callaghan, 1993. Interest-ingly, Wedick was also the single police witness who seemed to have more than a nodding acquaintance with serious theatre.
[5] Basically, sought a warrant.
[6] Swift, op .cit., p.292. Like the use of a summary warrant for the origi-nal arrest, the privilege claim is inexplicable in ordinary terms. Taken together the two very clearly suggest that either the State was abusing the law or else that it took the background to the *Rose Tattoo* case very seri-ously indeed. It has usually been taken for granted that the former was the case; while not entirely disagreeing, this book will later suggest that the truth is most likely to be a combination of the two.
[7] As, it should really be pointed out, very much of it seemingly remains, 45 years later.

11. Privilege
[1] The Commissioner was on leave, his place being taken in his absence by his deputy, Garrett Brennan. The Minister and Secretary at the Justice Ministry were, respectively, Oscar Traynor and Thomas J. Coyne. Both men will feature prominently at a later stage in this book.
[2] *Evening Herald*, July 15 1957.
[3] Gray, *The Irish Answer*, p.246
[4] Simpson, writing of the period five years later, would by and large give a deliberately upbeat slant to his account, but all the contemporary evi-dence (as well as common sense) suggests that he had quite a different attitude at the time.

[5] Reported by Anna Manahan on the *Joe Duffy Show*, RTÉ radio, January 2000.

[6] As Binchy recalled on the 1979 RTÉ *Eyewitness* television programme.

[7] There is a fascinating if rather pointless study waiting to be made on the importance of corsets as sublimated sex objects in the Ireland of that period. They feature in many of the *Rose Tattoo* myths. The League of Decency was also exercised with advertisements for women's underwear, while Archbishop McQuaid was apparently given to scrutinising such advertising with a magnifying glass.

[8] A transposition with a sensational case, involving another army officer, from three years earlier.

12. Appeals and Alarums

[1] *Irish Law Reports*, quoted in O'Callaghan.

[2] Swift, p.294.

[3] Simpson, p.163.

[4] Swift, p.294.

[5] *Irish Times*, 28 May 1958.

[6] Gray, *The Irish Answer*.

[7] Official State attempts to stem the tide were somewhat complicated by the fact that no one except the Hierarchy and its allies could see said tide.

[8] *Irish Times*, 28 April 1958. This Equity meeting, rather than the earlier Tóstal festival, was the true source of the modern Dublin Theatre Festival.

[9] Simpson, p.163.

[10] *Daily Telegraph*, 4 June 1958.

13. Endgame

[1] Quotations from O'Flynn's summing up are taken from the *Irish Law Reports* and from the *Irish Times* of June 10th.

[2] The prosecution evidence had, of course, failed to address the actual presentation of the play at all, but had concentrated exclusively on its contents.

[3] Italics in original.

[4] Italics in original.

⁵ This is one of the more fascinating asides in the judgement: read in context, it seems to suggest that O'Flynn (like many others) may have suspected that the police had been ordered to find 'dirt' in the play. If so it is the only reference in the judgement, even indirectly, to the prosecution's extreme sensitivity about the matter of police orders.

⁶ Simpson and Swift always sensed that Wedick was the most sympathetic of the police witnesses and that he was uncomfortable with what he was doing. His report – which the prosecution was so anxious to keep out of the hands of the defence – is among the released Government papers. Compared to the other police evidence it is relatively innocuous and sometimes seems to be struggling to find something incriminating to say about the play. Perhaps the best indication of this is its mention of Alvaro's calling a group of rowdy children 'little buggers' – something that could be heard 100 times a day anywhere in Ireland in an entirely non-sexual context.

⁷ This was the very case which the Attorney General had suggested on 9 May, 1957 might be used as a precedent to quash the play.

⁸ Author's italics.

14. Aftermath

¹ *Evening News*, 9 June 1958. The profanity charge, of course, was a goalpost that had been not so much moved as smuggled off the pitch long ago.

² *Daily Mail*, 10 June 1958.

³ *Daily Express*, 10 June 1958.

⁴ The *Evening Mail* was read mainly in Dublin, while the *Irish Times* was of course regarded as the newspaper of Protestants and liberals.

⁵ As indeed the *Irish Times* did throughout that whole era, when it was frequently a lone sane public voice.

⁶ W.B. Stanford to Alan Simpson, 10 June 1958, PTA.

⁷ Simpson to WB Stanford, 17 June 1958, PTA.

⁸Stanford to Simpson, 19 June 1958. Interestingly, Government willingness to abuse procedure is simply taken for granted.

⁹ In reality, whether the Cathaoirleach knew it or not, this was simply untrue: the Department of Justice had been directly responsible for the entire affair.

[10] *Seanad Éireann Debates*, vol. 49, p.657.

[11] The State did take careful note of Stanford's interest, however: a handwritten copy of the text of his Senate query, with nothing to identify what it is, is among the released State papers. This lack of identification has suggested to some (including the *Irish Times*) that the released document records the thinking of someone in the Justice Department. It doesn't but it does indicate that the Department was still keeping an eye on the matter.

[12] Notably the world première of Dominic Behan's *Posterity Be Damned* in 1959, though even that play – which dared to imply that killing and dying for Ireland were not the be-all and end-all of existence – caused controversy.

[13] Behan donated his royalties to the Pike defence fund.

[14] Conversions correct as of June 2001 (Central Statistics Office).

[15] Simpson to the Secretary of the Arts Council, 14 November 1959 (Pike Archive, TCD).

[16] Himself a dubious author for his Fursey books, which satirised Holy Catholic Ireland via historical fantasy.

[17] Arts Council Secretary to Simpson, 20 November 1959 (Pike Archive, TCD).

[18] In her autobiography, *Stage By Stage*.

15. Papers

[1] Usage of this term with reference to the 1950s risks being misleading, since there was – certainly in Ireland but more generally too – no such thing then as an identifiable Catholic Left; but the term 'conservative Catholics', which is the only real alternative, does not adequately describe the tight core of highly politicised individuals and groups, both clerical and lay, who worked assiduously throughout the era to ensure that the legal and societal norms of Irish life reflected the worldview of the Catholic Church.

[2] Two of these men, oddly enough, would play central roles during the Arms Trials over a decade later. Ó Caoimh, by then President of the High Court and presiding over the first trial, would cause a sensation when he withdrew from the case after six days, causing a retrial; Berry (who had been in the Department of Justice since 1927) would be the

man who – as much as any other single individual – was responsible for exposing the attempt to import arms for the IRA.

[3] Formerly in charge of Ireland's wartime censorship – the only period in which theatre censorship in Ireland had officially existed.

[4] Since this was three days before the play even opened at the Pike, it is in itself indisputable proof of one of Swift's most deeply held convictions: that (*pace* Tennessee Williams's own belief) it was not any feature of the Pike's production which set the fireworks off.

[5] Biographical details from Fianna Fáil Press Office.

[6] Berry to P.P. O'Donoghue, 9 May 1957, NAI SR 18/31.

[7] Author's italics.

[8] Cooney letter, 6 June 1957, Dublin Diocesan Archives (DDA).

[9] Ibid.

[10] We know of only some such attempts, but if others had been successful they would certainly have been brought up in court.

[11] He may of course have learned of it from other sources, but the man behind Brady's intervention only informed the Archbishop on June 6th.

[12] This lack of meaningful legislation – and the furore that any attempt to introduce new legislation might cause – was one good reason why the State stayed well away from action against theatres.

[13] O'Donoghue to Attorney General, 9 May 1957, NAI SR 18/31.

16. The Seven-point Memo

[1] While the present writer is no expert in these matters, a study of other Department of Justice documents of the period has convinced him that the author of the memo was Thomas J. Coyne. The memo shows Coyne's style and eye for detail. At any rate it seems certain that the author was *either* Coyne or Berry and while there are similar advisory documents by Coyne in the files there is nothing comparable by Berry.

[2] This would apply to Coyne but also to Berry, whose career in the Department of Justice had begun under Kevin O'Higgins. By the time he retired, he would have served under 14 separate Justice Ministers.

[3] No document verifying this assertion about O'Donoghue's view has been released. It should be noted, too, that the police reports seem to be regarded as simply confirming the Department's existing view of the play's 'indecency' – a view based, at this point, on no more than Brady's

say-so and, now, a clear desire to find a pretext on which to stop performances.

[4] Author's italics.

[5] Author's italics.

[6] Internal Department of Justice memo, unsigned and undated, NAI SR 18/31.

[7] The Garda copy, which the State entered as evidence in court, was bought only on May 22nd. There is no indication that the State possessed any other copy, though Brady had been loaned one.

[8] Certainly Carolyn Swift has no doubts. For 40-odd years after Longford reneged on his contract with the Pike, she held his behaviour against him. The author was with her when she realised what must really have happened. 'The poor man!' was all she said. 'The poor man!'

[9] Iremonger transcript, 24 May 1957, NAI SR 18/31. Iremonger, best known as a poet, was probably extremely relieved to be able to make this report. It seems particularly cruel that he should have been dragged into the affair: he had a great interest in theatre and had been on the 'Artistic Advisory Board' announced by the Pike when it opened. A friend of Simpson's and Swift's, he never – for understandable reasons – mentioned his small (but innocent) part in the case to them.

[10] Chief Superintendent 'A' to the Garda Deputy Commissioner, 4 June 1957, NAI SR 18/31.

[11] Note added to above.

[12] At one point the State even considered banning daily newspapers which quoted too much of the court proceedings – a remarkably self-serving exercise which it was fully empowered to do under the terms of the Censorship of Publications Act.

17. Paydirt?

[1] McQuaid to Fr Tuohy, 21 October 1957, DDA.

[2] Further acquaintance with McQuaid's style of correspondence would show that he had a certain fondness for such gnomic statements, which could be taken by the recipient as suggesting some secret knowledge on the Archbishop's part. It was at worst a small, harmless vanity, with no sinister meaning necessarily attached.

[3] Cooney to Mangan, 25 May 1956, DDA. A helpful footnote is appended to the *Herald* ad reading 'NOTE: The title of the play is *omitted in the Herald* advert. I venture to say, the Herald deliberately omitted it.' (Emphasis in original.)

[4] *Evening Herald*, 28 May 1956.

[5] Cooney to Mangan, 28 May 1956, DDA.

[6] *Evening Herald*, probably 3 June 1956.

[7] Cooney to Mangan, June 3rd 1956, McQuaid Archives (MA). *The Respectable Prostitute* did not in fact run for its extra week, so the police investigation (if indeed it ever took place) occurred at a very late stage in its actual run. Taken in conjunction with the police treatment of *I am a Camera* following complaints and other seemingly unrelated references to similar police actions, it is difficult not to see suggestions of an informal pattern whereby the police felt obliged to do *something* about complaints but did not wish to push matters in an area which, for lack of theatre censorship (and political will) was legally tricky.

[8] There seems to be some confusion about whether police records for the period still exists and if so where they are located and whether they are open to researchers. Certainly their location could not be tracked down, so Cooney's claim is unsupported – the police may simply have been fobbing him off.

[9] DDA. The letter is signed, but the Knight's surname cannot be deciphered.

[10] The proposed extension of the run, planned on the hoof because of its unexpected success, fell through because the cast had previous commitments.

[11] Cooney to Mangan, 22 June 1957, DDA.

18. The Plot Thickens

[1] Question marks as in original.

[2] Though O'Farrell's name crops up several times in documents relating to Cooney's actions now and though the two were clearly acting as a team, no further personal details on this individual occur in any of the papers we found: even his first name is unknown beyond this single occurrence of its initial.

[3] Cooney to Mangan, 1 June 1957 DDA.

⁴ 'Where the hell did he get that stuff about your family?' I asked Kate Binchy in 2001. 'Is any of it true? Was your mother hysterical?' 'Hardly,' she said. 'Probably just rumour. Dublin ran on rumours then, you know.'

⁵ This claim seems to be sheer nonsense.

⁶ From brief notes added by Mangan to both letters it was clear that they had originally been accompanied by publications which Cooney found objectionable; in both cases Mangan had forwarded the material to the Censorship Board and asked Cooney to deal directly with them in future. '[A]dvised Mr C.', Mangan wrote on the second letter, 'to send in future such literature to Mr B. MacMahon.' MacMahon was the permanent Secretary to the Censorship Board and will figure later in our story.

⁷ Quoted in Cooney to Mangan, 22 June 1957, DDA.

19. Concerned Citizens

¹ After the mid-1950s the Knights kept a particularly close eye on the Department of Justice. Indeed, Dr McQuaid obviously had a number of well-placed contacts in State circles, since one of the most striking things about his papers is the presence in them of documents which are clearly private State papers and which Dr McQuaid (whatever his position within the Catholic Church) had no business possessing. Some of these State documents are copies of items which do not appear in the relevant files in the National Archives themselves.

² And many of whom were also (as seems to have been the normal course of things under McQuaid) themselves Knights.

³ O'Sullivan to McQuaid, 9 March 1955.

⁴ He foiled attempts to erect the astonishing Christ the King statue in Dún Laoghaire for years because of the former, while having a rather sweet life of Jesus for little children effectively banned because of the latter.

⁵ Wm J. Fitzpatrick to Dr O'Connell, 20 March 1955.

⁶ E.g. 'I am reliably informed that Mr O'Sullivan is egotistical and rather fanatical. He is the sort of person who might ruin a good cause.' Jim Kavanagh to J. Ardle MacArdle, 24 March 1958, MA.

[7] Remarkable letters are so relatively common in the McQuaid papers that after a while one feels almost a need to remind oneself how uncommon some of them are.

[8] Among other surviving letters one in the National Archives from Mr O'Sullivan to Eamon de Valera suggests that Mrs Byrne was not exaggerating his literary style in the slightest.

[9] Mrs Byrne to Fr Diffney, 20 March 1958, DDA.

[10] Ibid.

[11] With a certain irony, perhaps, the Fethard-on-sea boycott had begun on May 12th, the same day as the first performance of *The Rose Tattoo*.

20. Another Country

[1] Gray, *Ireland This Century*.

[2] O'Sullivan, *Seán Lemass*, p.137

[3] Perhaps the best-known example of where this could lead was, again, the Mother and Child débâcle, which so damaged the Church when the Hierarchy's covert meddling was exposed by Noel Browne. The Hierarchy's resistance to the scheme was stoked by some senior medical figures who regarded the proposed State scheme as a threat to their independence, social status and fees.

[4] Much fascinating detail on such practices can be found in the McQuaid papers, which are apart from anything else a sort of goldmine for conspiracy theorists.

[5] This was de Valera's version of the Mother and Child Scheme, watered-down in accordance with the Hierarchy's wishes. At a delicate stage in negotiations the Hierarchy had written a public letter condemning the scheme, which they had delivered to the newspapers along with an embargo on publication. One of the newspapers was, of course, the *Irish Press* and Vivion de Valera had quickly alerted his father – as was, presumably, their Lordships' intention, the entire exercise being really no more than a ploy to show the State just how far they were prepared to go to get their way.

[6] The McQuaid papers give a far better idea of the actual degree of public response, since those letters objecting to particular plays or books which were planted by the Knights of Columbanus were sometimes forwarded

to the Archbishop with covering letters giving details of the relevant campaign.

[7] This genuinely controversial production, which had inspired walkouts and complaints due to its subject matter, had of course had no action at all taken against it.

[8] As late as 1968 he was writing to Vivion de Valera to complain about an item in the *Evening Press* which contained the line 'The important thing about Mary is that her son turned out well.' Dr McQuaid expressed his shock at what he termed 'In effect … blasphemy.' (McQuaid to Vivion de Valera, 11 January 1968 (DDA).

21. A Bloodless Coup

[1] Adams's book is an academic one and readers of academic books will of course appreciate that many of them give this impression at the best of times.

[2] Bolster, *The Knights of St Columbanus*,p.50.

[3] Adams, p.37. This was a political rather than a sectarian incident – the papers were English.

[4] Adams, p.39.

[5] Yeats described the legislation as 'Medieval' noting that '[t]here is that taint of hypocrisy about the whole proceeding.' Adams, p.49.

[6] Who wrote that '[t]he Irish Free State, through the publicity given to its Censorship Bill … has become … a butt for the wits of the world. To what must we attribute the Bill? It is, I think, a consequence of arrested growth; or, in other words, moral infantilism.' Ezra Pound took the trouble to write to the *Irish Times* from Italy with the view that 'the idiocy of humanity obviously knows no limits but the text of your proposed censorship Bill adds yet another clause to the axiom.' Adams, pp.48–49.

[7] Adams, p.73. The *Catholic Bulletin* greeted Doyle's appointment with the charming claim that 'empty asses with warm imaginations have a friend among the Censors now.'

[8] For *Stephen Hero* – *Ulysses*, in spite of legend, was never banned by the State.

[9] Adams, p.99.

[10] Details of the Magennis stitch-up are taken from John Cooney's *John Charles McQuaid.*

[11] Bolster, op. cit., p.51.

[12] Cooney, *John Charles McQuaid* , p.201.

[13] This ban was particularly unpleasant as it led to the unfortunate old couple themselves being seen as fair game for some very nasty treatment, including a visit by several priests who forced the Tailor to go on his knees and burn his personal copy of Cross's book in his own fireplace.

[14] In his introduction to the 1964 reprint of the book.

[15] Cooney, *John Charles McQuaid,* p.200.

[16] The official State record of the debate – which was widely reported in the press – was actually (very probably illegally) censored by the State. In the course of the debate the insane suggestion had been made that the Seanad records should be banned because pornographers would buy it in order to get hold of sections from *The Tailor and Ansty* which had been read into the record as a demonstration of the book's innocence. Though this suggestion was heavily defeated in a vote, the records when they appeared nonetheless did not feature the relevant material.

[17] Adams, p.110.

[18] Ibid., p.111.

[19] Ibid., p.219 (note 29).

[20] Bolster, op. cit., p.93.

22. Being Constructive

[1] There was a three-year time lag, for instance, before the report for 1952 was issued.

[2] No reports at all were published for the Board's most contentious years, 1954–57 and Brian MacMahon would later tell Adams that no reports for these years had even been prepared, because the Minister had not asked for them.

[3] Even the scrupulously straight-faced Adams, though seemingly unaware of Magennis's deviousness of the previous year, is forced to admit that there was 'a certain irony' in this.

[4] The Archbishop kept a close eye on even minor appointments: Pigott's Professorship was a plum job.

[5] It is not known how many others on this particular Board were Knights, though certainly Shields was (Bolster, p.65). It can only be said with certainty that Professor Wigham, as a Protestant, was not.

[6] Since the Catholic Church denied the viability of all moral codes but its own, this of course was quite frankly a hardly disguised codeword in that era for 'Catholic'.

[7] The abusive nature of the Board's public communications via letters to the newspapers had caused a great deal of the animosity against it. Adams – very gingerly – identifies MacMahon (one of his own primary sources) as the actual author of these letters, which the Board Secretary (who indeed wrote and signed them) invariably stipulated were being written on the instruction of the Board itself. That MacMahon had actually composed the letters had always been widely believed.

[8] The pro-censorship lobby seemed to confirm or deny these frequently made charges depending entirely on the circumstances.

[9] Blanshard, p.72.

[10] Cf. the *Irish Times*, 1 July 1957, which reports the address given by Dr Philbin, to Dr McQuaid's Dublin Institute of Catholic Sociology, in which the Bishop said it was necessary 'to point out that a concerted effort was being made by the religious minority to secure a dominating position in our public life'. References to this pernicious fantasy are to be found in much Irish Catholic writing of the time. In so far as it is possible to make out the details of the supposed plot, it seems to have centred on those hotbeds of wild iniquity, Trinity College and the *Irish Times*.

[11] Adams, p.118.

[12] On 24 May, 1945 McQuaid wrote to Boland of his 'pleasure' in nominating Deery to the Board; a week later Boland replied that he would – also 'with pleasure' – act on the recommendation (DDA).

[13] Quoted in Adams, p.148.

[14] Deery to McQuaid, 23 April 1956, MA.

[15] Cooney, *John Charles McQuaid*, p.242.

[16] Even the Board's address is helpfully given.

[17] The report notes that some Councils already manage this with the co-operation of local Garda Superintendents and Customs Officers.

[18] 'Particular attention', it is stressed, 'should be paid to undesirable Juvenile Literature' – this referred particularly to American crime comics, against which a campaign of complaints is mooted. The 'so-called "Correspondence Columns"' of women's magazines are also singled out as potential lurking-places for sin.

[19] 'It is important to secure the co-operation of the County Librarian.'

[20] Needless to say, this was hardly a reference to actual *literary* taste, but to 'moral' tone.

[21] Author's italics. The Order's methods of 'influencing' people were not always genteel. The unfortunate shopkeepers, the report directs, should be 'encouraged' to stock 'home produced and Catholic periodicals in greater variety'.

[22] Report of the Publications Committee of the Knights of St Columbanus, McQuaid Papers (DDA).

[23] These and the following figures are derived from Adams, who in turn derived them from the State's own records.

[24] Adams, p.119.

[25] Adams ascribes the fall to a severe drop in the number of books being forwarded by customs officers, whose always-contentious role in the censorship had attracted much criticism. Since the 1945 'reforms' customs officials were actually empowered to confiscate books from the personal property of individual travellers, a practice which remained legal until at least the 1960s.

23. A Low Ebb

[1] Cooney, p.242.

[2] Butler had actually gone to the meeting at the invitation of Owen Sheehy Skeffington to meet Paul Blanshard. But when he heard Peadar O'Curry, editor of the *Standard*, read a one-sided paper on Communist persecution of the Catholic Church in Yugoslavia, he felt obliged to bring up the rather sensitive subject of the Church-approved (indeed, many of the worst incidents were organised by priests) Catholic massacres of Orthodox Serbs during the Second World War. This in turn ruffled the feathers of the Nuncio, who was in the audience incognito, and he left in a huff. Within a day the Irish edition of the *Sunday Express* had turned this into: 'QUESTION FROM MAN IN AUDIENCE STARTS DIPLOMATIC ROW. THE POPE'S ENVOY WALKS OUT. GOVERNMENT TO DISCUSS "INSULT" TO NUNCIO. AFFRONT TO THE HOLY SEE'S REPRESENTATIVE IN A CATHOLIC COUNTRY' (quoted in Hannah Sheehy Skeffington, *Skeff*, p.156). There followed a widespread and astonishingly virulent

campaign against the unfortunate Butler, who had in fact not been allowed to speak beyond an opening sentence in the first place.

[3] The *Sunday Independent*'s review was headed, in approximately 40-point type, 'Mr Blanchard should stay at home' (*Sunday Independent*, 5 June 1955).

[4] The boy concerned had been beaten with a brush handle by two Christian Brothers and his arm had been broken. When Independent TD Peadar Cowan, one of the few politicians to show any consistent interest in the Industrial Schools, raised the case in the Dáil, the Minister, Mr Moylan, said that 'Accidents would happen in the best regulated families.' (*Irish Times*, 24 April 1954.)

[5] References to the League in State archives are invariably far less than flattering – though some are extremely funny, in a malicious sort of way.

[6] The actual lesson which Archbishop McQuaid himself drew from the incident was (typically) that he must gain control of the FAI (Cooney, p.314).

[7] Simply as a matter of course it must be presumed that some of those present were there on behalf of Archbishop McQuaid, who kept a close eye on all such public meetings.

[8] Sheehy Skeffington, *Skeff*, p.135.

[9] MacArdle was one of many feminist Republicans, long-term supporters of de Valera, who had been disillusioned by what they saw as his sell-out of women in his 1937 Constitution.

[10] Interestingly the Archbishop's denial of responsibility in the affair to some of the Protestant doctors involved – he 'was adamant that he had nothing to do with the affair and only knew what he had read in the newspapers' (Cooney, p.244) – precisely echoes his later comments on the *Rose Tattoo* case. If it is difficult to fully accept Dr McQuaid's word in this instance – and many have found it so – it is really his own fault.

[11] O'Reilly described the Witnesses as 'subversive, anti-Catholic, anti-Protestant, anti-Jewish and anti-Establishment' (Bolster, p.118).

[12] In a telling indication of where actual power lay, the whole court rose to its feet when Dr Rogers entered the room.

[13] Keogh, *Twentieth Century Ireland*.

[14] O'Sullivan, *Seán Lemass*, p.129.

24. Incautiously Rampant

[1] Founded in 1951 and regarded with suspicion by many in the arts ever since.

[2] It was a report by Bodkin which had been instrumental in persuading a reluctant State to found the Council in the first place.

[3] Ó'Faoláin had been elected to the Association's Provisional Board on its launch in 1948, along with Christo Gore-Grimes, Owen Sheehy Skeffington and Michael Yeats – a sort of Satanic rogue's gallery for McQuaid and the Knights of Columbanus.

[4] Quoted in Harmon, p.209.

[5] McQuaid, note (dated 23 December) added to Costello to McQuaid, 20 December 1956, DDA.

[6] *Irish Times*, 25 February 1957.

[7] *Irish Times*, 3 March 1956.

[8] *Irish Times*, early March 1956 (clipping undated).

[9] MacMahon to Coyne, 6 April 1956, DDA.

[10] MacMahon to Coyne, 12 April 1956, DDA.

[11] Liam Martin to McQuaid, 7 April 1956, DDA.

[12] McQuaid note on Deery's call, 13 April 1956, DDA. One can only imagine McQuaid's horror at the very idea.

[13] Quoted in Adams, p.150.

[14] It should be borne in mind that these two words, so often linked by the Catholic Right at the time, were not simply regarded as almost synonymous but as being highly pejorative terms.

[15] Letter circulated, along with petition form, to prospective signatories, dated 'March 1956', NAI S.2321.

[16] Covering note from Sweetman to Taoiseach's Department, dated 4 April 1956. Handwritten note added 'Seen by the Taoiseach 9/4/56', NAI S.2321.

[17] Association of Civil Liberty petition form, 1956, NAI S.2321.

[18] Deale to Costello, 6 July 1956, NAI S.2321.

25. The Villian of the Piece

[1] The Right's view of Coyne is particularly evident in MacMahon to McQuaid, 22 March 1960, and O'Flynn to McQuaid, 7 March 1958 (DDA). Interestingly the supposedly confidential proceedings of the new

Board were being leaked to O'Flynn, presumably by MacMahon, who remained Secretary. O'Flynn promptly reported them to McQuaid.

[2] Coyne's important wartime role is examined in detail in Ó Drisceoil, *Censorship in Ireland 1939-45.*

[3] The two made up when the war ended.

[4] 'An Irishman's Diary', *Irish Times*, 19 May 1945.

[5] Ó Drisceoil, p.52.

[6] Though there were (probably correct) suggestions that the Government used the censorship for its own ends – as when Sir John Keane accused it (in the Senate in 1940) of suppressing reports of an incident in Co. Cork where a factory owned by a Fianna Fáil supporter poisoned the river Blackwater with effluent.

[7] Though the activities of sections of the Catholic Right in wartime Ireland have been dismissed as the work of a lunatic extremist fringe, some of its central figures had close ongoing ties, then and afterwards, with mainstream elements in both Church and State. The fact that a fringe was lunatic did not bar it from influence in that era.

[8] Interestingly, MacMahon's letter (22 March 1960) was a response to McQuaid's sending him (as Secretary of the Board) a copy of *Weekend* magazine which had been sent to the Archbishop by a Mr Cooney – quite possibly Joseph J. Cooney of the League of Decency, who was drawing such matters to the Archbishop's attention well into the late 1960s.

[9] Coyne to McQuaid, 11 April 1960, DDA.

[10] Coyne's brother was a prominent Jesuit.

[11] Ironically because during the Emergency the two men had exasperated each other: when Ó Faoláin had threatened to move to Belfast and publish *The Bell* from there rather than continue to submit to Coyne's censorship, Coyne 'commented that he refrained from saying that he wished he would'. (Ó Drisceoil, p.185).

[12] Ibid.

[13] McQuaid to Coyne, 6 April 1960, DDA.

[14] McQuaid to Coyne, 13 April 1960, DDA.

[15] McQuaid to Coyne, 13 April 1960, DDA.

[16] In a February 1956 letter from Board Chairman Fr Deery to McQuaid as well as Coyne's already-mentioned calls to MacMahon.

[17] Memo from M. Ó Muimhneachain of the Taoiseach's office to Coyne, 10 July 1956, NAI S.2321. An appended handwritten note reads 'I understand that Mr Coyne would (?) like to speak to the Taoiseach or to forward written observations, when he has examined this matter.'

[18] Coyne report to the Taoiseach's Office, 3 September 1956, NAI S. 2321.

[19] By the Appeals Board, of which the Knights seem never to have been able to achieve control and towards which they felt a proportionate depth of resentment.

[20] Author's italics.

[21] One of Magennis's few failures with the 1945 'reforms' had been his failure to gain a foothold on the Censorship Appeal Board – he had originally suggested that a permanent place on this should be reserved for a member of the Censorship Board itself.

[22] *Irish Times*, 7 November 1956 (NAI).

[23] Draft letter from Costello's office to Deale, 5 September 1956, NAI S.2321.

[24] MacMahon to McQuaid, 22 March 1960, DDA.

[25] Deery to McQuaid, 9 February 1956, DDA.

26. Deep Waters

[1] Traynor to de Valera, 4 February 1958, NAI S.2321.

[2] Deery to McQuaid, 9 February 1956, DDA. Author's italics.

[3] When the author (as an experiment) read Dr Lucey's comments to Carolyn Swift in March, 2001, challenging her to guess their origin, she cited several obvious liberal candidates. When told the actual source, she simply refused to believe it until shown the document involved.

[4] Reported in the *Irish Independent*, 8 March 1956; cited in Traynor, *Memorandum for the Government*, 20 February 1958, NAI S.2321.

[5] Cf. Raftery & O'Sullivan, *Suffer the Little Children* – though Dr McQuaid's own papers bear testimony to his seemingly bottomless knowledge of just about everything going on in (and outside) the Church in Ireland.

27. Bust-up

[1] Adams, p.222n.

[2] Ibid., p.120.

[3] Ibid., p.222n.

[4] Ibid., p.120.

[5] Pigott press release, December 1957. Professor Pigott, though an intelligent man, seems genuinely never to have grasped that this was precisely what many people regarded as being the proper function of the Censorship Board.

[6] Adams, p.125.

[7] Adams, p.125.

[8] Ibid.

[9] Traynor had gone to the Department with the Secretary of the FAI, Joe Wickham, and they'd had a testy and rather confrontational interview with – of all people – Thomas J. Coyne.

[10] Seán Lemass, for instance, was himself a Knight – though it must be doubted that the more zealous of his brethren considered him a truly loyal one.

[11] Pigott press statement, *Irish Independent*, 5 December 1957.

28. Stand-off

[1] In this it would seem they were largely correct, but only technically: all architects, after all, do their jobs on the instructions of those who employ them.

[2] McMahon to Traynor, 4 June (?) 1957, Censorship Board file, DDA.

[3] Adams, p.126.

[4] Ibid.

[5] Ibid.

29. Mr Traynor and Professor Pigott

[1] Adams, p.121. Adams's version of events is taken largely from the press release issued by Pigott the following December. While obviously biased, this for long remained (in the absence of disclosure of the relevant archives) the fullest available version of the actual sequence of events.

[2] McQuaid handwritten note of meeting with Pigott, 3 September 1957 (DDA).

[3] Indicating that, whatever the public story might be, the Knights were at least partly aware of the true story behind the 1956 appointments.

[4] Pigott press statement.

[5] Ibid.

[6] O'Flynn to McQuaid, 12 April 1958 (DDA).

[7] Undated (1958) document 'For Minister's Information', NAI S.2321.

[8] In his/their *Memorandum to the Government* during the Campaign Against Evil Literature.

30. Protest and Protect

[1] Indeed, one can spend a long time in the National Archives of Ireland even today without learning anything at all about the real nature of the row on the Censorship Board.

[2] At least the serious sources: a grotesquely funny series of documents in the National Archives details the attempts made in autumn 1957 by Mr O'Sullivan of the League of Decency to see either the Taoiseach or the Minister for Justice, so as to personally show them some of the filth freely available in Dublin. O'Sullivan went to the extent of hand-delivering to the Taoiseach's office a parcel of 33 'obscene' magazines which included such hardcore publications as the *Daily Sketch*, *Popular Photography* and *Lilliput* magazine.

[3] Traynor, *Memorandum for the Government*, 20 February 1958, NAI S. 2321.

[4] The newspaper's report on both was kept by the Government.

[5] *Irish Independent*, 7 December 1957.

[6] Chaplain of St Joseph's Catholic Boys' Brigade to de Valera, 20 December 1957, NAI.

[7] CYMS resolution, conveyed to Government on 4 February 1958, NAI S.2321.

[8] By a most extraordinary coincidence, the very date of McQuaid's initial speech.

[9] The archives contain a particularly fine account (from the *Tipperary Star* of 2 February 1958) of a meeting of the North Tipperary VEC which seems to have been wholly given over to the subject.

[10] Traynor, *Memorandum for the Government*, 20 February 1958, NAI S.2321.

[11] Department of the Taoiseach memo (initials of signatory indecipherable) 13 January 1958, NAI S.2321.

¹² Ibid.

¹³ *Irish Press*, 28 January 1958, clipping kept in NAI S.2321. At the meeting where Traynor's response was read, Senator Tunney remarked that 'it was extraordinary that some of the people who were now making such an outcry ... made no comment on the thousands of young people who had to emigrate to other countries where they would be exposed to as bad and even worse literature.'

¹⁴ Letter of the Standing Committee of the Hierarchy, 30 January 1958, NAI S.2321.

¹⁵ *Irish Independent*, 1 February 1958, clipping filed in NAI. Reading such homilies, it is difficult not to wonder how much some of these men knew about events going on in Church institutions within their own dioceses.

¹⁶ It is a good indication of the Knights' secretiveness that even the Minister for Justice could not definitely establish whether someone was a member.

¹⁷ Traynor to de Valera, 4 February 1958, NAI S.2321.

¹⁸ Unsigned and undated document, NAI S.2321. This curious document is not half as candid as it seems and its intended recipient (unless Traynor wished to mislead de Valera somewhat) is something of a puzzle.

¹⁹ O'Flynn to McQuaid, 19 May 1958, DDA. The file in the archives contains an official transcript of Blowick's attempt to question Traynor in the Dáil on July 10th. The transcript conjures up the image of an angry gnat attempting to rouse a particularly smug stone wall. (Copy of pages from *Dáil Debates*, Vol. 170, No. 3, NAI S.2321.)

²⁰ Ibid., 20 January 1958, DDA.

²¹ Ibid., 23 April 1958, 1 May 1958, 19 May 1958, DDA. Interestingly enough two identical copies of a summary of this correspondence can be found in the McQuaid papers and the National Archives.

²² Ibid., 20 January 1958, DDA.

²³ Ibid., 20 January 1958, DDA.

²⁴ Ibid., 7 March 1958. There is no official record of some of these arrangements, which (at least as reported by O'Flynn) seem in some cases to have been outside the terms of the Act.

²⁵ 'We have already been at work on the Tóstal plays and have plans to intensify the campaign.' 20 Jan 1958, DDA.

[26] Ibid., 23 April 1958, DDA.

31. Defenders of the State
[1] O'Flynn to McQuaid, 7 March 1958, DDA.
[2] Memo, Department of the Taoiseach, 13 February 1958, NAI S.2321.
[3] Undated notification to Oscar Traynor, NAI S.2321.
[4] Undated (1958) document 'For Minister's Information', NAI S.2321.
[5] Ibid.
[6] De Valera to Traynor, 31 January 1958, NAI S.2321.
[7] Traynor Submission to Government, 20 February 1958, NAI S.2321.
[8] Which of course it essentially was – but the Devil, as ever, lay in the detail and the detail is conspicuously not given.
[9] This would not be at all the opinion of Brian MacMahon when he wrote his bitter diatribe to McQuaid in 1960. MacMahon would have a great deal to say about Conroy's Blueshirt past, political ambition and lack of scruple and would assert unequivocally that he was 'Coyne's man'. (MacMahon to McQuaid, 22 March 1960, DDA.)
[10] Author's italics.
[11] Author's italics.
[12] The text of Lucey's address was actually included as an appendix to the *Memorandum.*
[13] With such few public complaints, the reader may wonder where all the books banned in those years came from. The answer is the Revenue Commissioners, who were empowered to seize suspected books on importation and with whom the Knightly cabal on the Board (on the evidence of O'Flynn's letters to McQuaid) would seem to have had close contacts at senior levels. Tim Pat Coogan's *De Valera* contains anecdotal evidence suggesting just how arbitrary such seizures could be.

32. The Response to the Standing Committee
[1] Separate copies of which were sent to the Bishops of Raphoe and Achonry a fortnight later.
[2] Of which perhaps the most beautiful example is perhaps the letter's reference to the Board infighting of early 1957 as 'difficulties' of which 'I think Their Lordships are aware'.

[3] Coyne to McQuaid, 20 May 1958; O'Flynn to McQuaid, 7 June 1958, DDA. Interestingly O'Flynn seems to know of Coyne's letter. He warns the Archbishop – sight unseen – not to believe the letter's contents. The interesting thing is that O'Flynn seems to have heard of this letter from someone who both saw Coyne write it (O'Flynn comments on its length) and knew its destination.

[4] Coyne found two of them 'objectionable' and was sure they would have been banned by the new Board *if* they'd been submitted through the proper channels; the third he regarded 'as being the sort of bawdy which no one but the very young and immature could be corrupted by and I can't imagine a responsible parent leaving it lying about'. (Coyne to McQuaid, 20 May 1958, DDA.)

[5] McQuaid to Burke-Savage, 14 December 1959, DDA.

[6] Coyne to McQuaid, 14 December 1960.

33. Ar Ais Arís

[1] Given the desperate lack of prosecution evidence it must be presumed that, had legitimate complainants existed, the State would have produced them as witnesses in court.

[2] NAI SR 18/31.

[3] A fact well-illustrated by the account of the case given in Lionel Pilkington's *Theatre and the State in Twentieth-Century Ireland*, at the time of writing the only book to have made use of the released file.

34. May 1957: Take Two

[1] Certainly written by a Fianna Fáil supporter, possibly Traynor himself – though not Coyne, since we have it on the later authority of the Knights (who seem to have regarded Coyne and Traynor's ability to work together across party lines as something of a mystery) that Coyne was a Fine Gael supporter.

[2] NAI, S.2321.

[3] Peter Berry to P.P. O'Donoghue, 9 May 1957, NAI SR 18/31.

[4] The seven-point memo, May 1957, NAI SR 18/31.

[5] Of a sort that Seán Brady himself was very possibly unaware of.

[6] Compare the Hierarchy's move during the sometimes fraught Mother and Infant Scheme negotiations only a few years before: at a particularly

sensitive moment, when it looked as though de Valera meant to defy their wishes over some elements of the scheme, their Lordships (without informing him) wrote a statement condemning the Government's proposals, which was delivered to the newspapers for publication. The statement was accompanied, however, by a temporary embargo on publication. One of the papers to which the document was given was, naturally, the *Irish Press*. As their Lordships presumably intended, Vivion de Valera immediately informed his father of what was happening; the Government, having reconsidered, came to heel. The statement was never published. One might also compare McQuaid's opening salvo in the Evil Literature campaign itself.

[7] Cooney to Mangan, 6 June 1957, MA.

[8] In his press statement and elsewhere Pigott would claim that rumours about Comyn and Figgis's links to the Civil Liberty Association were already rife around Dublin even before their official appointment to the Board.

[9] NAI SR 18/31.

35. Action

[1] In 1957 Coyne was very possibly the only person in the State apparatus with any experience at all of theatre censorship.

[2] Itemised list of documents sent by Deputy Commissioner's Office to Chief State Solicitor, 22 May 1957, NAI SR 18/31.

[3] The list sent with the file mentions the Department's instructions to Brennan, Ward's report on his call to the Pike and a minute from Brennan to the Department as being among its contents. All are missing from the file as released.

[4] Swift, p.254. See Chapter 7 above.

[5] And this was the Justice Department's opinion in the case of *printed* obscenity, where the law was recent and at least reasonably clear: the dubious and ancient law found to excuse a move against the Pike had never even been tested in a modern court.

[6] In countries where this is allowed – and in many where theoretically it is not – they may also expect to be beaten.

[7] This was indeed a prerogative of the Attorney General's office, but one used only very rarely and then only in exceptional circumstances. Simp-

son himself could recall its happening only once before, after a judge had interfered in the case of a drunk driver who had killed someone (Simpson, p.159).

36. Last Thoughts on Licensed Premises
[1] This is simple common sense: the Knights' seemingly endless campaigns of organised written complaints would hardly have been necessary if genuine large-scale outrage had existed; they can only have been designed to supply the want of the real thing.

[2] 'Ever since the Liberals scored a victory in Court over the Rose Tattoo, the authorities are slow and hesitant in taking any action' (O'Flynn to McQuaid, 15 March 1962). The slowness of the authorities in taking action *before* the move on the Pike is not mentioned.

Bibliography

A: PUBLISHED WORKS

BOOKS

Adams, Michael *Censorship: The Irish Experience* (Sceptre, 1968)

Blanshard, Paul *The Irish and Catholic Power: An American Interpretation* (Derek Verschoyle, 1954)

Bolster, Evelyn *The Knights of St Columbanus* (Gill & Macmillan, 1979)

Brown, Terence *Ireland: a Social and Cultural History* (Fontana, 1981)

Browne, Noel *Against The Tide* (Gill & Macmillan, 1986)

Carlson, Julia *Banned In Ireland* (Routledge, 1990)

Coogan, Tim Pat *De Valera: Long Fellow, Long Shadow* (Hutchinson, 1993)

Cooney, John *John Charles McQuaid, Ruler of Catholic Ireland* (O'Brien Press, 1999)

Cooney, John *The Crozier and the Dáil* (Mercier Press,1986)

Cowell, John *No Profit But the Name: The Longfords and the Gate Theatre* (O'Brien Press, 1988)

Fallon, Brian *An Age of Innocence* (Gill & Macmillan, 1998)

Fitz-Simon, Christopher *The Boys* (Gill & Macmillan, 1994)

Gray, Tony *Ireland This Century* (Little, Brown, 1994)

Gray, Tony *The Irish Answer* (Heinemann, 1966)

Gray, Tony *The Lost Years* (Little, Brown, 1997)

Harmon, Maurice *Seán O Faoláin: a Life* (Constable, 1994)

Hartnoll, Phyllis (ed.) *Concise Oxford Companion to the Theatre* (OUP, 1972)

Hickey, Des and Smith, Gus *A Paler Shade of Green* (Gill & Macmillan, 1984)

Hogan, Robert *'Since O'Casey' and Other Essays on Irish Drama* (Colin Smythe/Barnes and Noble, 1983)

Irish Times *The Irish Times Book of the Century* (Irish Times Books, 1999)

Inglis, Tom *Moral Monopoly: The Rise and Fall of the Catholic Church in Modern Ireland* (UCD, 1998)

Keogh, Dermot *Ireland and the Vatican* (Cork University Press, 1995)

Keogh, Dermot *Twentieth Century Ireland* (Gill & Macmillan, 1994)

Lee, JJ *Ireland 1912-1985: Politics and Society* (Cambridge, 1989)

Lee, JJ (ed.) *Ireland 1945-70* (Gill & Macmillan, 1979)

Manning, Maurice *James Dillon* (Wolfhound, 2000)

Murray, Christopher *Twentieth Century Irish Drama* (Manchester University Press, 1997)

O'Brien, Conor Cruise *Ancestral Voices* (Poolbeg Press, 1994)

O'Brien, Conor Cruise *States of Ireland* (Hutchinson, 1972)

O'Brien, John A. *The Vanishing Irish* (WH Allen, 1954)

Ó Drisceoil, Donal *Censorship in Ireland 1939-45* (Cork University Press,1996)

O'Faoláin, Seán *The Irish: A Character Study* (Devin-Adair, 1949)

O'Farrell, Padraic *Green and Chaste and Foolish* (Gill & Macmillan, 1994)

Ó hAodha, Micheál *The Importance of being Micheál* (Brandon, 1990)

O'Sullivan, Michael *Brendan Behan* (Blackwater, 1997)

O'Sullivan, Michael *Seán Lemass* (Blackwater, 1994)

Pilkington, Lionel *Theatre and the State in Twentieth Century Ireland: Cultivating the People* (Routledge, 2001)

Raftery, Mary & O'Reilly, Eoin, *Suffer the Little Children* (New Island, 1999)

Roche, Anthony *Contemporary Irish Drama* (Gill & Macmillan, 1994)

Ryan, Phyllis *The Company I Kept* (Town House, 1996)

Sheehy, Michael *Is Ireland Dying?* (Hollis & Carter, 1968)

Sheehy Skeffington, Hannah *Skeff: A Life of Owen Sheehy Skeffington* (Lilliput, 1991)

Simpson, Alan *Beckett and Behan and a Theatre in Dublin* (Routledge & Kegan Paul, 1962)

Swift, Carolyn *Stage By Stage* (Poolbeg, 1985)

Williams, Tennessee *The Rose Tattoo* (Secker & Warburg, 1951)

NEWSPAPERS AND PERIODICALS

The Irish Independent
The Irish Press
The Irish Times
The Evening Herald
The Evening Press
The Evening Mail
The Times
The Manchester Guardian
The Observer
The Standard
Model Housekeeping
The Stage

B: UNPUBLISHED WORKS/PAPERS

O'Callaghan, Órlaith *Theatre and the Modern Irish State: A Case Study of the Pike Theatre Club* (MA Thesis, UCC, 1995)

(Ms O'Callaghan also provided access to the large collection of research material she compiled as background to her thesis, saving an enormous amount of time and effort in duplicating her work.)

Mitchell, Jennifer Elizabeth *What Contribution Did the Pike Theatre Make to Theatre in Ireland in the 1950s?* (MA Thesis, UCD, 2000)

Pike Theatre Archives (Trinity College Dublin)

Pike Beckett Archives (Trinity College Dublin)

McQuaid Papers (Dublin Diocesan Archives, Drumcondra)

Personal and unpublished papers, drafts and manuscripts of Ms Carolyn Swift

GOVERNMENT PAPERS

Department of Justice files, 1957 & 1958 (National Archives, Dublin)

Attorney General's files, 1957 & 1958 (National Archives, Dublin)

Department of the Taoiseach's files, 1957 & 1958 (National Archives, Dublin)

C: VIDEO AND AUDIO

RTÉ Television *Eyewitness* programme, 1979 (soundtrack tape)

RTÉ Radio *Joe Duffy Show*, January 4th, 5th, 6th 2000

RTÉ videotaped interviews with Carolyn Swift, 1999

RTÉ Television *Seven Ages* series

Index

Index

Index